CHILD PSYCHOLOGY

CHILD PSYCHOLOGY

Dr. Asha Rani

CENTRUM PRESS
NEW DELHI-110002 (INDIA)

CENTRUM PRESS

H.O.: 4360/4, Ansari Road, Daryaganj,
New Delhi-110002 (India)
Tel: 23278000, 23261597, 23255577, 23286875

B.O.: No. 1015, Ist Main Road, BSK IIIrd Stage,
IIIrd Phase, IIIrd Block, Bangalore-560085 (INDIA)
Tel: 080-41723429

Email: centrumpress@gmail.com
Visit us at: www.centrumpress.com

Child Psychology

First Edition, 2011

ISBN 978-93-80921-60-0

PRINTED IN INDIA

Printed at Tarun Offset Printers, Delhi-110053

Contents

	Preface	*(vii)*
1.	Introduction	1
2.	Child Development	11
3.	Growth, Development and Maturation	56
4.	Nature and Principles of Human Growth and Development	71
5.	Intellectual and Mental Development	87
6.	Emotional Development	100
7.	Sexual Development	110
8.	Social Development	123
9.	Learning, Maturation and Manual Skill	155
10.	Perceptual Development	228
11.	Personality Development	239
	Bibliography	293
	Index	295

Preface

Many parents shudder at the idea of showing their child to a child psychologist. What! My child is not crazy! Why does he need to see a psychologist? And then the old school of thought so prevalent in our society. Child psychology is one of the many branches of psychology and one of the most frequently studied specialty areas. This particular branch focuses on the mind and behaviour of children from prenatal development through adolescence. Child psychology deals not only with how children grow physically, but with their mental, emotional and social development as well. Historically, children were often viewed simply as smaller versions of adults. When Jean Piaget suggested that children actually *think differently* than adults, Albert Einstein proclaimed that the discovery was "so simple that only a genius could have thought of it."

Today, psychologists recognize that child psychology is unique and complex, but many differ in terms of the unique perspective they take when approaching development. Experts also differ in their responses to some of the bigger questions in child psychology, such as whether early experiences matter more than later ones or whether nature or nurture plays a greater role in certain aspects of development. When you think of development, what comes to mind? If you are like most people, you probably think about the internal factors that influence how a child grows, such as genetics and personal characteristics. However, development involves much more than the influences that arise from within an individual. Environmental factors such as social relationships and the culture in which we live also play essential roles.

Some of the major contexts that we need to consider in our analysis of child psychology include the relationships with peers and adults have an effect on how children think, learn and develop. Families, schools and peer groups all make up an important part of the social context. The culture a child lives in contributes a set of values, customs, shared assumptions and ways of living that influence development throughout the lifespan. Culture may play a role in how children relate to their parents, the type of education they receive and the type of child care that is provided. Social class can also play a major role in child development. Socioeconomic status (often abbreviated as SES), is based upon a number of different factors including how much education people have, how much money they earn, the job they hold and where they live. Children raised in households with a high socioeconomic status tend to have greater access to opportunities, while those from households with lower socioeconomic status may have less access to such things as health care, quality nutrition and education. Such factors can have a major impact on child psychology. Remember, all three of these contexts are constantly interacting. While a child may have fewer opportunities due to a low socioeconomic status, enriching social relationships and strong cultural ties may help correct this imbalance. Child psychology encompasses a wide range of topics, from the genetic influences on behaviour to the social pressures on development.

This book provides deep insight to various dimensions of issues relating to development of this subject.

—Dr. Asha Rani & Dr. Punam Singh

1

Introduction

Every child enters a competitive world in which he or she will be compared with other children. Social acceptance will depend on the child's ability to form and maintain alliances with other children and key adults such as teachers, coaches, and counsellors. One of the tasks for parents is to help their children navigate through a maze of obstacles and threats. A good parent teaches survival skills and provides reassurance that the taunts and threats of teasers and bullies are not as serious as they sometimes seem. At the same time, the good parent is alert to the possibility of real danger and intervenes strategically whenever threats do become serious.

Child psychology is an eclectic assembly of ideas, miscellaneous observation, opinions, fears and irrational beliefs. If psychologists, physicians, and educators are confused, what about parents? The best parents are pragmatic and not theorists. They stay involved with their children, follow some basic guidelines they learned and tend to do whatever works. Good parents improvise childcare with a combination of innate generosity, common sense, love and concessions to the demands of modern life.

Child psychology is one of the many branches of psychology and one of the most frequently studied speciality areas. This particular branch focuses on the mind and behaviour of children from prenatal development through adolescence. Child psychology deals not only with how children grow physically, but with their mental, emotional and social development as well.

Historically, children were often viewed simply as smaller versions of adults. When Jean Piaget suggested that children actually *think differently* than adults, Albert Einstein proclaimed that the discovery was "so simple that only a genius could have thought of it."

Today, psychologists recognize that child psychology is unique and complex, but many differ in terms of the unique perspective they take when approaching development. Experts also differ in their responses to some of the bigger questions in child psychology, such as whether early experiences matter more than later ones or whether nature or nurture plays a greater role in certain aspects of development.

The Different Contexts of Child Psychology

When you think of development, what comes to mind? If you are like most people, you probably think about the internal factors that influence how a child grows, such as genetics and personal characteristics. However, development involves much more than the influences that arise from within an individual. Environmental factors such as social relationships and the culture in which we live also play essential roles.

Some of the major contexts that we need to consider in our analysis of child psychology include:

- The Social Context: Relationships with peers and adults have an effect on how children think, learn and develop. Families, schools and peer groups all make up an important part of the social context.
- The Cultural Context: The culture a child lives in contributes a set of values, customs, shared assumptions and ways of living that influence development throughout the lifespan. Culture may play a role in how children relate to their parents, the type of education they receive and the type of child care that is provided.
- The Socioeconomic Context: Social class can also play a major role in child development. Socioeconomic status (often abbreviated as SES), is based upon a number of different factors including how much education people have, how much money they earn, the job they hold and

where they live. Children raised in households with a high socioeconomic status tend to have greater access to opportunities, while those from households with lower socioeconomic status may have less access to such things as health care, quality nutrition and education. Such factors can have a major impact on child psychology.

Remember, all three of these contexts are constantly interacting. While a child may have fewer opportunities due to a low socioeconomic status, enriching social relationships and strong cultural ties may help correct this imbalance.

Topics Within Child Psychology

Child psychology encompasses a wide range of topics, from the genetic influences on behaviour to the social pressures on development. The following are just some of the major subjects that are essential to the study of child psychology:

- Genetics
- Prenatal Development
- Social Growth
- Personality Development
- Language
- Gender Roles
- Cognitive Development
- Sexual Development.

Methods of Study

Psychologists use a variety of methods to test out a theory or hypothesis. The starting point of any scientific study is a question or questions. Questions lead to the formation of a theory. Question child psychologists might ask are: Why did the child demonstrate the particular behaviour at the specific time he or she did? How did the child come to produce such a behaviour at such times? And what is the functional significance or survival value of the produced behaviour?

These questions focus on features of learning and development, motivation and evolutionary adaptation. Answers might bring up suggestions or theories about the way children were brought up by their parents, the influence of their peers and others in their life and/or their lifestyle. A theory can then produce a hypothesis and once a hypothesis is formed, the psychologist will design a study (or method) to test it out.

The main methods psychologists use are:

- Experiments-these are the most controlled form of psychological study, used to try to prove that one thing causes another. Experiments test a specific hypothesis in controlled conditions that enable psychologists to focus on exactly the things they are investigating. The disadvantages of experiments is that they can be in some instances artificial and when people are involved, the experimenter may unintentionally insinuate the purpose of the experiment in which they are taking part.
- Observation-In an observation the psychologists does just that: observes what is going on, asks questions about what has been observed and reaches a conclusion based on these observations. Although less artificial than an experiment the disadvantages of observations are that there is no control over what is happening and not all observations may be accurate.
- Surveys-Surveys include interviews that are conducted personally, questionnaires that can be distributed more widely, opinion polls and market research. Surveys can cover a wide range of subjects and obtain a lot of information but they are unlikely to get an in-depth response. Questions may be interpreted in several different ways.
- Tests-Psychological or psychometric tests consist of a series of questions that the person who is being tested answers. These answers will then be analysed carefully to reveal information about the interviewee. Intelligence tests are an example. Tests are useful in sorting out the differences between children in a particular setting but could be biased against particular individuals or groups.
- Case studies-Case studies will focus exclusively on an individual case. This will make for a detailed observation recording the child's behaviour and reactions. Case

studies can last for a day or over a period of years (longtitudinal studies). A lot of information can be obtained from Case Studies but it isn't easy to generalise from one individual to a representative group. Another disadvantage is that the researcher might get over involved.

Research Methods in Psychology Study

A common method for studying development in infants and children is longitudinal studies in which a specific group of children is studied over a period of years. Cross-sectional methods are also a popular way of studying child development; this involves studying different groups of children who for instance share the same age but who may come from a different educational or ethnic background; any differences between groups might be attributed to the child's lifestyle rather than age. Or as another example, in order to compare different ages, different sample groups will be studied in specific situations and differences can be attributed to age differences rather than any other variable. Before designing a study, the advantages and disadvantages of the various methods should be taken into account and a method fitting of testing a particular hypothesis should be chosen.

Basic Instincts Temperaments and Instinct among Children

Instinct is the inherent inclination of a living organism toward a particular behaviour. The fixed action patterns are unlearned and inherited. The stimuli can be variable due to imprinting in a sensitive period or also genetically fixed. Examples of instinctual fixed action patterns can be observed in the behaviour of animals, which perform various activities (sometimes complex) that are not based upon prior experience, such as reproduction, and feeding among insects. Sea turtles, hatched on a beach, automatically move toward the ocean, and honeybees communicate by dance the direction of a food source, all without formal instruction. Other examples include animal fighting, animal courtship behaviour, internal escape functions, and building of nests. Another term for the same concept is innate behaviour.

Instinctual actions-in contrast to actions based on learning which are served by memory and which provide individually stored successful reactions built upon experience-have no learning curve, they are hard-wired and ready to use without learning. Some instinctual behaviours depend on maturational processes to appear.

Biological predispositions are innate biologically vectored behaviours that can be easily learned. For example in one hour, a baby colt can learn to stand, walk, glide, skip, hop and run. A biological predisposition may also mean that a person, because of his/her genetic makeup, is more prone to certain conditions or disease. Learning is required to fine tune the neurological wiring reflex like behaviour. True reflexes can be distinguished from instincts by their seat in the nervous system; reflexes are controlled by spinal or other peripheral ganglia, but instincts are the province of the brain. In a situation when two instincts contradict each other, an animal may resort to a displacement activity.

Some sociobiologists and ethologists have attempted to comprehend human and animal social behaviour in terms of instincts. Psychoanalysts have stated that *instinct* refers to human motivational forces (such as sex and aggression), sometimes represented as *life instinct* and *death instinct*. This use of the term *motivational forces* has mainly been replaced by the term *instinctual drives*.

Instincts in humans can also be seen in what are called *instinctive reflexes*. Reflexes, such as the Babinski Reflex (fanning of the toes when the foot is stroked), are seen in babies and are indicative of stages of development. These reflexes can truly be considered instinctive because they are generally free of environmental influences or conditioning.

Additional human traits that have been looked at as instincts are: sleeping, disgust, face perception, language acquisitions, "fight or flight" and "subjugate or be subjugated". Some experiments in human and primate societies have also come to the conclusion that a sense of fairness could be considered instinctual, with humans and apes willing to harm their own interests in protesting unfair treatment of self or others. Many scientists consider that it is instinctual in children to put everything in their mouths, because this is how they tell their immune system about the environment and the surroundings, what the immune system should adapt to. Other sociologists argue that humans have no instincts, defining them as a "complex pattern of behaviour present in every specimen of a particular species, that is innate, and that cannot be overridden." Said sociologists argue that drives such as sex and hunger cannot be considered instincts, as they can be overridden. This definitory argument is present in many introductory sociology and biology textbooks, but is still hotly debated.

Psychologist Abraham Maslow argued that humans no longer have *instincts* because we have the ability to override them in certain situations. He felt that what is called instinct is often imprecisely defined, and really amounts to strong *drives*. For Maslow, an instinct is something which cannot be overridden, and therefore while it may have applied to humans in the past it no longer does.

In the book An Instinct for Dragons anthropologist David E. Jones suggests a hypothesis that humans just like monkeys have inherited instinctive reactions to snakes, large cats and birds of prey. Folklore dragons have features that are combinations of these three, which would explain why dragons with similar features occur in stories from independent cultures on all continents. Other authors have suggested that especially under the influence of drugs or in dreams, this instinct may give raise to fantasies about dragons, snakes, spiders, which makes these symbols popular in drug culture. The traditional mainstream explanation to the folklore dragons does however not rely on human instinct, but on the assumption that fossil remains of dinosaurus gave raise to similar speculations all over the world.

Newborns also exhibit many reflex responses to external stimulation and these patterns and reflexes help the baby to manage their energy resources as well as their responses to what is around them.

Just after birth, there is often a short spell where the baby is attentive, looking at and responding to people. Sleep patterns of a newborn vary. Research has identified six different states of infant awareness:

- Quiet or deep sleep: Baby will have eyes closed with no eye movements and no activity apart from occasional jerky movements; regular breathing.
- Active or light sleep: Baby's eyes are closed but rapid eye movements can be observed; breathing may be irregular, activity level is low.
- Drowsiness: Baby's eyes may open and close but appea dull when open; there is delayed response to stimulation and activity level varies.
- Alert inactivity: Baby's eyes are open and bright; his/her attention will focus on outside stimuli such as a ceiling light or something bright.
- Alert activity: Baby's eyes are open; activity level is high. Baby will react to stimulation and show increased startles and motor activity.
- Crying: Intense crying that is hard to stop; high levels of motor activity.

A newborn will exhibit several reflexive responses. Some will last for life. The presence or absence of reflexes and their developmental course will give information about the baby's neural responses. For instance when the doctor runs a thumb along the left side of baby's spinal column, the baby should reflexively bent to the left. If this reflex occurs on one side but not the other it is possible the nerves are damaged on the side that shows no reflexive reaction.

Other reflexes a newborn will show include:

- Rooting Reflex: Stroke a newborn's cheek next to the side of his mouth and baby will turn his head to that side and search with his mouth.
- Moro Reflex: Baby will thrust arms outward, open hands, arch back and stretch legs outward before clenching fists across chest in reaction to a sudden sound or the loss of head support.
- Palmar or hand grasp: Baby will grasp a finger or rod with his finger.
- Stepping Reflex: Support baby in upright position with bare feet on flat surface and baby will make rhythmic stepping movements. This reflex disappears in two to three months.

- Swimming Reflex: Hold baby horizontally on stomach in water and baby will alternate arm and leg movements, exhaling through mouth. This reflex disappears at six months.
- Plantar or toe grasp: Press finger against ball of baby's foot and he will curl all toes under. This reflex disappears between eight and twelve months.

Although reflexes are usually automatic, it has been found that environmental factors do affect their appearance for instance a satiated baby may not show a rooting response.

Development in Baby's First Month-oilstones in Infant's Development

All babies will develop differently however research helps give a general indication of the different stages of development in infants and approximately when these stages might be seen.

As well as the different stages of development, research also helps suggest when these stages might be seen.

Just after birth baby's birth weight will drop and this is regained when baby is approximately ten days old.

Newborns will sleep and eat whenever they need it. Some babies sleep as much as twenty hours a day, waking randomly, others might need less sleep and may spend time crying instead.

During the first month the baby will begin to recognise mother's voice and smell.

Sight and Hearing during the First Few Months of Life

A newborn will turn his head from side to side when lying on his stomach; he will exhibit poor head control when lifted and display alternating movements of his legs when on stomach as if trying to crawl. At this stage too, baby will automatically grasp and hold onto a finger.

Familiar sounds may elicit some response in baby for instance he might respond to music or a TV program his mother watched regularly while he was in her womb. He will be comforted by familiar voices and should be left to sleep with a background of general household sounds. Baby will turn head towards voices, from birth.

Baby can see from birth but a newborn has difficulty focusing beyond nine inches (22 cm). Adults should make regular eye contact with baby. Over the first few weeks baby's sight will sharpen until at about six to eight months, he will see the world almost as well as an adult does.

Baby's hearing is fully mature at the end of the first month. By two months baby will be able to focus both eyes and track a moving object. (Some do this earlier). Also at two months baby will see colour differences more clearly.

How Adults can Help Baby's Development

Studies have shown babies prefer human faces to patterns; keep your face close to the newborn so he or she can study your features. When baby is one month old, almost anything passed in front of his face will transfix him. Hold shiny, colourful objects in front of baby and move them up and down. This should attract his attention and encourage his interest in colours. Hang eye-catching mobiles where baby can see them.

Always be sure to support baby's neck when he is being lifted. Talk to baby continuously while he is awake during the first weeks and months. He will love the different tones in voices. During his first month baby may also try to mimic the faces you make and lip movements. Vocal interactions are crucial in the development of baby so even if you feel silly talking to him in public, just do it.

2

Child Development

Child development refers to the biological and psychological changes that occur in human beings between birth and the end of adolescence, as the individual progresses from dependency to increasing autonomy. Because these developmental changes may be strongly influenced by genetic factors and events during prenatal life, genetics and prenatal development are usually included as part of the study of child development. Related terms include developmental psychology, referring to development throughout the lifespan, and pediatrics, the branch of medicine relating to the care of children. Developmental change may occur as a result of genetically-controlled processes known as maturation, or as a result of environmental factors and learning, but most commonly involves an interaction between the two.

There are various definitions of periods in a child's development, since each period is a continuum with individual differences regarding start and ending.

Some age-related development periods and examples of defined intervals are: newborn (ages 0–1 month); infant (ages 1 month – 1 year); toddler (ages 1–3 years); preschooler (ages 4–6years); school-aged child (ages 6–13 years); adolescent (ages 13–20). However, organizations like Zero to Three and the World Association for Infant Mental Health use the term infant as a broad category, including children from birth to age 3, a logical decision considering that the Latin derivation of the word infant refers to those who have no speech. The optimal development of children is considered vital to society and so it is important to understand the social, cognitive, emotional, and educational development of children. Increased research and interest in this field has resulted in new theories and strategies, with specific regard to practice that promotes development within the school system. In addition there are also some theories that seek to describe a sequence of states that compose child development

Prenatal Development

Prenatal or antenatal development is the process in which an embryo or fetus (or *foetus*) gestates during pregnancy, from fertilization until birth. Often, the terms fetal development, foetal development, or embryology are used in a similar sense.

After fertilization the embryogenesis starts. In humans, when embryogenesis finishes, by the end of the 10th week of gestational age, the precursors of all the major organs of the body have been created. Therefore, the following period, the fetal period, is described both topically on one hand, i.e. by organ, and strictly chronologically on the other, by a list of major occurrences by weeks of gestational age.

- The perinatal period (from Greek *peri*, "about, around" and Latin *nasci* "to be born") is "around the time of birth", specifically from 22 completed weeks (154 days) of gestation (the time when birth weight is normally 500 g) to 7 completed days after birth.
- The antepartum period (from Latin *ante* "before" and *parere* "to give birth") is literally equivalent to prenatal (from Latin *pre*-"before" and *nasci* "to be born"). Practically, however, *antepartum* usually refers to the period between the 24th/26th week of gestational age until birth, for example in antepartum hemorrhage.

Fertilization

When semen is deposited in the vagina, the spermatozoa travel through the cervix and body of the uterus and into the Fallopian tubes. Fertilization of the ovum (egg cell) usually takes place in the Fallopian tube. Many sperm must cooperate to penetrate the thick protective shell-like barrier that surrounds the ovum. The first sperm that penetrates fully into the egg donates its genetic material (DNA). The egg then polarizes, repelling any additional sperm. The resulting combination is called a zygote. The term "conception" refers variably to either fertilization or to formation of the conceptus after uterine implantation, and this terminology is controversial.

Prior to fertilization, each ovum contains a complete human genome, including a single X but no Y chromosome. Likewise, each spermatozoon contains a complete set of autosomes and a single sex chromosome, either X or Y. The resulting zygote is similar to the majority of somatic cells because it contains two copies of the genome in a diploid set of chromosomes. One set of chromosomes came from the nucleus of the ovum and the second set from the nucleus of the sperm. If the spermatozoon contributes a Y chromosome then the zygote will develop as a male. Unlike the X chromosome, the Y chromosome contains very little genetic information. However it does contain a gene, SRY, which will switch on androgen production at a later stage, leading to the development of a male body type. In contrast, the mitochondrial genetic information of the zygote comes entirely from the mother via the ovum.

Embryonic Period

The embryonic period in humans begins at fertilization (12-24hrs after ovulation, generally between the 2nd and 3rd week of gestational age) and continues until the end of the 10th week of gestation (8th week by embryonic age).

The zygote spends the next few days travelling down the Fallopian tube. Meanwhile it divides several times to form a ball of cells called a morula. Further cellular division is accompanied by the formation of a small cavity between the cells. This stage is called a blastocyst. Up to this point there is no growth in the overall size of the embryo, so each division produces successively smaller cells.

The blastocyst reaches the uterus at roughly the fifth day after fertilization. It is here that lysis of the zona pellucida, a glycoprotein shell, occurs. This is required so that the trophectoderm cells, which give rise to extra-embryonic structures such as the placenta, of the blastocyst can come into contact with the luminal epithelial cells of the endometrium. (Contrast this with zona hatching, an event that occurs *in vitro* by a different mechanism, but with a similar result). It then adheres to the uterine lining and becomes embedded in the endometrial cell layer. This process is also called implantation. In most successful pregnancies, the conceptus implants 8 to 10 days after ovulation. The inner cell mass forms the embryo, while the outer cell layers form the membranes and placenta. Together, the embryo and its membranes are referred to as a conceptus, or the "products of conception".

Rapid growth occurs and the embryo's main external features begin to take form. This process is called differentiation, which produces the varied cell types (such as blood cells, kidney cells, and nerve cells). A spontaneous abortion, or miscarriage, in the first trimester of pregnancy is usually due to major genetic mistakes or abnormalities in the developing embryo. During this critical period (most of the first trimester), the developing embryo is also susceptible to toxic exposures, such as:

- Alcohol, certain drugs, and other toxins that cause birth defects, such as Fetal alcohol syndrome
- Infection (such as rubella or cytomegalovirus)
- Radiation from x-rays or radiation therapy
- Nutritional deficiencies such as lack of folate which contributes to spina bifida.

Generally, if a structure pre-dates another structure in evolutionary terms, then it often appears earlier than the other in an embryo; this general observation is sometimes summarized by the phrase "ontogeny recapitulates phylogeny." For example, the backbone is a common structure among all vertebrates such as fish, reptiles and mammals, and the backbone also appears as one of the earliest structures laid out in all vertebrate embryos. The cerebrum in humans, which is the most sophisticated part of the brain, develops last. The concept of recapitulation is not absolute, but it is recognized as being partly applicable to development of the human embryo.

Gestational Age vs. Embryonic Age

Gestational age is the time that has passed since the onset of the last menstruation, which generally or as standard occurs 2 weeks before the actual fertilization. *Embryonic age*, in contrast measures the actual age of the embryo or fetus from the time of fertilization. Nevertheless, menstruation has historically been the only means of estimating embryonal/fetal age, and is still the presumed measure if not else specified. However, the actual duration between last menstruation and fertilization may in fact differ from the standard 2 weeks by several days. Thus, the first week of embryonic age is already week three counting with gestational age.

Furthermore, the number of the week is one more than the actual age of the embryo/fetus. For example, the embryo is 0 whole weeks old during the 1st week after fertilization.

The following table summarizes the various expression systems during week number x of gestation.

	Weeknumber	**Reached age (whole weeks)**
Gestational	x	x-1
Embryonic	x-2	x-3

Week 1-2

Gestational age: 0 to 1 (whole) weeks old. 1–14 days from last menstruation.

Embryonic age: -2 to -1 weeks old. That is, week 1-2 of gestational age are merely theoretical extrapolations of embryonic age, since the fertilization hasn't actually occurred yet.

Week 3

Gestational age: 2 (whole) weeks old. 15–21 days from last menstruation.

Embryonic age: Week nr 1. 0 (whole) weeks old. 1–7 days from fertilization.

- Fertilization of the ovum to form a zygote. (day 1 of fert.)
- The zygote undergoes mitotic cellular divisions, but does not increase in size. This mitosis is also known as cleavage. A hollow cavity forms marking the blastocyst stage. (day 1.5-3 of fert.)
- The blastocyst contains only a thin rim of trophoblast cells and a clump of cells at one end known as the "embryonic pole" which include embryonic stem cells.

- The embryo hatches from its protein shell (zona pellucida) and performs implantation onto the endometrial lining of the mother's uterus. (day 5-6 of fert.)
- If separation into identical twins occurs, 1/3 of the time it will happen before day 5.

Week 4

Gestational age: 3 weeks old. 22–28 days from last menstruation.

Embryonic age: Week nr 2. 1 week old. 8–14 days from fertilization.

- Trophoblast cells surrounding the embryonic cells proliferate and invade deeper into the uterine lining. They will eventually form the placenta and embryonic membranes. The blastocyst is fully implanted day 7-12 of fert.
- Formation of the yolk sac.
- The embryonic cells flatten into a disk, two cells thick.
- If separation into identical twins occurs, 2/3 of the time it will happen between days 5 and 9. If it happens after day 9, there is a significant risk of the twins being conjoined.
- Primitive streak develops. (day 13 of fert.)
- Primary stem villi appear. (day 13 of fert.)

Week 5

Gestational age: 4 weeks old. 29–35 days from last menstruation.

Embryonic age: Week nr 3. 2 weeks old. 15–21 days from fertilization.

- A notochord forms in the centre of the embryonic disk. (day 16 of fert.)
- Gastrulation commences. (day 16 of fert.)
- A neural groove (future spinal cord) forms over the notochord with a brain bulge at one end. Neuromeres appear. (day 18 of fert.)
- Somites, the divisions of the future vertebra, form. (day 20 of fert.)

- Primitive heart tube is forming. Vasculature begins to develop in embryonic disc. (day 20 of fert.)

Week 6

Gestational age: 5 weeks old. 36–42 days from last menstruation.

Embryonic age: Week nr 4. 3 weeks old. 22–28 days from fertilization.

- The embryo measures 4 mm (1/8 inch) in length and begins to curve into a C shape.
- The heart bulges, further develops, and begins to beat in a regular rhythm. Septum primum appear.
- Branchial arches, grooves which will form structures of the face and neck, form.
- The neural tube closes.
- The ears begin to form as otic pits.
- Arm buds and a tail are visible.
- Pulmonary primordium, the first traits of the lung appear.
- Hepatic plate, the first traits of the liver appear.
- Buccopharyngeal membrane ruptures. This is the future mouth.
- Cystic diverticulum, which will become the gallbladder, and dorsal pancreatic bud, which will become the pancreas appear.
- Urorectal septum begins to form. Thus, the rectal and urinary passageways become separated.
- Anterior and posterior horns differentiate in the spinal cord
- Spleen appears.
- Ureteric buds appear.

Week 7

Gestational age: 6 weeks old. 43–49 days from last menstruation.

Embryonic age: Week nr 5. 4 weeks old. 29–35 days from fertilization.

- The embryo measures 8 mm (1/4 inch) in length.
- Lens pits and optic cups form the start of the developing eye.
- Nasal pits form.
- The brain divides into 5 vesicles, including the early telencephalon.
- Leg buds form and hands form as flat paddles on the arms.
- Rudimentary blood moves through primitive vessels connecting to the yolk sac and chorionic membranes.
- The metanephros, precursor of the definitive kidney, starts to develop.

Week 8

Gestational age: 7 weeks old. 50–56 days from last menstruation.

Embryonic age: Week nr 6. 5 weeks old. 36–42 days from fertilization.

- The embryo measures 13 mm (1/2 inch) in length.
- Lungs begin to form.
- The brain continues to develop.
- Arms and legs have lengthened with foot and hand areas distinguishable.
- The hands and feet have digits, but may still be webbed.
- The gonadal ridge begins to be perceptible.
- The lymphatic system begins to develop.
- Main development of external genitalia starts.

Week 9

Gestational age: 8 weeks old. 57–63 days from last menstruation.

Embryonic age: Week nr 7. 6 weeks old. 43–49 days from fertilization.

- The embryo measures 18 mm (3/4 inch) in length.
- Fetal heart tone (the sound of the heart beat) can be heard using doppler.
- Nipples and hair follicles begin to form.

- Location of the elbows and toes are visible.
- Spontaneous limb movements may be detected by ultrasound.
- All essential organs have at least begun
- The vitelline duct normally closes.

Fetal Period

The fetal period begins at the end of the 10th week of gestation (8th week of development). Since the precursors of all the major organs are created by this time, the fetal period is described both by organ and by a list of changes by weeks of gestational age.

Because the precursors of the organs are formed, fetus also is not as sensitive to damage from environmental exposures as the embryo. Instead, toxic exposures often cause physiological abnormalities or minor congenital malformation.

Changes by Organ

Each organ has its own development.

- Development of circulatory system
  - o Heart development
- Development of digestive system
  - o Tooth development
- Development of endocrine system
- Development of integumentary system
- Development of lymphatic system
- Development of muscular system
- Development of nervous system
- Development of the urinary and reproductive system
  - o Development of the reproductive system
    - * Development of the gonads
- Development of respiratory system.

Changes by Weeks of Gestation

From the 8th week until birth (around 38 weeks), the developing organism is called a fetus. The fetus is not as sensitive to damage from environmental exposures as the embryo, and toxic exposures often cause physiological abnormalities or minor congenital malformation. All major structures are already formed in the fetus, but they continue to grow and develop.

Weeks 10-12

Gestational age: 9–11 weeks old.

Embryonic age: Weeks nr 8-10. 7–9 weeks old.

- Embryo measures 30 mm-8 cm (1.2-3.2 inches) in length.
- Ventral and dorsal pancreatic buds fuse during the 8th week
- Intestines rotate.
- Facial features continue to develop.
- The eyelids are more developed.
- The external features of the ear begin to take their final shape.
- The head comprises nearly half of the fetus' size.
- The face is well formed
- The eyelids close and will not reopen until about the 28th week.
- Tooth buds, which will form the baby teeth, appear.
- The limbs are long and thin.
- The fetus can make a fist with its fingers.
- Genitals appear well differentiated.
- Red blood cells are produced in the liver.

Weeks 13 to 16

Gestational age: 12–15 weeks old.

Embryonic age: Weeks nr 11-14. 10–13 weeks old.

- The fetus reaches a length of about 15 cm (6 inches).
- A fine hair called lanugo develops on the head.
- Fetal skin is almost transparent.
- More muscle tissue and bones have developed, and the bones become harder.
- The fetus makes active movements.
- Sucking motions are made with the mouth.

- Meconium is made in the intestinal tract.
- The liver and pancreas produce fluid secretions.
- From week 13, sex prediction by obstetric ultrasonography is almost 100% accurate.
- At week 15, main development of external genitalia is finished.

Week 19

Gestational age: 18 weeks old.

Embryonic age: Week nr 17. 16 weeks old.

- The fetus reaches a length of 20 cm (8 inches).
- Lanugo covers the entire body.
- Eyebrows and eyelashes appear.
- Nails appear on fingers and toes.
- The fetus is more active with increased muscle development.
- "Quickening" usually occurs (the mother and others can feel the fetus moving).
- The fetal heartbeat can be heard with a stethoscope.

Week 23

Gestational age: 22 weeks old.

Embryonic age: Week nr 21. 20 weeks old.

- The fetus reaches a length of 28 cm (11.2 inches).
- The fetus weighs about 725 g (1 lb 10 oz).
- Eyebrows and eyelashes are well formed.
- All of the eye components are developed.
- The fetus has a hand and startle reflex.
- Footprints and fingerprints continue forming.
- Alveoli (air sacs) are forming in lungs.

Week 27

Gestational age: 26 weeks old.

Embryonic age: Week nr 25. 24 weeks old.

- The fetus reaches a length of 38 cm (15 inches).
- The fetus weighs about 1.2 kg (2 lb 11 oz).

- The brain develops rapidly.
- The nervous system develops enough to control some body functions.
- The eyelids open and close.
- The cochleae are now developed, though the myelin sheaths in neural portion of the auditory system will continue to develop until 18 months after birth.
- The respiratory system, while immature, has developed to the point where gas exchange is possible.

Week 31

Gestational age: 30 weeks old.

Embryonic age: Week nr 29. 28 weeks old.

- The fetus reaches a length of about 38–43 cm (15-17 inches).
- The fetus weighs about 2 kg (3 lb 0 oz).
- The amount of body fat rapidly increases.
- Rhythmic breathing movements occur, but lungs are not fully mature.
- Thalamic brain connections, which mediate sensory input, form.
- Bones are fully developed, but are still soft and pliable.
- The fetus begins storing iron, calcium, and phosphorus.

Week 35

Gestational age: 34 weeks old.

Embryonic age: Week nr 33. 32 weeks old.

- The fetus reaches a length of about 40–48 cm (16-19 inches).
- The fetus weighs about 2.5 to 3 kg (5 lb 12 oz to 6 lb 12 oz).
- Lanugo begins to disappear.
- Body fat increases.
- Fingernails reach the end of the fingertips.
- A baby born at 36 weeks has a high chance of survival, but may require medical interventions.

Weeks 36 to 39

Gestational age: 35–38 weeks old.

Embryonic age: Weeks nr 34-37. 33–36 weeks old.

- The fetus is considered full-term at the end of the 37th week of gestational age.
- It may be 48 to 53 cm (19 to 21 inches) in length.
- The lanugo is gone except on the upper arms and shoulders.
- Fingernails extend beyond fingertips.
- Small breast buds are present on both sexes.
- Head hair is now coarse and thickest.

The development is continued postnatally with adaptation to extrauterine life and child development stages.

Infant

An infant or baby is the very young offspring of humans. A newborn is an infant who is within hours, days, or up to a few weeks from birth. In medical contexts, newborn or neonate (from Latin, *neonatus*, newborn) refers to an infant in the first 28 days of life (from birth up to 4 weeks after birth, less than a month old). The term "newborn" includes premature infants, postmature infants and full term newborns. The term infant is derived from the Latin word *infans*, meaning "unable to speak" or "speechless." It is typically applied to children between the ages of 1 month and 12 months; however, definitions vary between birth and 3 years of age. "Infant" is also a legal term referring to any child under the age of legal adulthood.

Physical Characteristics

A newborn's shoulders and hips are narrow, the abdomen protrudes slightly, and the arms and legs are relatively short. In the developed world, the average birth weight of a full-term newborn is approximately 7 ½ lbs. (3.2 kg), but is typically in the range of 5.5–10 pounds (2.7–4.6 kg). The average total body length is 14–20 inches (35.6–50.8 cm), although premature newborns may be much smaller. The Apgar score is a measure of a newborn's transition from the uterus during the first minutes of life.

A newborn's head is very large in proportion to the rest of the body, and the cranium is enormous relative to his or her face. While the adult human skull is about 1/8 of the total body length, the newborn's is about 1/4. At birth, many regions of the newborn's skull have not yet been converted to bone, leaving "soft spots" known as fontanels.

The two largest are the diamond-shaped anterior fontanel, located at the top front portion of the head, and the smaller triangular-shaped posterior fontanel, which lies at the back of the head. Later in the child's life, these bones will fuse together in a natural process. A protein called noggin is responsible for the delay in an infant's skull fusion.

During labour and birth, the infant's skull changes shape to fit through the birth canal, sometimes causing the child to be born with a misshapen or elongated head. It will usually return to normal on its own within a few days or weeks. Special exercises sometimes advised by physicians may assist the process.

Some newborns have a fine, downy body hair called lanugo. It may be particularly noticeable on the back, shoulders, forehead, ears and face of premature infants. Lanugo disappears within a few weeks. Infants may be born with full heads of hair; others, particularly white infants, may have very fine hair or may even be bald. Amongst fair-skinned parents, this fine hair may be blond, even if the parents are not. The scalp may also be temporarily bruised or swollen, especially in hairless newborns, and the area around the eyes may be puffy.

Newborns' digestive tracts, which of course have never been used prior to birth, are filled with a greenish-black, sticky material called meconium. This has the function of standing in for fecal material and allows the intestines to develop to the point where they can process milk immediately on birth. This material is passed by the child in the first few days.

Immediately after birth, a newborn's skin is often grayish to dusky blue in colour. As soon as the newborn begins to breathe, usually within a minute or two, the skin's colour returns to its normal tone. Newborns are wet, covered in streaks of blood, and coated with a white substance known as vernix caseosa, which is hypothesised to act as an antibacterial barrier.

The newborn may also have Mongolian spots, various other birthmarks, or peeling skin, particularly on the wrists, hands, ankles, and feet.

A newborn's genitals are enlarged and reddened, with male infants having an unusually large scrotum. The breasts may also be enlarged, even in male infants. This is caused by naturally occurring maternal hormones and is a temporary condition. Females (and even males) may actually discharge milk from their nipples (sometimes called witch's milk), and/ or a bloody or milky-like substance from the vagina. In either case, this is considered normal and will disappear in time.

The umbilical cord of a newborn is bluish-white in colour. After birth, the umbilical cord is normally cut, leaving a 1–2 inch stub. The umbilical stub will dry out, shrivel, darken, and spontaneously fall off within about 3 weeks. Occasionally, hospitals may apply triple dye to the umbilical stub to prevent infection, which may temporarily colour the stub and surrounding skin purple.

Internal Physiological Changes at Birth

Upon its entry to the air-breathing world, without the nutrition and oxygenation from the umbilical cord, the newborn must begin to adjust to life outside the uterus.

Newborns can feel all different sensations, but respond most enthusiastically to soft stroking, cuddling and caressing. Gentle rocking back and forth often calms a crying infant, as do massages and warm baths. Newborns may comfort themselves by sucking their thumb, or a pacifier. The need to suckle is instinctive and allows newborns to feed.

Newborn infants have unremarkable vision, being able to focus on objects only about 18 inches (45 cm) directly in front of their face. While this may not be much, it is all that is needed for the infant to look at the mother's eyes or areola when breastfeeding. Depth perception does not develop until the infant is mobile. Generally, a newborn cries when wanting to feed. When a newborn is not sleeping, or feeding, or crying, he or she may spend a lot of time staring at random objects. Usually anything that is shiny, has sharp contrasting colors, or has complex patterns will catch an infant's eye. However, the newborn has a preference for looking at other human faces above all else.

While still inside the mother, the infant could hear many internal noises, such as the mother's heartbeat, as well as many external noises including human voices, music and most other sounds. Therefore, although a newborn's ears may have some catarrh and fluid, he or she can hear sound from before birth. Newborns usually respond to a female voice over a male voice. This may explain why people will unknowingly raise the pitch of their voice when talking to newborns (this voice change is called motherese). The sound of other human voices, especially the mother's, can have a calming or soothing effect on the newborn. Conversely, loud or sudden noises will startle and scare a newborn. Newborns have been shown to prefer sounds that were a regular feature of their prenatal environment, for example, the theme tune of a television programme that their mother watched regularly.

Newborns can respond to different tastes, including sweet, sour, bitter, and salty substances, with a preference toward sweets. It has been shown that neonates show a preference for the smell of foods that their mother ate regularly.

Care and Feeding

Infants cry as a form of basic instinctive communication. A crying infant may be trying to express a variety of feelings including hunger, discomfort, overstimulation, boredom, wanting something, or loneliness.

Breastfeeding is the recommended method of feeding by all major infant health organizations. If breastfeeding is not possible or desired, bottle feeding is done with expressed breast-milk or with infant formula. Infants are born with a sucking reflex allowing them to extract the milk from the nipples of the breasts or the nipple of the baby bottle, as well as an instinctive behaviour known as *rooting* with which they seek out the nipple. Sometimes a wet nurse is hired to feed the infant, although this is rare, especially in developed countries.

As infants grow, food supplements are added. Many parents choose commercial, ready-made baby foods to supplement breast milk or formula for the child, while others adapt their usual meals for the dietary needs of their child. Whole cow's milk can be used at one year, but lower-fat milk should not be provided until the child is 2 to 3 years old. Until they are toilet-trained, infants in industrialized countries wear diapers. Children need more sleep than adults—up to 18 hours for newborn babies, with a declining rate as the child ages. Until babies learn to walk, they are carried in the arms, held in slings or baby carriers, or transported in baby carriages or strollers. Most industrialized countries have laws requiring child safety seats for infants in motor vehicles.

Infant Mortality

Infant mortality is the death of an infant in the first year of life. Major causes of infant mortality include dehydration, infection, congenital malformation and SIDS.

This epidemiological indicator is recognized as a very important measure of the level of health care in a country because it is directly linked with the health status of infants, children, and pregnant women as well as access to medical care, socioeconomic conditions, and public health practices.

Emotional Development

Attachment theory is primarily an evolutionary and ethological theory whereby the infant or child *seeks proximity* to a *specified attachment figure* in situations of alarm or distress for the purpose of survival. The forming of attachments is considered to be the foundation of the infant/child's capacity to form and conduct relationships throughout life. Attachment is not the same as love and/or affection although they often go together. Attachment and attachment behaviours tend to develop between the age of 6 months and 3 years. Infants become attached to adults who are sensitive and responsive in social interactions with the infant, and who remain as consistent caregivers for some time. Parental responses lead to the development of patterns of attachment which in turn lead to 'internal working models' which will guide the individual's feelings, thoughts, and expectations in later relationships. There are a number of attachment 'styles' namely 'secure', 'anxious-ambivalent', 'anxious-avoidant', (all 'organized') and 'disorganized', some of which are more problematic than others.

A lack of attachment or a seriously disrupted capacity for attachment could potentially amount to serious disorders.

Todler

A toddler is a young child of 1 to 3 years of age. During the toddler stage, the child learns a great deal about social roles, develops motor skills, and first starts to use language.

Toddler (1-3 Years Old)

Physiological Changes

- Abdominal breathing, respiratory rate slows
- Heart rate slows further 110-90 per minute
- Blood pressure increases 99/64 mmHg
- Brain develops to 90% of its adult size
- Middle ear infections still common
- Stomach secretions become more acidic
- Urinary and anal sphincter control becomes possible with complete myelination of the spinal cord
- In immune system, IgG and IgM Ab product becomes mature at 2 years of age.

Toddler Profile

- Gains weight only about 5 lbs. appetite decreases accordingly.

2 Years

- Doubles birth height
- Chest circumference greater than HC
- New teeth.

1/2-3 Years

- All 20 deciduous teeth are generally present
- Subcutaneous tissue or baby fat begins to disappear as child changes from a plump baby to a leaner, more muscular child.

Body Contour

- Tends to have prominent abdomen since his abdominal muscle are not yet strong to support abdominal contents.

- Has lordosis because he is a beginning walker. As he walks longer, this will correct itself naturally.

Developmental Milestones

Physical Development

18 Months

- Growth has decreased and appetite lessened- "physiologic anorexia"
- Anterior fontanel usually closed
- Circumference protrudes, larger than chest circumference.

2 Years

- Weight: about 11–13 kg
- Height: about 80–82 cm
- Teeth: 12 temporary.

2 1/2 Years

- Teeth: full set of 20 temporary
- Decreased need for naps.

Motor Development

14 Months

- Walks well alone with wide based gait
- Creeps upstairs
- Builds of two blocks
- Drinks from a cup, uses spoon
- Enjoys throwing objects picking them up.

18 Months

- Walks sideways and backwards, runs well, falls easily
- Climbs stairs or up on furnitures
- Scribbles vigorously, attempting a straight line
- Drinks well from a cup, still spills with a spoon.

2 Years

- Gross motor skills quite well refined, can walk up and

down stairs on both feet, one step at a time while holding on to a rail
- Builds tower of five cubes
- Control of spoon well-developed
- Toilet trained during day time.

Vocalization and Socialization

15 Months

- Can use 10-15 words
- Says "no" (see holophrasis)
- Indicates when diaper is wet.

18 Months

- Uses phrases composed of adjectives and nouns
- Begins to have temper tantrums
- Very ritualistic, has favourite toy or blanket, thumb-sucking may be at peak.

2 Years

- Vocabulary of about 350 words
- Obey simple commands
- Helps undress self and put on simple clothes
- Shows sign of increased autonomy and individuality
- Does not share possessions, everything "mine".

2 1/2 Years

·Begins to see self as separate individual; still sees other children as "objects".

Major Learning Events

Toilet Training

1. Psychologic readiness
2. Process training
3. Parental response.

Play (Parallel Play)

- Child plays alongside other children but not with them
- Mostly free and spontaneous, no rules or regulations

- Attention span very short and change of toys occur at frequent intervals
- Start Imitation and make-believe play begins by end of the second year.

Games: Throwing and Retrieving Objects

Suggested toys: Play furniture, dishes, cooking utensils, play telephone, puzzles with large pieces, pedal propelled toys, rocking horse, clay crayons, finger paints, pounding toys, blocks, push-pull toys, balls

Walking

To *toddle* is to walk unsteadily; the term *cruising* is sometimes used for toddlers who cannot toddle but must hold onto something while walking.

On average, a child begins walking between 9 and 14 months of age. The age at which children start to walk can generally be determined by their gender, physical attributes and family genes. Small, light children usually walk earlier than heavy, large children.

Language

Talking is the next milestone of which parents are typically aware. A toddler's first word most often occurs around 12 months, but again this is only an average. The child will then continue to steadily add to his or her vocabulary until around the age of 18 months when language increases rapidly. He or she may learn as many as 7-9 new words a day. Around this time, toddlers generally know about 50 words. At 21 months is when toddlers begin to incorporate two word phrases into their vocabulary, such as "I go", "mama give", and "baby play". Before going to sleep they often engage in a monologue called crib talk in which they practice conversational skills. At this age, children are becoming very proficient at conveying their wants and needs to their parents in a verbal fashion.

Emotions and Self

There are several other important milestones that are achieved in this time period that parents tend to not emphasize as much as walking and talking. Gaining the ability to point at whatever it is the child wants you to see shows huge psychological gains in a toddler. This generally happens before a child's first birthday.

This age is sometimes referred to as 'the terrible twos', because of the temper tantrums for which they are famous. This stage can begin as early as nine months old depending on the child and environment. Toddlers tend to have temper tantrums because they have such strong emotions but do not know how to express themselves the way that older children and adults do. They also throw tantrums to let others know that they are free and can do what they want. The toddler is discovering that they are a separate being from their parent and are testing their boundaries in learning the way the world around them works. Although the toddler is in their exploratory phase, it is also important to understand that the methods used by the parents for communicating with the toddler can either set off a tantrum or calm the situation. This time between the ages of two and five when they are reaching for independence repeats itself during adolescence.

Self-awareness is another milestone that helps parents understand how a toddler is reacting. Around 18 months of age, a child will begin to recognize himself or herself as a separate physical being with his/her own thoughts and actions. A parent can test if this milestone has been reached by noticing if the toddler recognizes that their reflection in a mirror is in fact themselves. One way to test this is to put lipstick on the child's forehead and show them their own reflection. Upon seeing the out-of-the-ordinary mark, if the child reaches to her own forehead, the child has achieved this important milestone. Along with self recognition comes feelings of embarrassment and pride that the child had not previously experienced.

Toilet Training

Although there is a growing movement of parents who choose to help their babies use the toilet from birth, most children in the United States are toilet trained while they are toddlers. In most Western countries, toilet training can begin as early as 9 months (as soon as the child starts to walk) for some, while others are not ready to begin toilet training until they are up to three years old. Two important indicators of toilet training readiness are whether a child understands the concept of using the toilet and whether they have any control over excreting waste (parents who use elimination communication do not have to wait for these readiness signs to help their babies use the potty). This can be a frustrating time for parents. Some toddlers can learn this task in a week, while some take up to eight or nine months.

Preschooler

Preschoolers are constantly on the move, exploring their world with exuberance, curiosity, and a seemingly endless source of energy. A child's capacity for learning in this stage is enormous. Preschool-age children learn and develop from every experience, relationship, and adventure they encounter. Having the space and opportunity to explore objects and play environments helps preschool children develop their imagination and master the motor, cognitive, language, and social skills that are essential for future development.

How well children will learn and develop and how well they will do in school depends on a number of things, including the children's health and physical well-being, their social and emotional preparation and their language skills and general knowledge of the world.

Good Health and Physical Well-Being

Seeing to it that your preschool child has nutritious food, enough exercise and regular medical care gives him* a good start in life and lessens the chances that he will have serious health problems or trouble learning later on.

Food

Preschoolers require a healthy diet. After your child is born, she requires nutritious food to keep her healthy. School-aged children can concentrate better in class if they eat balanced meals that include servings of breads and cereals; fruits and vegetables; meat, poultry and fish and meat alternatives (such as eggs and dried beans and peas); and milk, cheese and yogurt. You should see to it that your child does not eat too many fatty foods and sweets. Children aged 2–5 generally can eat the same foods as adults but in smaller portions. Your child's doctor or medical clinic adviser can provide you with advice on what to feed a baby or a toddler who under the age of 2.

Exercise

Preschoolers need opportunities to exercise. To learn to control and coordinate the large muscles in his arms and legs, your child needs to throw and catch balls, run, jump, climb and dance to music. To learn to control and coordinate the small muscles in his hands and fingers, he needs to colour with crayons, put together puzzles, use blunt-tipped— safety— scissors, zip his jacket and grasp small objects such as coins. If you suspect that your child has a disability, see a doctor as soon as possible. Early intervention can help your child to develop to his full potential.

Social and Emotional Preparation

Children start school with different degrees of social and emotional maturity. These qualities take time and practice to learn. Give your child opportunities at home to begin to develop the following positive qualities.

- Confidence: Children must feel good about themselves and believe they can succeed. Confident children are more willing to attempt new tasks—and try again if they don't succeed the first time.
- Independence: Children must learn to do things for themselves.
- Motivation: Children must want to learn.
- Curiosity: Children are naturally curious and must remain so to get the most out of learning opportunities.
- Persistence: Children must learn to finish what they start.
- Cooperation: Children must be able to get along with others and learn to share and take turns.
- Self-control: Children must learn that there are good and bad ways to express anger. They must understand that some behaviours, such as hitting and biting, are not acceptable.
- Empathy: Children must have an interest in others and understand how others feel.

Here are some things that you can do to help your child develop these qualities.

- Show your child that you care about him and that you are dependable. Children who feel loved are more likely to be confident. Your child must believe that, no matter what, someone will look out for him. Give your baby or toddler plenty of attention, encouragement, hugs and lap time.
- Set a good example. Children imitate what they see others do and what they hear others say. When you exercise and eat nourishing food, your child is more likely to do so as well. When you treat others with respect, your child probably will, too. If you share things with others, your child also will learn to be thoughtful of others' feelings.
- Provide opportunities for repetition. It takes practice for a child to crawl, pronounce new words or drink from a cup. Your child doesn't get bored when she repeats things. Instead, by repeating things until she learns them, your child builds the confidence she needs to try new things.
- Use appropriate discipline. All children need to have limits set for them. Children whose parents give them firm but loving discipline generally develop better social skills and do better in school than do children whose parents set too few or too many limits. Here are some ideas.
- Direct your child's activities, but don't be too bossy.
- Give reasons when you ask your child to do something. Say, for example, "Please move your truck from the stairs so no one falls over it"—not, "Move it because I said so."
- Listen to your child to find out how he feels and whether he needs special support.
- Show love and respect when you are angry with your child. Criticize your child's behaviour but not the child. Say, for example, "I love you, but it's not okay for you to draw pictures on the walls. I get angry when you do that."

- Help your child make choices and work out problems. You might ask your 4-year-old, for example, "What can we do to keep your brother from knocking over your blocks?"
- Be positive and encouraging. Praise your child for a job well done. Smiles and encouragement go much further to shape good behaviour than harsh punishment.
- Let your child do many things by herself. Young children need to be watched closely. However, they learn to be independent and to develop confidence by doing tasks such as dressing themselves and putting their toys away. It's important to let your child make choices, rather than deciding everything for her.
- Encourage your child to play with other children and to be with adults who are not family members. Preschoolers need social opportunities to learn to see the point of view of others. Young children are more likely to get along with teachers and classmates if they have had experiences with different adults and children.
- Show a positive attitude toward learning and toward school. Children come into this world with a powerful need to discover and to explore. If your child is to keep her curiosity, you need to encourage it. Showing enthusiasm for what your child does ("You've drawn a great picture!") helps to make her proud of her achievements.

Children also become excited about starting school when their parents show excitement about this big step. As your child gets ready to enter kindergarten, talk to him about school. Talk about the exciting things that he will do in kindergarten, such as making art projects, singing and playing games. Be enthusiastic as you describe all the important things that he will learn from his teacher—how to read, how to how to count and how to measure and weigh things.

Language and General Knowledge

Children can develop language skills only if they have many opportunities to talk, listen and use language to solve problems and learn about the world.

Long before your child enters school, you can do many things to help her develop language. You can:

- Give your child opportunities to play. Play is how children learn. It is the natural way for them to explore, to become creative, to learn to make up and tell stories and to develop social skills. Play also helps children learn to solve problems—for example, if her wagon tips over, a child must figure out how to get it upright again. When they stack up blocks, children learn about colors, numbers, geometry, shapes and balance. Playing with others helps children learn how to negotiate.
- Support and guide your child as she learns a new activity. Parents can help children learn how to do new things by "scaffolding," or guiding their efforts. For example, as you and your toddler put together a puzzle, you might point to a piece and say, "I think this is the piece we need for this space. Why don't you try it?" Then have the child pick up the piece and place it correctly. As the child becomes more aware of how the pieces fit into the puzzle, you can gradually withdraw your support.
- Talk to your child, beginning at birth. Your baby needs to hear your voice. Voices from a television or radio can't take the place of your voice, because they don't respond to your baby's coos and babbles.

Your child needs to know that when he makes a certain sound, for example, "mamamamamama," that his mother will respond—she will smile and talk back to him. The more you talk to your baby, the more he will learn and the more he will have to talk about as he gets older. Everyday activities provide opportunities to talk, sometimes in detail, about what's happening around him. As you give your child a bath, for example, you might say, "First let's stick the plug in the drain. Now let's turn on the water. Do you want your rubber duck? That's a good idea. Look, the duck is yellow, just like the rubber duck we saw on 'Sesame Street.'"

Listen to Your Child

Children have their own special thoughts and feelings, joys and sorrows, hopes and fears. As your child's language skills develop, encourage her to talk about her thoughts and feelings. Listening is the best way to learn what's on her mind and to discover what she knows and doesn't know and how she thinks and learns. It also shows your child that her feelings and thoughts are valuable.

Ask your child questions, particularly questions that require him to give more than a "yes" or "no" response. If, as you walk with your toddler in a park, he stops to pick up leaves, you might point out how the leaves are the same and how they are different. With an older child, you might ask, "What else grows on trees?"

Answer your child's questions. Asking questions is a good way for your child to learn to compare and to classify things—different kinds of dogs, different foods and so forth. Answer your child's questions thoughtfully and, whenever possible, encourage her to answer her own questions. If you don't know the answer to a question, say so. Together with your child, try to find the answer.

Read aloud to your child every day. Children of all ages love to be read to—even babies as young as six weeks. Although your child doesn't understand the story or poem that you read, reading together gives her a chance to learn about language and enjoy the sound of your voice. You don't have to be an excellent reader for your child to enjoy reading aloud together. Just by allowing her to connect reading with the warm experiences of being with you, you can create in her a lifelong love of reading.

Be aware of your child's television viewing. Good television programs can introduce children to new worlds and promote learning, but poor programs or too much TV watching can be harmful. It's up to you to decide how much TV and what kinds of shows your child should watch.

Be realistic about your child's abilities and interests. Set high standards and encourage your child to try new things. Children who aren't challenged become bored. But children who are pushed along too quickly or who are asked to do things that don't interest them can become frustrated and unhappy.

Provide opportunities for your child to do and see new things. The more varied the experiences that she has, the more she will learn about the world. No matter where you live, your community can provide new experiences. Go for walks in your neighbourhood or go places on the bus. Visit museums, libraries, zoos and other places of interest.

If you live in the city, spend a day in the country. If you live in the country, spend a day in the city. Let your child hear and make music, dance and paint. Let her participate in activities that help to develop her imaginations and let her express her ideas and feelings. The activities in the next section of this booklet can provide your children with these opportunities.

School-Aged Child

Five, six and seven-year-old children are often excited about going to school and their new responsibilities. Their parents are still the most important persons in their lives.

With school-age children, it is important to set limits and let children know what is expected of them. Do this with a soft voice. Be patient and kind. Provide clear and consistent discipline. Each child needs to feel special and cared about in your care. Children in this stage are very enjoyable. They like to be helpful, especially to adults.

Physical Development-Growth is slow but steady. They have gained control of their major muscles. Most children have a good sense of balance. They can stand on one foot and walk on a balance beam. They enjoy performing physical tricks. They enjoy testing muscle strength and skills. They like to skip, run, tumble, and dance to music. They can catch small balls. They can manage buttons and zippers. They can learn to tie their shoelaces. They can print their names. They can copy designs and shapes including numbers and letters. They use utensils and tools correctly with supervision.

Social and Emotional Development-They think of themselves more than others until about age seven or eight. They play well in groups but may need some time to play alone. Many children have a best friend and an enemy. They tend to prefer playmates of the same sex. Children often tell on each other. This is done for two reasons: to help them understand the rules and to get an adult's attention. They do not like criticism or failure. It is best to have each child compete against himself or herself not other children. They can be helpful with small chores. They have a strong need for love and attention from their parents. They are beginning to care about the feelings and needs of others. They may enjoy taking care of and playing with younger children. To them, "good" and "bad" are what parents and teachers approve or disapprove of. They are starting to develop a moral sense such as understanding honesty. They begin to develop a sense of humour and may enjoy nonsense rhymes, songs, and riddles. They become upset when their behaviour or school work is criticized or ignored.

Intellectual Development- They can tell left from right. Their ability to speak and express themselves develops rapidly. This is important for success in school. They talk to each other about themselves and their families. During play, they practice using the words and language they learn in school. They start to understand time and days of the week. They like silly rhymes, riddles, and jokes. Their attention span is longer. They can follow more involved stories. They are learning letters and words. By six, most can read words or combinations of words.

Older School-Age Children

Physical Development- They are very active with lots of energy. Their fine motor and large motor skills have become much better.

Social/Emotional Development- They have a strong need to feel accepted and worthwhile. They show their ability to be independent by being disobedient, using back-talk and being rebellious. They prefer individual achievements over competition. They like encouragement and suggestions over competition. They still look to adults for approval. They begin to take responsibility for their own actions. They like to join organized groups. They prefer to be with members of their own sex. They look up to and imitate older youth. They are beginning to build and understand friendship. They want to be accepted by the peer group.

Intellectual Development- They need opportunities to share thoughts and reactions. They see things as either "black or white." They have interests which change often. They are easily motivated and eager to try new things. They usually do best when the work is done in small pieces. They need guidance from adults to stay at a task to achieve their best.

Physical Development

School-age children typically have fairly smooth and strong motor skills. However, their coordination (especially eye-hand), endurance, balance, and physical tolerance vary.

Fine motor skills may also vary widely and influence a child's ability to write neatly, dress appropriately, and perform certain chores, such as making beds or doing dishes.

There will be significant differences in height, weight, and build among children of this age range. It is important to remember that genetic background, as well as nutrition and exercise, may influence a child's growth.

There can also be a big difference in the age at which children begin to develop secondary sexual characteristics. For girls, secondary sex characteristics include:

- Breast development
- Underarm and pubic hair growth.

For boys, they include:

- Growth of underarm, chest, and pubic hair
- Growth of testicles and penis.

Language Development

Early school-age children should be able to consistently use simple, but complete sentences that average five to seven words. As the child progresses through the elementary years, grammar and pronunciation become normal. Children use more complex sentences as they grow.

Language delays may be due to hearing or intelligence problems. In addition, children who are unable to express themselves well may be more likely to have aggressive behaviour or temper tantrums.

A 6-year-old child normally can follow a series of three commands in a row. By age 10, most children can follow five commands in a row. Children with a problem in this area may try to cover it up with backtalk or clowning around. They will rarely ask for help because they are afraid of being teased.

Behaviour

Frequent physical complaints (such as sore throats, tummy aches, arm or leg pain) may simply be due to a child's increased body awareness. Although there is often no physical evidence for such complaints, the complaints should be investigated to rule out possible health conditions, and to assure the child that the parent is concerned about his or her well-being.

Peer acceptance becomes increasingly important during the school-age years. Children may engage in certain behaviours to be part of "the group." Talking about these behaviours with your child will allow the child to feel accepted in the group, without crossing the boundaries of the family's behaviour standards.

Friendships at this age tend to be mainly with members of the same sex. In fact, younger school-age children typically talk about members of the opposite sex as being "strange" or "awful." Children become less negative about the opposite sex as they get closer to adolescence.

Lying, cheating, and stealing are all examples of behaviours that school-age children may "try on" as they learn how to negotiate the expectations and rules placed on them by family, friends, school, and society. Parents should deal with these behaviours privately (so that the child's friends don't tease them), apply a punishment that is related to the behaviour, and show forgiveness.

An ability to pay attention is important for success both at school and at home. A 6-year-old should be able to focus on an appropriate task for at least 15 minutes. By age 9, a child should be able to focus attention for about an hour.

It is important for the child to learn how to deal with failure or frustration without losing self-esteem or developing a sense of inferiority.

Safety

Safety is important for school-age children.

- School-age children are highly active and need strenuous physical activity, peer approval, and more daring and adventurous behaviours.

- Children should be taught to play sports in appropriate, safe, supervised areas, with proper equipment and rules. Bicycles, skateboards, in-line skates, and other types of recreational sports equipment should fit the child. They should be used only while following traffic and pedestrian rules, and while using safety equipment such as knee, elbow, wrist pads/braces, and helmets. Sports equipment should not be used in darkness or extreme weather conditions.
- Swimming and water safety lessons may help prevent drowning.
- Safety instruction regarding matches, lighters, barbecues, stoves, and open fires can prevent major burns.
- Wearing seat belts remains the most important way to prevent major injury or death from a motor vehicle accident.

Parenting Tips

- If your child's physical development appears to be outside the norm, talk to your health care provider.
- If language skills appear to be lagging, request a speech and language evaluation.
- Maintain close communication with teachers, other school personnel, and parents of friends to be aware of potential problems as they arise.
- Encourage children to express themselves openly and talk about concerns without fear of punishment.
- While encouraging children to participate in a variety of social and physical experiences, parents should be careful not to over-schedule a child's free time. Free play or simple, quiet time is important for the child not to feel constantly pushed to perform.
- Children today are exposed, through the media and their peers, to a vast array of issues dealing with violence, sexuality, and substance abusesubstance abuse. Discuss these issues openly with your children to share concerns or correct misconceptions. Setting limits may be necessary to ensure children will be

exposed to such issues only when they are developmentally ready.

- Encourage children to participate in constructive activities such as sports, clubs, arts, music, and scouts. Staying sedentary at this age increases the risk of lifetime obesity. However, it is important not to over-schedule your child. Try to find a balance between family time, school work, free play, and structured activities.
- School-age children should participate in family chores such as setting the table and cleaning up.

Adolescent

Adolescence (from Latin: *adolescere* meaning "to grow up") is a transitional stage of physical and mental human development generally occurring between puberty and legal adulthood (age of majority), but largely characterized as beginning and ending with the teenage stage. According to Erik Erikson's stages of human development, for example, a young adult is generally a person between the ages of 20 and 40, whereas an adolescent is a person between the ages of 13 and 19. Historically, puberty has been heavily associated with teenagers and the onset of adolescent development. However, the start of puberty has had somewhat of an increase in preadolescence (particularly females, as seen with early and precocious puberty), and adolescence has had an occasional extension beyond the teenage years (typically males) compared to previous generations. These changes have made it more difficult to rigidly define the time frame in which adolescence occurs.

The end of adolescence and the beginning of adulthood varies by country and by function, and furthermore even within a single nation-state or culture there can be different ages at which an individual is considered to be (chronologically and legally) mature enough to be entrusted by society with certain tasks. Such milestones include, but are not limited to, driving a vehicle, having legal sexual relations, serving in the armed forces or on a jury, purchasing and drinking alcohol, voting, entering into contracts, completing certain levels of education, and marrying.

Adolescence is usually accompanied by an increased independence allowed by the parents or legal guardians and less supervision, contrary to the preadolescence stage.

In many societies, adolescence was not recognized as a phase of life. Most societies simply distinguished between childhood and adulthood. Stanley Hall is generally credited with "discovering" adolescence with his 1904 study "Adolescence" in which he describes the developmental phase now recognized as adolescence. Hall attributed the new stage to social changes at the turn of the 20th century. Child labor laws kept individuals under 16 out of the work force, and universal education laws kept them in secondary school, thus prolonging the period of dependence — a dependence that allowed them to address psychological tasks they might have ignored when they took on adult roles straight out of childhood.

Puberty

Puberty is a period of several years in which rapid physical growth and psychological changes occur, culminating in sexual maturity. The average onset of puberty is at 10 for girls and age 12 for boys. Every person's individual timetable for puberty is influenced primarily by heredity, although environmental factors, such as diet and exercise, also exert some influence. These factors can also contribute to precocious puberty and delayed puberty.

Puberty begins with a surge in hormone production, which in turn causes a number of physical changes. It is also the stage of life in which a child develops secondary sex characteristics (for example, a deeper voice and larger adam's apple in boys, and development of breasts and more curved and prominent hips in girls) as his or her hormonal balance shifts strongly towards an adult state. This is triggered by the pituitary gland, which secretes a surge of hormonal agents into the blood stream, initiating a chain reaction. The male and female gonads are subsequently activated, which puts them into a state of rapid growth and development; the triggered gonads now commence the mass production of the necessary chemicals. The testes primarily release testosterone, and the ovaries predominantly dispense estrogen. The production of these hormones increases gradually until sexual maturation is met. Some boys may develop gynecomastia due to an imbalance of sex hormones, tissue responsiveness or obesity. Put simply, puberty is the time when a child's body starts changing into an adult's body.

Facial hair in males normally appears in a specific order during puberty: The first facial hair to appear tends to grow at the corners of the upper lip, typically between 14 to 16 years of age. It then spreads to form a moustache over the entire upper lip. This is followed by the appearance of hair on the upper part of the cheeks, and the area under the lower lip. The hair eventually spreads to the sides and lower border of the chin, and the rest of the lower face to form a full beard. As with most human biological processes, this specific order may vary among some individuals. Facial hair is often present in late adolescence, around ages 17 and 18, but may not appear until significantly later. Some men do not develop full facial hair for 10 years after puberty. Facial hair will continue to get coarser, darker and thicker for another 2–4 years after puberty.

The major landmark of puberty for males is the first ejaculation, which occurs, on average, at age 13. For females, it is menarche, the onset of menstruation, which occurs, on average, between ages 12 and 13. The age of menarche is influenced by heredity, but a girl's diet and lifestyle contribute as well. Regardless of genes, a girl must have certain proportion of body fat to attain menarche. Consequently, girls who have a high-fat diet and who are not physically active begin menstruating earlier, on average, than girls whose diet contains less fat and whose activities involve fat reducing exercise (e.g. ballet and gymnastics). Girls who experience malnutrition or are in societies in which children are expected to perform physical labor also begin menstruating at later ages.

The timing of puberty can have important psychological and social consequences. Early maturing boys are usually taller and stronger than their friends. They have the advantage in capturing the attention of potential partners and in becoming hand-picked for sports. Pubescent boys often tend to have a good body image, are more confident, secure, and more independent. Late maturing boys can be less confident because of poor body image when comparing themselves to already developed friends and peers. However, early puberty is not always positive for boys; early sexual maturation in boys can be accompanied by increased aggressiveness due to the surge of hormones that affect them. Because they appear older than their peers, pubescent boys may face increased social pressure to conform to adult norms; society may view them as more emotionally advanced, despite the fact that their cognitive and social development may lag behind their appearance. Studies have shown that early maturing boys are more likely to be sexually active and are more likely to participate in risky behaviours.

For girls, early maturation can sometimes lead to increased self-consciousness, though a typical aspect in maturing females. Because of their bodies developing in advance, pubescent girls can become more insecure. Consequently, girls that reach sexual maturation early are more likely than their peers to develop eating disorders. Nearly half of all American high school girls' diet is to lose weight. In addition, girls may have to deal with sexual advances from older boys before they are emotionally and mentally mature. In addition to having earlier sexual experiences and more unwanted pregnancies than late maturing girls, early maturing girls are more exposed to alcohol and drug abuse. Those who have had such experiences tend to perform less well in school than their "inexperienced" age peers.

Girls have usually reached full physical development by ages 15–17, while boys usually complete puberty by ages 16–18. Any increase in height beyond these ages is uncommon. Girls attain reproductive maturity about 4 years after the first physical changes of puberty appear. In contrast, boys accelerate more slowly but continue to grow for about 6 years after the first visible pubertal changes. Teenage and early adult males may continue to gain natural muscle growth even after puberty.

Psychology of Adolescent

Adolescence is characterized by a number of cognitive, emotional, physical and attitudinal changes, which can be a cause of conflict on one hand and positive personality development on the other.

The home environment and parents are still important for the behaviours and choices of adolescents. Adolescents who have a good relationship with their parents are less likely to engage in various risk behaviours, such as smoking, drinking, fighting, and/or sexual intercourse. In conflict with their parents, adolescents are more flexible than younger children, but more hostile and rigid compared to adults. The topics of conflicts between adolescents and their parents are often about the extent to which parents can control and supervise the adolescent, for instance conflicts about chores, schoolwork, curfew, and the adolescent's right to privacy.

For the first time in their lives adolescents may start to view their friends, their peer group, as more important and influential than their parents or guardians. Peer groups offer its members the opportunity to develop various social skills, such as empathy, sharing and leadership. Peer groups can have positive influences on an individual, for instance on academic motivation and performance, but they can also have negative influences and lead to an increase in experimentation with drugs, drinking, vandalism, and stealing. Susceptibility to peer pressure increases during early adolescence, peaks around age 14, and declines thereafter.

In the search for a unique social identity for themselves, adolescents are frequently confused about what is 'right' and what is 'wrong.' G. Stanley Hall denoted this period as one of "Storm and Stress" and, according to him, conflict at this developmental stage is normal and not unusual. Margaret Mead, on the other hand, attributed the behaviour of adolescents to their culture and upbringing.

Adolescence is also a time for rapid cognitive development. Piaget describes adolescence as the stage of life in which the individual's thoughts start taking more of an abstract form and the egocentric thoughts decrease. This allows the individual to think and reason in a wider perspective. A combination of behavioural and fMRI studies have demonstrated development of executive functions, that is, cognitive skills that enable the control and coordination of thoughts and behaviour, which are generally associated with the prefrontal cortex. The thoughts, ideas and concepts developed at this period of life greatly influence one's future life, playing a major role in character and personality formation.

Adolescent psychology is associated with notable changes in mood sometimes known as mood swings.

Positive psychology is sometimes brought up when addressing adolescent psychology as well. This approach towards adolescents refers to providing them with motivation to become socially acceptable and notable individuals, since many adolescents find themselves bored, indecisive and/or unmotivated.

Struggles with adolescent identity and depression usually set in when an adolescent experiences a loss. The most important loss in their lives is the changing relationship between the adolescent and their parents. Adolescents may also experience strife in their relationships with friends. This may be due to the activities their friends take part in, such as smoking, which causes adolescents to feel as though participating in such activities themselves is likely essential to maintaining these friendships. Teen depression can be extremely intense at times because of physical and hormonal changes but emotional instability is part of adolescence. Their changing mind, body and relationships often present themselves as stressful and that change, they assume, is something to be feared. Sleep deprivation has also been linked to adolescent depression, particularly in the teen years.

Views of family relationships during adolescence are changing. The old view of family relationships during adolescence put an emphasis on conflict and disengagement and thought storm and stress was normal and even inevitable. However, the new view puts emphasis on transformation or relationships and maintenance of connectedness.

Sexuality

Adolescent sexuality refers to sexual feelings, behaviour and development in adolescents and is a stage of human sexuality. Sexuality and sexual desire usually begins to intensify along with the onset of puberty. The expression of sexual desire among adolescents (or anyone, for that matter), might be influenced by family values and the culture and religion they have grown up in (or as a backlash to such), social engineering, social control, taboos, and other kinds of social mores.

In contemporary society, adolescents also face some risks as their sexuality begins to transform. Whilst some of these such as emotional distress (fear of abuse or exploitation) and sexually transmitted diseases (including HIV/AIDS) may not necessarily be inherent to adolescence, others such as pregnancy (through failure or non-use of contraceptives) are seen as social problems in most western societies. In terms of sexual identity, while all sexual orientations found in adults are also represented among adolescents, statistically the suicide rate amongst LGBT adolescents is up to four times higher than that of their heterosexual peers.

According to anthropologist Margaret Mead and psychologist Albert Bandura, the turmoil found in adolescence in Western society has a cultural rather than a physical cause; they reported that societies where young women engaged in free sexual activity had no such adolescent turmoil.

In a 2008 study conducted by YouGov for Channel 4, 20% of 14"17-year-olds surveyed revealed that they had their first sexual experience at 13 or under. Another study from 2002 found that those aged 15–44 reported that the average age of first sexual intercourse was 17.0 for males and 17.3 for females.

The age of consent to sexual activity varies widely between international jurisdictions, ranging from 12 to 21 years.

Culture

In commerce, this generation is seen as an important target. Mobile phones, contemporary popular music, movies, television programs, websites, sports, video games and clothes are heavily marketed and often popular amongst adolescents.

In the past (and still in some cultures) there were ceremonies that celebrated adulthood, typically occurring during adolescence. *Seijin shiki* (literally "adult ceremony") is a Japanese example of this. Upanayanam is a coming of age ceremony for males in the Hindu world. In Judaism, 13-year-old boys and 12-year-old girls become Bar or Bat Mitzvah, respectively, and often have a celebration to mark this coming of age. Among some denominations of Christianity, the rite or sacrament of Confirmation is received by adolescents and may be considered the time at which adolescents become members of the church in their own right (there is also a Confirmation ceremony in some Reform Jewish temples, although the bar or bat mitzvah ceremony appears to have precedence). In United

States, girls will often have a "sweet sixteen" party to celebrate turning the aforementioned age, a tradition similar to the quinceañera in Latin culture. In modern western society, events such as getting your first driver's license, high school and later on college graduation and first career related job are thought of as being more significant markers in transition to adulthood.

Adolescents have also been an important factor in many movements for positive social change around the world. The popular history of adolescents participating in these movements may perhaps start with Joan of Arc, and extend to present times with popular youth activism, student activism, and other efforts to make the youth voice heard.

Legal Issues, Rights and Privileges

Internationally, those who reach a certain age (often 18, though this varies) are legally considered to have reached the age of majority and are regarded as adults and are held to be responsible for their actions. People below this age are considered minors or children. A person below the age of majority may gain adult rights through legal emancipation.

Those who are under the age of consent, or legal responsibility, may be considered too young to be held accountable for criminal action. This is called *doli incapax* or the defence of infancy. The age of criminal responsibility varies from 7 in India to 18 in Belgium. After reaching the initial age, there may be levels of responsibility dictated by age and type of offence, and crimes committed by minors may be tried in a juvenile court.

The legal working age in Western countries is usually 14 to 16, depending on the number of hours and type of employment. In the United Kingdom and Canada, for example, young people between 14 and 16 can work at certain types of light work with some restrictions to allow for schooling; while youths over 16 can work full-time (excluding night work). Many countries also specify a minimum school leaving age, ranging from 10 to 18, at which a person is legally allowed to leave compulsory education.

The age of consent to sexual activity varies widely between jurisdictions, ranging from 13 to 21 years, the average age is

16. In a 2008 study of 14 to 17-year-olds conducted by YouGov for Channel 4, it was revealed that one in three 15-year-olds were sexually active.

Sexual intercourse with a person below the local age of consent is usually treated as the crime of statutory rape. Some jurisdictions allow an exemption where both partners are close in age; for example, a 16-year-old and an 18-year-old. The age at which people are allowed to marry also varies, from 17 in Yemen to 22 for males and 20 for females in China. In Western countries, people are typically allowed to marry at 18, although they are sometimes allowed to marry at a younger age with parental or court consent. In developing countries, the legal marriageable age does not always correspond with the age at which people actually marry; for example, the legal age for marriage in Ethiopia is 18 for both males and females, but in rural areas most girls are married by age 16.

In most democratic countries, a citizen is eligible to vote at 18. For example, in the United States, the Twenty-sixth amendment decreased the voting age from 21 to 18. In a minority of countries, the voting age is 17 (for example, Indonesia) or 16 (for example, Brazil). By contrast, some countries have a minimum voting age of 21 (for example, Singapore) whereas the minimum age in Uzbekistan is 25. Age of candidacy is the minimum age at which a person can legally qualify to hold certain elected government offices. In most countries, a person must be 18 or over to stand for elected office, but some countries such as the United States and Italy have further restrictions depending on the type of office.

The sale of selected items such as cigarettes, alcohol, and videos with violent or pornographic content is also restricted by age in most countries. In the U.S, the minimum age to buy an R-rated movie, M-rated game or an album with a parental advisory label is 17 (in some states 18 or even 21). In practice, it is common that young people engage in underage smoking or drinking, and in some cultures this is tolerated to a certain degree. In the United States, teenagers are allowed to drive between 14–18 (each state sets its own minimum driving age of which a curfew may be imposed), in the US, adolescents 17 years of age can serve in the military. In Europe it is more common for the driving age to be higher (usually 18) while the drinking age is lower than that of the US (usually 16 or 18). In Canada, the drinking age is 18 in some areas and 19 in other areas. In Australia, universally the minimum drinking age is 18, unless a person is in a private residence or is under parental supervision in a licensed premises.

The driving age varies from state to state but the more common system is a graduated system of "L plates" (a learning license that requires supervision from a licensed driver) from age 16, red "P plates" (probationary license) at 17, green "P plates" at 18 and finally a full license, i.e. for most people around the age of 20.

The legal gambling age also depends on the jurisdiction, although it is typically 18.

The minimum age for donating blood in the U.S is 17 although it may be 16 with parental permission in some states such as New York, New Jersey, and Pennsylvania.

Suitable age and discretion is a legal definition of maturity.

A number of social scientists, including anthropologist Margaret Mead and sociologist Mike Males, have noted the contradictory treatment of laws affecting adolescents in the United States. As Males has noted, the US Supreme Court has, "explicitly ruled that policy-makers may impose adult responsibilities and punishments on individual youths as if they were adults at the same time laws and policies abrogate adolescents' rights en masse as if they were children."

The issue of youth activism affecting political, social, educational, and moral circumstances is of growing significance around the world. Youth-led organizations around the world have fought for social justice, the youth vote seeking to gain teenagers the right to vote, to secure more youth rights, and demanding better schools through student activism.

Since the advent of the Convention on the Rights of the Child in 1989 (children defined as under 18), almost every country (except the U.S. & Somalia) in the world has become voluntarily legally committed to advancing an anti-discriminatory stance towards young people of all ages. This is a legally binding document which secures youth participation throughout society while acting against unchecked child labor, child soldiers, child prostitution, and pornography.

Nutritional Values among Children

Children's needs for calories change as they grow. The Estimated Average Requirements (EARs) are based on the requirements (and the activity levels) of the UK population, and give an idea of calorie requirements at different ages.

Needs for calories can also change according to time of year, how active the child is, what size the child is, whether they are a boy or a girl, whether they are going through a growth spurt, and whether they are ill or well. The EAR for girls is generally lower because they have a smaller frame.

Children need a healthy and varied diet to help them grow, which includes protein, carbohydrates and fats, as well as plenty of fruit and vegetables.

The numbers of calories given are approximate, and calorie needs do depend on a number of things, but taking in too many calories can lead to obesity.

Babies

Babies from birth to six months should, as far as possible, exclusively be fed breast milk. The EAR for boys is 545-690 kcal (calories) per day, and for girls, 515-645 kcal per day, the figures rising as the babies grow and become more active as they approach their first half year.

From seven to 12 months, the EAR for boys is 825 to 920 kcal per day, and for girls 765 to 865 kcal per day.

Toddlers

Toddlers are considerably more active than babies are, as they learn to walk and their play becomes more active. They can also have fast growth spurts. The EAR for boys aged one to three years is around 1230 kcal per day, and for girls around 1165 kcal per day. Children of this age should have full fat milk, and not have a diet that is too high in fibre or low in fat, as this may not include enough calories or nutrients.

Pre-school Children

Pre-school children can be very active, and are learning, growing and developing fast. The EAR for boys aged four to six years is 1715 kcal per day, and for girls 1545 per day.

School-age Children

Once children have started school, they may be taking part in regular games and PE sessions, as well as playing in the playground. They are still growing as well, and for some children, their bodies may be changing as they begin to approach puberty, though other children may not go through puberty until their teens. The EAR for boys aged seven to 10 years is 1970 kcal per day, and for girls, 1740 kcal per day.

Teenagers

Teenagers may need more calories than adults of the same size because they are still growing. Teenagers who are very active, for example those who play sport regularly, or who walk or cycle long distances to school, will need even more.

The EAR for boys aged 11 to 14 years is 2220 kcal per day, and for girls, 1845 kcal per day. The EAR for boys aged 15 to 18 years is 2755 kcal per day, and for girls, 2110 kcal per day. After the age of 18, the EAR for adults is 2550 kcal per day for men, and 1910-1940 kcal per day for women.

3

Growth, Development and Maturation

Adolescence is the period of growth that bridges childhood and adulthood. This period includes puberty, or the development of sexual maturity. The physical changes of puberty result in both males and females being able to create babies. Adolescence begins when a child is 10 to 12 years old. It ends between the ages of 18 and 21.

Adolescence does not mean just physical growth. It also means emotional, social, and mental growth. Most teenagers complete puberty when they are 16 to 18 years old. This is an important time for young people to form their own identities, separate from their families, and prepare for their future as members of society.

The exact age a child enters puberty depends on a number of different things, such as a person's genes, nutrition, and gender. During puberty, various endocrine glands produce hormones that cause body changes and the development of secondary sex characteristics.

- In girls, the ovaries begin to increase production of estrogen and other female hormones.
- In boys, the testicles increase production of testosterone.

The adrenal glands produce hormones that cause increased armpit sweating, body odor, acne, and armpit and pubic hair. This process is called adrenarche. An underarm deodorant or antiperspirant often becomes necessary during this time.

Puberty in Girls

Breast development is the main sign that a girl is entering puberty. The first menstrual period (menarche) usually follows within about 2 years.

Before the first menstrual period, a girl will normally have:

- An increase in height
- An increase in hip size
- Clear or whitish vaginal secretions
- Pubic, armpit, and leg hair growth.

Menstrual cycles occur over about one month (28 to 32 days). At first, the menstrual periods may be irregular. A girl may go 2 months between periods, or may have two periods in 1 month. Over time, they become more regular. Keeping track of when the period occurs and how long it lasts can help you predict when you should have your next menstrual period. After menstruation starts, the ovaries begin to produce and release eggs, which have been stored in the ovaries since birth. About every month after menstruation starts, an ovary releases an egg, called an ovum. The egg travels down a Fallopian tube, which connects the ovary to the womb.

When the egg reaches the womb, the lining becomes thick with blood and fluid. This happens so that if the egg is fertilized, it can grow and develop in the lining to produce a baby. (It is important to remember that fertility comes before emotional maturity and pregnancy can occur before an adolescent is prepared for parenthood.)

If the egg does not meet with sperm from a male and is not fertilized, it dissolves. The thickened lining falls off and forms menstrual blood flow, which passes out of the body through the vagina. In between the menstrual periods, there may be a clear or whitish vaginal discharge. This is normal.

During or just before each period, the girl may feel moody or emotional, and her body may feel puffy or swollen (bloated). PMS (premenstrual syndrome) may begin to develop, especially as the girl gets older. In girls, puberty is usually complete by age 17. Any increases in height beyond this age are uncommon. Although full physical maturity has been reached at this time, educational and emotional maturity remain ongoing.

Puberty in Boys

The first sign of puberty in boys is enlargement of both testicles. Afterwards, boys will normally experience:

- Faster growth, especially height
- Hair growth under the arms, on the face, and in the pubic area
- Increased shoulder width
- Growth of the penis, scrotum (accompanied by reddening and folding of the skin), and testes
- Nighttime ejaculations (nocturnal emissions or "wet dreams")
- Voice changes.

The testes constantly produce sperm. While some sperm can be stored in a structure called the epididymis, the stored sperm are occasionally released as part of the normal process to make room for new sperm. This can occur automatically during sleep (nocturnal emissions) or following masturbation or sexual intercourse. Nocturnal emissions are a normal part of puberty.

Heredity and Environment

Heredity is the passing of traits to offspring (from its parent or ancestors). This is the process by which an offspring cell or organism acquires or becomes predisposed to the characteristics of its parent cell or organism. Through heredity, variations exhibited by individuals can accumulate and cause a species to evolve. The study of heredity in biology is called genetics, which includes the field of epigenetics.

Ancients had a variety of ideas about heredity: Theophrastus proposed that male flowers caused female flowers to ripen; Hippocrates speculated that "seeds" were produced by various body parts and transmitted to offspring at the time of conception, and Aristotle thought that male and female semen mixed at conception. Aeschylus, in 458 BC, proposed the male as the parent, with the female as a "nurse for the young life sown within her."

Various hereditary mechanisms were envisaged without being properly tested or quantified. These included blending inheritance and the inheritance of acquired traits. Nevertheless, people were able to develop domestic breeds of animals as well as crops through artificial selection. The inheritance of acquired traits also formed a part of early Lamarckian ideas on evolution.

In the 9th century AD, the Afro-Arab writer Al-Jahiz considered the effects of the environment on the likelihood of an animal to survive, and first described the struggle for existence. His ideas on the struggle for existence in the *Book of Animals* have been summarized as follows:

> *"Animals engage in a struggle for existence; for resources, to avoid being eaten and to breed. Environmental factors influence organisms to develop new characteristics to ensure survival, thus transforming into new species. Animals that survive to breed can pass on their successful characteristics to offspring."*

In 1000 AD, the Arab physician, Abu al-Qasim al-Zahrawi (known as Albucasis in the West), wrote the first clear description of haemophilia, a hereditary genetic disorder, in his *Al-Tasrif*. In this work, he wrote of an Andalusian family whose males died of bleeding after minor injuries.

During the 18th century, Dutch microscopist Antonie van Leeuwenhoek (1632–1723) discovered "animalcules" in the sperm of humans and other animals. Some scientists speculated they saw a "little man" (homunculus) inside each sperm. These scientists formed a school of thought known as the "spermists." They contended the only contributions of the female to the next generation were the womb in which the homunculus grew, and prenatal influences of the womb. An opposing school of thought, the ovists, believed that the future human was in the egg, and that sperm merely stimulated the growth of the egg. Ovists thought women carried eggs containing boy and girl children, and that the gender of the offspring was determined well before conception.

Pangenesis was an idea that males and females formed "pangenes" in every organ. These pangenes subsequently moved through their blood to the genitals and then to the children. The concept originated with the ancient Greeks, and influenced biology until as recently as a century ago. The terms "blood relative," "bloodline," "full-blooded," and "royal blood" are relics of pangenesis. Francis Galton, Charles Darwin's cousin, experimentally tested and disproved pangenesis during the 1870s.

Modern Development of Genetics and Heredity

In the 1930s, work by Fisher and others resulted in a combination of Mendelian and biometric schools into the modern evolutionary synthesis. The modern synthesis bridged the gap between experimental geneticists and naturalists; and between both and palaeontologists, stating that:

1. All evolutionary phenomena can be explained in a way consistent with known genetic mechanisms and the observational evidence of naturalists.
2. Evolution is gradual: small genetic changes, recombination ordered by natural selection. Discontinuities amongst species (or other taxa) are explained as originating gradually through geographical separation and extinction (not saltation).
3. Selection is overwhelmingly the main mechanism of change; even slight advantages are important when continued. The object of selection is the phenotype in its surrounding environment. The role of genetic drift is equivocal; though strongly supported initially by Dobzhansky, it was downgraded later as results from ecological genetics were obtained.
4. The primacy of population thinking: the genetic diversity carried in natural populations is a key factor in evolution. The strength of natural selection in the wild was greater than expected; the effect of ecological factors such as niche occupation and the significance of barriers to gene flow are all important.
5. In palaeontology, the ability to explain historical observations by extrapolation from micro to macro-evolution is proposed. Historical contingency means explanations at different levels may exist. Gradualism does not mean constant rate of change.

The idea that speciation occurs after populations are reproductively isolated has been much debated. In plants, polyploidy must be included in any view of speciation. Formulations such as 'evolution consists primarily of changes in the frequencies of alleles between one generation and another' were proposed rather later. The traditional view is that developmental biology ('evo-devo') played little part in the synthesis, but an account of Gavin de Beer's work by Stephen Jay Gould suggests he may be an exception.

Almost all aspects of the synthesis have been challenged at times, with varying degrees of success. There is no doubt, however, that the synthesis was a great landmark in evolutionary biology. It cleared up many confusions, and was directly responsible for stimulating a great deal of research in the post-World War II era.

Trofim Lysenko however caused a backlash of what is now called Lysenkoism in the Soviet Union when he emphasised Lamarckian ideas on the inheritance of acquired traits. This movement affected agricultural research and led to food shortages in the 1960s and seriously affected the USSR.

Nature Versus Nurture

"Nature versus nurture" is a term coined by the English Victorian polymath Francis Galton (although Shakespeare had long since contrasted the terms in his play, The Tempest: 4.1) in regarding the influence of heredity and environment on social careers. Galton was influenced by the book The Origin of Species written by his cousin, Charles Darwin. The concept embodied in the phrase has been criticized for its binary simplification of two tightly interwoven parameters, as for example an environment of wealth, education and social privilege are often historically passed to genetic offspring.

The nature versus nurture debates concern the relative importance of an individual's innate qualities ("nature", i.e. nativism, or innatism) versus personal experiences ("nurture", i.e. empiricism or behaviourism) in determining or causing individual differences in physical and behavioural traits.

The view that humans acquire all or almost all their behavioural traits from "nurture" is known as tabula rasa ("blank slate"). This question was once considered to be an appropriate division of developmental influences, but since both types of factors are known to play such interacting roles in development, many modern psychologists consider the question naive-representing an outdated state of knowledge. Psychologist Donald Hebb is said to have once answered a journalist's question of "which, nature or nurture, contributes more to personality?" by asking in response, "Which contributes more to the area of a rectangle, its length or its width?" That is, the idea that *either* nature *or* nurture explains a creature's behaviour is a sort of single cause fallacy.

In the social and political sciences, the nature versus nurture debate may be contrasted with the structure versus agency debate (i.e. socialisation versus individual autonomy). For a discussion of nature versus nurture in language and other human universals.

Scientific Approach

To disentangle the effects of genes and environment, behavioural geneticists perform adoption and twin studies. Behavioural geneticists do not generally use the term "nurture" to explain that portion of the variance for a given trait (such as IQ or the Big Five personality traits) that can be attributed to environmental effects. Instead, two different types of environmental effects are distinguished: shared family factors (i.e., those shared by siblings, making them more similar) and nonshared factors (i.e., those that uniquely affect individuals, making siblings different). To express the portion of the variance due to the "nature" component, behavioural geneticists generally refer to the heritability of a trait.

With regard to the Big Five personality traits as well as adult IQ in the general U.S. population, the portion of the overall variance that can be attributed to shared family effects is often negligible. On the other hand, most traits are thought to be at least partially heritable. In this context, the "nature" component of the variance is generally thought to be more important than that ascribed to the influence of family upbringing.

In her Pulitzer Prize-nominated book *The Nurture Assumption*, author Judith Harris argues that "nurture," as traditionally defined in terms of family upbringing does not effectively explain the variance for most traits (such as adult

IQ and the Big Five personality traits) in the general population of the United States. On the contrary, Harris suggests that either peer groups or random environmental factors (i.e., those that are independent of family upbringing) are more important than family environmental effects.

Although "nurture" has historically been referred to as the care given to children by the parents, with the mother playing a role of particular importance, this term is now regarded by some as any environmental (not genetic) factor in the contemporary *nature versus nurture* debate. Thus the definition of "nurture" has expanded to include influences on development arising from prenatal, parental, extended family, and peer experiences, and extending to influences such as media, marketing, and socio-economic status. Indeed, a substantial source of environmental input to human nature may arise from stochastic variations in prenatal development.

Heritability Estimates

While there are many examples of single-gene-locus traits, current thinking in biology discredits the notion that genes alone can determine most complex traits. At the molecular level, DNA interacts with signals from other genes and from the environment. At the level of individuals, particular genes influence the development of a trait in the context of a particular environment. Thus, measurements of the degree to which a trait is influenced by genes versus environment will depend on the particular environment and genes examined. In many cases, it has been found that genes may have a substantial contribution, including psychological traits such as intelligence and personality. Yet these traits may be largely influenced by environment in other circumstances, such as environmental deprivation.

A researcher seeking to quantify the influence of genes or environment on a trait needs to be able to separate the effects of one factor away from that of another. This kind of research often begins with attempts to calculate the heritability of a trait. Heritability quantifies the extent to which variation among individuals in a trait is due to variation in the genes those individuals carry. In animals where breeding and environments can be controlled experimentally, heritability can be determined relatively easily. Such experiments would be unethical for human research. This problem can be overcome by finding existing populations of humans that reflect the experimental setting the researcher wishes to create.

One way to determine the contribution of genes and environment to a trait is to study twins. In one kind of study, identical twins reared apart are compared to randomly selected pairs of people. The twins share identical genes, but different family environments. In another kind of twin study, identical twins reared together (who share family environment and genes) are compared to fraternal twins reared together (who also share family environment but only share half their genes). Another condition that permits the disassociation of genes and environment is adoption. In one kind of adoption study, biological siblings reared together (who share the same family environment and half their genes) are compared to adoptive siblings (who share their family environment but none of their genes).

Some have pointed out that environmental inputs affect the expression of genes. This is one explanation of how environment can influence the extent to which a genetic disposition will actually manifest. The interactions of genes with environment, called gene-environment interaction, are another component of the nature-nurture debate. A classic example of gene-environment interaction is the ability of a diet low in the amino acid phenylalanine to partially suppress the genetic disease phenylketonuria. Yet another complication to the nature-nurture debate is the existence of gene-environment correlations. These correlations indicate that individuals with certain genotypes are more likely to find themselves in certain environments. Thus, it appears that genes can shape (the selection or creation of) environments. Even using experiments like those described above, it can be very difficult to determine convincingly the relative contribution of genes and environment.

Interaction of Genes and Environment

In only a very few cases is it fair to say that a trait is due almost entirely to nature, or almost entirely to nurture. In the case of most diseases now strictly identified as genetic, such as Huntington's disease, there is a better than 99.9% correlation between having the identified gene and the disease and a similar correlation for not having either. On the other hand, Huntington's animal models live much longer or shorter lives depending on how they are cared for (animal husbandry).

At the other extreme, traits such as native language are environmentally determined: linguists have found that any child (if capable of learning a language at all) can learn any human language with equal facility. With virtually all biological and psychological traits, however, genes and environment work in concert, communicating back and forth to create the individual.

But even in the most clear-cut cases, extreme genetic or environmental conditions can overrule the other – if a child is born mute due to a genetic mutation, it will not learn to speak any language regardless of the environment; similarly, someone who is practically certain to eventually develop Huntington's disease according to their genotype may die in an unrelated accident (an environmental event) long before the disease will manifest itself.

Examples of environmental, interactional, and genetic traits are:

Predominantly Environmental	Interactional	Predominantly Genetic
Specific language	Height	Blood type
Specific religion	Weight	Eye colour
	Skin colour	

Steven Pinker (2004) likewise described several examples: concrete behavioural traits that patently depend on content provided by the home or culture—which language one speaks, which religion one practices, which political party one supports—are not heritable at all. But traits that reflect the underlying talents and temperaments —how proficient with language a person is, how religious, how liberal or conservative— are partially heritable.

When traits are determined by a complex interaction of genotype and environment it is possible to measure the heritability of a trait within a population. However, many non-scientists who encounter a report of a trait having a certain percentage heritability imagine non-interactional, additive contributions of genes and environment to the trait. As an analogy, some laypeople may think of the degree of a trait being made up of two "buckets", genes and environment, each able to hold a certain capacity of the trait. But even for intermediate heritabilities, a trait is always shaped by both genetic dispositions and the environments in which people develop, merely with greater and lesser plasticities associated with these heritability measures.

Heritability measures always refer to the degree of *variation between individuals in a population*. These statistics cannot be applied at the level of the individual. It is incorrect to say that since the heritability index of personality is about .6, you got 60% of your personality from your parents and 40% from the environment. To help to understand this, imagine that all humans were genetic clones. The heritability index for all traits would be zero (all variability between clonal individuals must be due to environmental factors). And, contrary to erroneous interpretations of the heritibility index, as societies become more egalitarian (everyone has more similar experiences) the heritability index goes up (as environments become more similar, variability between individuals is due more to genetic factors).

A highly genetically loaded trait (such as eye colour) still assumes environmental input within normal limits (a certain range of temperature, oxygen in the atmosphere, etc.). A more useful distinction than "nature vs. nurture" is "obligate vs. facultative" —under typical environmental ranges, what traits are more "obligate" (e.g., the nose —everyone has a nose) or more "facultative" (sensitive to environmental variations, such as specific language learned during infancy). Another useful distinction is between traits that are likely to be adaptations (such as the nose) and those that are byproducts of adaptations (such the white colour of bones), or are due to random variation (non-adaptive variation in, say, nose shape or size).

IQ Debate

Evidence suggests that family environmental factors may have an effect upon childhood IQ, accounting for up to a quarter of the variance. On the other hand, by late adolescence this correlation disappears, such that adoptive siblings are no more similar in IQ than strangers.

Moreover, adoption studies indicate that, by adulthood, adoptive siblings are no more similar in IQ than strangers (IQ correlation near zero), while full siblings show an IQ correlation of 0.6. Twin studies reinforce this pattern: monozygotic (identical) twins raised separately are highly similar in IQ (0.74), more so than dizygotic (fraternal) twins raised together (0.6) and much more than adoptive siblings (~0.0).

Personality Traits

Personality is a frequently cited example of a heritable trait that has been studied in twins and adoptions. Identical twins reared apart are far more similar in personality than randomly selected pairs of people. Likewise, identical twins are more similar than fraternal twins. Also, biological siblings are more similar in personality than adoptive siblings. Each observation suggests that personality is heritable to a certain extent. However, these same study designs allow for the examination of environment as well as genes. Adoption studies also directly measure the strength of shared family effects. Adopted siblings share only family environment. Unexpectedly, some adoption studies indicate that by adulthood the personalities of adopted siblings are no more similar than random pairs of strangers. This would mean that shared family effects on personality are zero by adulthood. As is the case with personality, non-shared environmental effects are often found to out-weigh shared environmental effects. That is, environmental effects that are typically thought to be life-shaping (such as family life) may have less of an impact than non-shared effects, which are harder to identify. One possible source of non-shared effects is the environment of pre-natal development. Random variations in the genetic program of development may be a substantial source of non-shared environment. These results suggest that "nurture" may not be the predominant factor in "environment".

Advanced Techniques

The power of quantitative studies of heritable traits has been expanded by the development of new techniques. *Developmental genetic analysis* examines the effects of genes over the course of a human lifespan. For example, early studies of intelligence, which mostly examined young children, found that heritability measures 40 to 50 percent. Subsequent developmental genetic analyses found that variance attributable to additive environmental effects is less apparent in older individuals, with estimated heritability of IQ being higher than that in adulthood. However, the high IQ heritability estimates are derived with questionable methodologies, according the work by Peter Schönemann..

Another advanced technique, *multivariate genetic analysis*, examines the genetic contribution to several traits that vary together. For example, multivariate genetic analysis has demonstrated that the genetic determinants of all specific cognitive abilities (e.g., memory, spatial reasoning, processing speed) overlap greatly, such that the genes associated with any specific cognitive ability will affect all others. Similarly, multivariate genetic analysis has found that genes that affect scholastic achievement completely overlap with the genes that affect cognitive ability.

Extremes analysis, examines the link between normal and pathological traits. For example, it is hypothesized that a given behavioural disorder may represent an extreme of a continuous distribution of a normal behaviour and hence an extreme of a continuous distribution of genetic and environmental variation. Depression, phobias, and reading disabilities have been examined in this context.

For a few highly heritable traits, some studies have identified loci associate with variance in that trait in some individuals. For example, research groups have identified loci that are associated with schizophrenia in subsets of patients with that diagnosis.

Moral Difficulties

Some observers believe that modern science tends to give too much weight to the nature side of the argument, in part because of social consciousness. Historically, much of this debate has had undertones of racist and eugenicist policies — the notion of race as a scientific truth has often been assumed as a prerequisite in various incarnations of the nature versus nurture debate. In the past, heredity was often used as "scientific" justification for various forms of discrimination and oppression along racial and class lines. Works published in the

United States since the 1960s that argue for the primacy of "nature" over "nurture" in determining certain characteristics, such as *The Bell Curve*, have been greeted with considerable controversy and scorn.

Philosophical Difficulties

Are the Traits Real?

It is sometimes a question whether the "trait" being measured is even a real thing. Much energy has been devoted to calculating the heritability of intelligence (usually the I.Q., or intelligence quotient), but there is still some disagreement as to what exactly "intelligence" is.

Biological Determinism

If genes do contribute substantially to the development of personal characteristics such as intelligence and personality, then many wonder if this implies that genes determine who we are.

Is the Problem Real?

Many scientists feel that the very question opposing nature to nurture is a fallacy. Already in 1951, Calvin Hall in his seminal chapter remarked that the discussion opposing nature and nurture was fruitless. If an environment is changed fundamentally, then the heritability of a character changes, too. Conversely, if the genetic composition of a population changes, then heritability will also change. As an example, we may use phenylketonuria (PKU), which causes brain damage and progressive mental retardation.

PKU can be treated by the elimination of phenylalanine from the diet. Hence, a character (PKU) that used to have a virtually perfect heritability is not heritable any more if modern medicine is available (the actual *allele* causing PKU would still be inherited, but the *phenotype* PKU would not be expressed any more). Similarly, within, say, an inbred strain of mice, no genetic variation is present and every character will have a zero heritability. If the complications of gene-environment interactions and correlations are added, then it appears to many that heritability, the epitome of the nature-nurture opposition, is "a station passed".

Myths about Identity

Within the debates surrounding cloning, for example, is the far-fetched contention that a Jesus or a Hitler could be "re-created" through genetic cloning. Current thinking finds this largely inaccurate, and discounts the possibility that the clone of anyone would grow up to be the same individual due to environmental variation. For example, like clones, identical twins are genetically identical, and unlike the hypothetical clones share the same family environment, yet they are not identical in personality and other traits.

History of the Nature Versus Nurture Debate

Traditionally, human nature has been thought of as not only inherited but divinely ordained. Whole ethnic groups were considered to be, by nature, superior or inferior. Since the late Middle Ages, intellectuals increasingly attributed differences among races, classes and genders to socialization (nurture), rather than to innate qualities (nature). In the 20th century, the Nazis pursued an agenda based on the concept of human nature as defined by one's race. The Communists, on the other hand, largely followed Marx's lead in defining the human identity as subject to social structures, not nature. In scientific circles, this conflict led to ongoing controversy of sociobiology and evolutionary psychology.

4

Nature and Principles of Human Growth and Development

Maslow's Hierarchy of Needs

Unlike others researchers in the earlier days of psychology, Abraham Maslow's based his theory of *human needs* on creative people who used all their talents, potential, and capabilities. His methodology differed from most other psychological researchers at the time in that these researchers mainly observed mentally unhealthy people.

Maslow (1970) felt that *human needs* were arranged in a hierarchical order that could be divided into two major groups: basic needs and metaneeds (higher order needs):

- Basic Needs are physiological, such as food, water, and sleep; and psychological, such as affection, security, and self-esteem. These basic needs are also called "deficiency needs" because if they are not met by an individual, then that person will strive to make up the deficiency.
- Metaneeds or *being needs* (growth needs). These include justice, goodness, beauty, order, unity, etc. Basic needs normally take priority over these meta needs. For example, a person who lacks food or water will not normally attend to justice or beauty needs.

These needs are normally listed in a hierarchical order in the form of a pyramid to show that the basic needs (bottom ones) must be met before the higher order needs:

- *Self-actualization* — know exactly who you are, where you are going, and what you want to accomplish. A state of well-being.
- *Esteem* — feeling of moving up in world, recognition, few doubts about self.
- *Belongingness and love* — belong to a group, close friends to confide with.
- *Safety* — feel free from immediate danger.
- *Physiological* — food, water, shelter, sex.

Maslow posited that people want and are forever striving to meet various goals. Because the lower level needs are more immediate and urgent, then they come into play as the source and direction of a person's goal if they are not satisfied. A need higher in the hierarchy will become a motive of behaviour as long as the needs below it have been satisfied. Unsatisfied lower needs will dominate unsatisfied higher needs and must be satisfied before the person can climb up the hierarchy.

Knowing where a person is located on the pyramid will aid you in determining effective motivators. For example, motivating a middle-class person (who is in range 4 of the hierarchy) with a certificate will have a far greater impact than using the same motivator to effect a minimum wage person from the ghetto who is desperately struggling to meet the first couple of needs.

It should be noted that almost no one stays in one particular hierarchy for an extended period. We constantly strive to move up, while at the same time various forces outside our control try to push us down. Those on top get pushed down for short time periods, i.e., death of a loved-one or an idea that does not work, while those on the bottom get pushed up, i.e., come across a small prize. Our goal as leaders therefore is to help people obtain the skills and knowledge that will push them up the hierarchy on a more permanent basis. People who have their basic needs met become much better workers as they are able to concentrate on fulfilling the visions put forth to them, rather than consistently struggling to make ends meet.

Criticisms and Strengths

Note however, that the above statements may be considered generalizations. Maslow's theory has often been criticized because we can find exceptions to it, such as the military, police, firefighters, etc. who will risk their safety for the well-being of others or parents who will sacrifice their basic needs for their children. However, there are very few theories that are not flawed in that once we start drilling down to individualistic levels, then the theory or generalization often starts to fall apart. For example, even Newton's theory of physics, which later became laws, fell apart once we were able to drill down to the atomic level.

Maslow's theory remains a classic because rather than looking at psychology as strictly the study of the mentally ill, his theory was based upon healthy persons. And being one of the first humanistic ones, it has its share of flaws.

Expansion of the Pyramid

In Maslow's (1971) later years, he become more interested in the higher order or metaneeds and tried to further distinguish them. Maslow theorized that the ultimate goal of life is self-actualization, which is almost never fully attained but rather is something we try to always strive for. He later theorized that this level does not stop, it goes on to self-transcendence, which carries us to the spiritual level, e.g. Gandhi, Mother Theresa, Dalai Lama, or even poets, such as Robert Frost. Maslow's self-transcendence level recognizes the human need for ethics, creativity, compassion and spirituality. Without this spiritual or transegoic sense, we are simply animals or machines.

This expansion of the higher order needs is shown here:

Note that the four meta needs (above the inner pyramid) can be pursued in any order, depending upon a person's wants or circumstances, as long as the basic needs have all been met:

- *Self-transcendence* — a transegoic level that emphasizes visionary intuition, altruism, and unity consciousness.
- *Self-actualization* — know exactly who you are, where you are going, and what you want to accomplish. A state of well-being.
- *Aesthetic* — to do things not simply for the outcome but because it's the reason you are here on earth — at peace, more curious about the inner workings of all things.

- *Cognitive* — to be free of the good opinion of others—learning for learning alone, contribute knowledge.
- *Esteem* — feeling of moving up in world, recognition, few doubts about self.
- *Belongingness and love* — belong to a group, close friends to confide with.
- *Safety* — feel free from immediate danger.
- *Physiological* — food, water, shelter, sex.

Note: Transegoic means a higher, psychic, or spiritual state of development. The trans *is related to transcendence, while the* ego *is based on Freud's work. We go from preEGOic levels to EGOic levels to transEGOic. The EGO in all three terms are used in the Jungian sense of consciousness as opposed to the unconscious. Ego equates with the personality.*

In addition, just as in his earlier model, we may be in a state of flux — we shift between levels (Maslow, 1968). For example there may be peak experiences for temporary self-actualizations and self-transcendence. These are our spiritual or creative moments.

Characteristics of self-actualizing people:

- Have better perceptions of reality and are comfortable with it.
- Accept themselves and their own natures.
- Lack of artificiality.
- They focus on problems outside themselves and are concerned with basic issues and eternal questions.
- They like privacy and tend to be detached.
- Rely on their own development and continued growth.
- Appreciate the basic pleasures of life (e.g. do not take blessings for granted).
- Have a deep feeling of kinship with others.
- Are deeply democratic and are not really aware of differences.
- Have strong ethical and moral standards.
- Are original, inventive, less constricted and fresher than others.

Going Beyond Maslow

While the research of Maslow's theory has undergone limited empirical scrutiny, it still remains quite popular due to its simplicity and being the start of the movement away from a totally behaviourist/reductionistic/mechanistic approach to a more humanistic one. In addition, a lot of concerns are directed at his methodology in that he picked a small number of people that he declared self-actualizing and came to the conclusion about self-actualization. However, he understood this and thought of his work as simply a method of pointing the way, rather than being the final say. In addition, he hoped that others would take up the cause and complete what he had begun. Which brings us to the next models. Other researchers have taken up his cause and furthered refined them, mostly in the area of organizations and work. Herzberg, Alderfer, and McGregor's research are all closely tied to Maslow's theory.

Herzberg's Hygiene and Motivational Factors

Frederick Herzberg was considered one of the most influential management consultants and professors of the modern postwar era. Herzberg was probably best known for his challenging thinking on work and motivation. He was considered both an icon and legend among visionaries such as Abraham Maslow, Peter Drucker, and Douglas MacGregor.

Herzberg (1966) is best known for his list of factors that are based on Maslow's Hierarchy of Needs, except his version is more closely related to the working environment:

Herzberg's Hygiene & Motivational Factors

Hygiene or Dissatisfiers:

- Working conditions
- Policies and administrative practices
- Salary and Benefits
- Supervision
- Status
- Job security
- Co-workers
- Personal life.

Motivators or Satisfiers:

- Recognition
- Achievement
- Advancement
- Growth
- Responsibility
- Job challenge.

Hygiene or dissatisfiers factors must be present in the job before motivators can be used to stimulate a person. That is, you cannot use motivators until all the hygiene factors are met. Herzberg's needs are specifically job related and reflect some of the distinct things that people want from their work as opposed to Maslow's Hierarchy of Needs which reflect all the needs in a person's life. Building on this model, Herzberg coined the term *job enrichment* — the process of redesigning work in order to build in motivators by increasing both the number of tasks that an employee performs and the control over those tasks. It is associated with the design of jobs and is an extension of job enlargement (an increase in the number of tasks that an employee performs).

McGregor's Theory X and Theory Y

Douglas McGregor (1957) developed a philosophical view of humankind with his Theory X and Theory Y — two opposing perceptions about how people view human behaviour at work and organizational life. McGregor felt that organizations and the managers within them followed either one or the other approach:

Theory X

- People have an inherent dislike for work and will avoid it whenever possible.
- People must be coerced, controlled, directed, or threatened with punishment in order to get them to achieve the organizational objectives.
- People prefer to be directed, do not want responsibility, and have little or no ambition.
- People seek security above all else.

In an organization with Theory X assumptions, management's role is to coerce and control employees.

Theory Y

- Work is as natural as play and rest.
- People will exercise self-direction if they are committed to the objectives (they are NOT lazy).
- Commitment to objectives is a function of the rewards associated with their achievement.
- People learn to accept and seek responsibility.
- Creativity, ingenuity, and imagination are widely distributed among the population. People are capable of using these abilities to solve an organizational problem.
- People have potential.

In an organization with Theory Y assumptions, management's role is to develop the potential in employees and help them to release that potential towards common goals. Theory X is the view that traditional management has taken towards the workforce. Most organizations are now taking the enlightened view of theory Y (even though they might not be very good at it). A *boss* can be viewed as taking the theory X approach, while a *leader* takes the theory Y approach. Notice that Maslow, Herzberg, and McGregor's theories all tie together:

- Herzberg's theory is a micro version of Maslow's theory that is focused in the work environment.
- McGregor's Theory X is based on workers caught in the lower levels (1 to 3) of Maslow's theory due to bad management practices, while his Theory Y is for workers who have gone above level 3 with the help of management.
- McGregor's Theory X is also based on workers caught in Herzberg's Hygiene Dissatisfiers, while Theory Y is based on workers who are in the Motivators or Satisfiers section.

Alderfer's Existence/Relatedness/Growth (ERG)

Clayton Alderfer's (1969) Existence/Relatedness/Growth (ERG) Theory of Needs postulates that there are three groups of needs:

- Existence-This group of needs is concerned with providing the basic requirements for material existence, such as physiological and safety needs. This need is satisfied by money earned in a job so that one may buy food, shelter, clothing, etc.
- Relationships-This group of needs centres upon the desire to establish and maintain interpersonal relationships. Since people normally spend approximately half of their waking hours on the job, this need is normally satisfied to some degree by their coworkers.
- Growth-These needs are met by personal development. A person's job, career, or profession provides significant satisfaction of growth needs.

Alderfer's ERG theory states that more than one need may be influential at the same time. If the gratification of a higher-level need is frustrated, the desire to satisfy a lower-level need will increase. He identifies this phenomenon as the "frustration & shy aggression dimension."

Its relevance on the job is that even when the upper-level needs are frustrated, the job still provides for the basic physiological needs upon which one would then be focused. If, at that point, something happens to threaten the job, the person's basic needs are significantly threatened. If there are no factors present to relieve the pressure, the person may become desperate and panicky.

Notice that Alderfer's ERG theory is built upon Maslow's, however it does differ. First he collapses it from five needs to three. And unlike Maslow, he did not see these needs as being a hierarchy in which one climbs up, but rather being more of a continuum:

Alderfer's ERG theory more of a continuum than a hierarchy

While there has not been a lot of research on Alderfer's theory, most contemporary theories and related studies tend to give it stronger support than Maslow's theory.

Vroom's Expectancy Theory

Vroom's Expectancy Theory (1964) states that an individual will act in a certain way based on the expectation (belief) that the act will be followed by a given outcome and on the attractiveness of that outcome to the individual. This motivational model has been modified by several people, to include Porter and Lawler (1968). Vroom's Expectancy Theory is written as a formula:

Valence x Expectancy x Instrumentality = Motivation

- Valence (Reward) = the amount of desire for a goal (What is the reward?)
- Expectancy (Performance) = the strength of belief that work related effort will result in the completion of the task (How hard will I have to work to reach the goal?)
- Instrumentality (Belief) = the belief that the reward will be received once the task is completed (Will they notice the effort I put forth?)

The product of valence, expectancy, and instrumentality is motivation. It can be thought of as the strength of the drive towards a goal. For example, if an employee wants to move up through the ranks, then promotion has a high valence for that employee. If the employee believes that high performance will result in good reviews, then the employee has a high expectancy. However, if the employee believes the company will not promote from within, then the employee has low instrumentality, and the employee will not be motivated to perform better.

Motor Development

Most infants develop motor abilities in the same order and at approximately the same age. In this sense, most agree that these abilities are genetically preprogrammed within all infants. The environment does play a role in the development, with an enriched environment often reducing the learning time and an impoverished one doing the opposite.

The following chart delineates the development of infants in sequential order. The ages shown are averages and it is normal for these to vary by a month or two in either direction.

2 months – able to lift head up on his own

3 months – can roll over

4 months – can sit propped up without falling over

6 months – is able to sit up without support

7 months – begins to stand while holding on to things for support

9 months – can begin to walk, still using support

10 months – is able to momentarily stand on her own without support

11 months – can stand alone with more confidence

12 months – begin walking alone without support

14 months – can walk backward without support

17 months – can walk up steps with little or no support

18 months – able to manipulate objects with feet while walking, such as kicking a ball.

Cognitive Development in Children

Probably the most cited theory in the cognitive development in children is Jean Piaget (1896-1980). As with all stage theories, *Piaget's Theory of Cognitive Development*, maintains that children go through specific stages as their intellect and ability to see relationships matures. These stages are completed in a fixed order with all children, even those in other countries. The age range, however can vary from child to child.

Sensorimotor Stage. This stage occurs between the ages of birth and two years of age, as infants begin to understand the information entering their sense and their ability to interact with the world. During this stage, the child learns to manipulate objects although they fail to understand the permanency of these objects if they are not within their current sensory perception. In other words, once an object is removed from the child's view, he or she is unable to understand that the object still exists.

The major achievement during this stage is that of *Object Permanency*, or the ability to understand that these objects do in fact continue to exist. This includes his ability to understand that when mom leaves the room, she will eventually return, resulting in an increased sense of safety and security. Object

Permanency occurs during the end of this stage and represents the child's ability to maintain a mental image of the object (or person) without the actual perception.

Preoperational Stage. The second stage begins after Object Permanency is achieved and occurs between the ages of two to seven years of age. During this stage, the development of language occurs at a rapid pace. Children learn how to interact with their environment in a more complex manner through the use of words and images. This stage is marked by Egocentrism, or the child's belief that everyone sees the world the same way that she does. The fail to understand the differences in perception and believe that inanimate objects have the same perceptions they do, such as seeing things, feeling, hearing and their sense of touch.

A second important factor in this stage is that of Conservation, which is the ability to understand that quantity does not change if the shape changes. In other words, if a short and wide glass of water is poured into a tall and thin glass. Children in this stage will perceive the taller glass as having more water due only because of it's height. This is due to the children's inability to understand *reversibility* and to focus on only one aspect of a stimulus (called *centration*), such as height, as opposed to understanding other aspects, such as glass width.

Concrete Operations Stage. Occurring between ages 7 and about 12, the third stage of cognitive development is marked by a gradual decrease in centristic thought and the increased ability to focus on more than one aspect of a stimulus. They can understand the concept of grouping, knowing that a small dog and a large dog are still both dogs, or that pennies, quarters, and dollar bills are part of the bigger concept of money.

They can only apply this new understanding to concrete objects (those they have actually experienced). In other words, imagined objects or those they have not seen, heard, or touched, continue to remain somewhat mystical to these children, and abstract thinking has yet to develop.

Formal Operations Stage. In the final stage of cognitive development (from age 12 and beyond), children begin to develop a more abstract view of the world. They are able to apply reversibility and conservation to both real and imagined situations. They also develop an increased understanding of the world and the idea of cause and effect. By the teenage years, they are able to develop their own theories about the world. This stage is achieved by most children, although failure to do so has been associated with lower intelligence.

Development of Speech and Language

Language Development Chart

Age of Child	*Typical Language Development*
6 Months	• Vocalization with intonation • Responds to his name • Responds to human voices without visual cues by turning his head and eyes • Responds appropriately to friendly and angry tones
12 Months	• Uses one or more words with meaning (this may be a fragment of a word) • Understands simple instructions, especially if vocal or physical cues are given • Practices inflection· Is aware of the social value of speech
18 Months	• Has vocabulary of approximately 5-20 words • Vocabulary made up chiefly of nouns • Some echolalia (repeating a word or phrase over and over) • Much jargon with emotional content • Is able to follow simple commands
24 Months	• Can name a number of objects common to his surroundings • Is able to use at least two prepositions, usually chosen from the following: in, on, under • Combines words into a short sentence-largely noun-verb combinations (mean) length of sentences is given as 1.2 words • Approximately 2/3 of what child says should be intelligible Vocabulary of approximately 150-300 words • Rhythm and fluency often poor • Volume and pitch of voice not yet well-controlled • Can use two pronouns correctly: I, me, you, although me and I are often confused • My and mine are beginning to emerge

	• Responds to such commands as "show me your eyes (nose, mouth, hair)"
36 Months	• Use pronouns I, you, me correctly • Is using some plurals and past tenses • Knows at least three prepositions, usually in, on, under • Knows chief parts of body and should be able to indicate these if not name • Handles three word sentences easily • Has in the neighbourhood of 900-1000 words • About 90% of what child says should be intelligible • Verbs begin to predominate • Understands most simple questions dealing with his environment and activities • Relates his experiences so that they can be followed with reason • Able to reason out such questions as "what must you do when you are sleepy, hungry, cool, or thirsty?" • Should be able to give his sex, name, age • Should not be expected to answer all questions even though he understands what is expected
48 Months	• Knows names of familiar animals • Can use at least four prepositions or can demonstrate his understanding of their meaning when given commands • Names common objects in picture books or magazines • Knows one or more colors • Can repeat 4 digits when they are given slowly • Can usually repeat words of four syllables • Demonstrates understanding of over and under • Has most vowels and diphthongs and the consonants p, b, m, w, n well established • Often indulges in make-believe • Extensive verbalization as he carries out activities • Understands such concepts as longer, larger, when a contrast is presented • Readily follows simple commands even thought the stimulus objects are not in sight

- Much repetition of words, phrases, syllables, and even sounds

60 Months
- Can use many descriptive words spontaneously-both adjectives and adverbs
- Knows common opposites: big-little, hard-soft, heave-light, etc.
- Has number concepts of 4 or more
- Can count to ten
- Speech should be completely intelligible, in spite of articulation problems
- Should have all vowels and the consonants, m, p, b, h, w, k, g, t, d, n, ng, y (yellow)
- Should be able to repeat sentences as long as nine words
- Should be able to define common objects in terms of use (hat, shoe, chair)
- Should be able to follow three commands given without interruptions
- Should know his age
- Should have simple time concepts: morning, afternoon, night, day, later, after, while
- Tomorrow, yesterday, today
- Should be using fairly long sentences and should use some compound and some complex sentences
- Speech on the whole should be grammatically correct

6 Years
- In addition to the above consonants these should be mastered: f, v, sh, zh, th, 1
- He should have concepts of 7
- Speech should be completely intelligible and socially useful
- Should be able to tell one a rather connected story about a picture, seeing relationships
- Between objects and happenings

7 Years
- Should have mastered the consonants s-z, r, voiceless th, ch, wh, and the soft g as in George
- Should handle opposite analogies easily: girl-boy, man-woman, flies-swims, blunt-sharp short-long, sweet-sour, etc.
- Understands such terms as: alike, different, beginning, end, etc.
- Should be able to tell time to quarter hour

	• Should be able to do simple reading and to write or print many words
8 Years	• Can relate rather involved accounts of events, many of which occurred at some time in the past
	• Complex and compound sentences should be used easily
	• Should be few lapses in grammatical constrictions-tense, pronouns, plurals
	• All speech sounds, including consonant blends should be established
	• Should be reading with considerable ease and now writing simple compositions
	• Social amenities should be present in his speech in appropriate situations
	• Control of rate, pitch, and volume are generally well and appropriately established
	• Can carry on conversation at rather adult level
	• Follows fairly complex directions with little repetition
	• Has well developed time and number concepts

Here are some tips to help develop speech communication in your child:

1. Ensure that your child is wearing appropriate amplification or other sensory aids during all waking hours of the day.
2. Talk to your child clearly, at a normal conversational level, and at close range.
3. Be aware of your child's interests, and talk to her about the features in the objects and events that are taking place while observing them.
4. Follow your child's focus of attention. Don't try to constantly lead or control topics of discussion.
5. Talk to your child about the routine situations in her life.
6. Talk about shared experiences and events and objects that are common to both of you.
7. Use different voice patterns when indicating various aspects of speech to your child.
8. Use intonation to mark important elements in utterances.

9. Allow your child plenty of time to respond during conversations.
10. Shift gradually the responsibility for being understood from you to the child as he acquires more spoken language.
11. Use mainly complete sentences when speaking.
12. Provide your child with the opportunity to acquire language by participating in activities which are common in life.
13. Maintain a close relationship with professionals in order to provide your child with the optimal opportunities to develop spoken language communication.
14. Be prepared to be the primary person responsible for the initial development of your child's spoken language.
15. Work in as many one-on-one situations as possible until your child has acquired reasonable communication skills.
16. Remember children who have learned in primarily one-on-one situations have to learn additional communication skills to interact appropriately in a group setting.
17. Remember to set aside time to just play with your child without concentrating on language development.
18. Don't begin formal teaching of vowels and consonants until ample time has been spent on the informal learning of spoken language.
19. Remember that speech production and reception are complex issues and give your child adequate time to learn them before you conclude that she can't handle them.
20. Use meaningful communication as a base for developing spoken language.
21. Optimize your child's contact with his hearing peers in order to enhance natural development of his spoken language skills.
22. Motivate your child to talk by ensuring that her experiences with the acquisition of spoken language are successful.
23. Adopt an alternative communication system only as a last resort.

5

Intellectual and Mental Development

The stages of intellectual development formulated by Piaget appear to be related to major developments in brain growth. The human brain is not fully developed until late adolescence or in the case of males sometimes early adulthood. We often expect children to think like adults when they are not yet capable of doing so. It is important that parents know what to expect from their child as they develop and to be sure that the expectations they may have for their child at a given age are realistic.

Piaget's Stages of Cognitive Development

Sensory Motor Period (0-24 months)

Developmental Stage & Approximate Age	Characteristic Behaviour
Reflexive Stage (0-2 months)	Simple reflex activity such as grasping, sucking.
Primary Circular Reactions (2-4 months)	Reflexive behaviours occur in stereotyped repetition such as opening and closing fingers repetitively.
Secondary Circular Reactions (4-8 months)	Repetition of change actions to reproduce interesting consequences such as kicking one's feet to more a mobile suspended over the crib.
Coordination of Secondary Reactions (8-12 months)	Responses become coordinated into more complex sequences. Actions take on an "intentional" character such as the infant reaches behind a screen to obtain a hidden object.

Tertiary Circular Reactions (12-18 months)	Discovery of new ways to produce the same consequence or obtain the same goal such as the infant may pull a pillow toward him in an attempt to get a toy resting on it.
Invention of New Means Through Mental Combination (18-24 months)	Evidence of an internal representational system. Symbolizing the problem-solving sequence before actually responding. Deferred imitation.

The Preoperational Period (2-7 years)

Developmental Stage & Approximate Age	Characteristic Behaviour
Preoperational Phase (2-4 years)	Increased use of verbal representation but speech is egocentric. The beginnings of symbolic rather than simple motor play. Transductive reasoning. Can think about something without the object being present by use of language.
Intuitive Phase (4-7 years)	Speech becomes more social, less egocentric. The child has an intuitive grasp of logical concepts in some areas. However, there is still a tendency to focus attention on one aspect of an object while ignoring others. Concepts formed are crude and irreversible. Easy to believe in magical increase, decrease, disappearance. Reality not firm. Perceptions dominate judgment. In moral-ethical realm, the child is not able to show principles underlying best behaviour. Rules of a game not develop, only uses simple do's and don'ts imposed by authority.

Period of Concrete Operations (7-12 years) Characteristic Behaviour: Evidence for organized, logical thought. There is the ability to perform multiple classification tasks, order objects in a logical sequence, and comprehend the principle of conservation. Thinking becomes less transductive and less egocentric. The child is capable of concrete problem-solving. Some reversibility now possible (quantities moved can be restored such as in arithmetic: 3+4 = 7 and 7-4 = 3, etc.) Class logic-finding bases to sort unlike objects into logical groups where previously it was on superficial perceived attribute such as colour. Categorical labels such as "number" or animal" now available.

Period of Formal Operations 12 years and onwards) Characteristic Behaviour: Thought becomes more abstract, incorporating the principles of formal logic. The ability to generate abstract propositions, multiple hypotheses and their possible outcomes is evident. Thinking becomes less tied to concrete reality. Formal logical systems can be acquired. Can handle proportions, algebraic manipulation, other purely abstract processes. If a + b = x then a = x-b. If ma/ca = IQ = 1.00 then Ma = CA. Prepositional logic, as-if and if-then steps. Can use aids such as axioms to transcend human.

The Necessity for a Balanced Diet in Children: Physical, Mental and Intellectual Development

A holistic approach is necessary to address the child's overall development, including physical, mental, emotional and behavioural development. Many factors impact on growth and development, but malnutrition impair both physical. Mental and intellectual development.

Childhood nutrition determines the risk for immediate health problems for example iron deficiency associated with poor school performance, eating disorders, obesity, under nutrition and dental caries. Nutritional status has long-term health implications as web, blamely obesity, coronary heart disease and osteoporosis.

Nutritional status of South African children

Studies indicate a wide range of percentages of children under any given anthropometrical cut point for under nutrition, with pockets of malnutrition, especially in rural areas. There is a low prevalence of wasting or acute malnutrition, but stunting (Low height-for-age) occurs in 20% and relative overweight in :: 17% of children. Critical periods of intense growth are during infancy, during adolescence. High nutritional demands during these periods make children particularly vulnerable to deficiency.

According to the SA V Aea results, 33% of children have marginal vitamin A status in 6 months to 6 year old children, with iron-deficiency anaemia (.Hb < 1 I g/dl) in 21 % of children and low red blood cell folate concentration in some groups. Multiple micro-nutrient deficiencies were described in rural black children, namely indications of vitamin A1 iron and folate deficiencies. Dietary intakes of SA children indicate mostly adequate energy and protein intakes, but low calcium, iron and zinc intakes. A wide range of vitamin A, C and folate intakes were found in studies.

Energy and nutrients for growth and development of children

Illness and competitive sport may increase nutritional requirements and decrease food intake of children. Children with allergies have low intakes of important food groups, for example milk may be excluded. Peer pressure has an effect on eating of snack foods. Self-imposed dieting by adolescents often leads to low intakes of nutrients.

Iron is required for optimal growth, skeletal development, cellular immunity and cognitive function.

Zinc is necessary for normal growth, skeletal development and neuropsychological function.

Calcium requirements of children are high due to high velocity of bone growth during infancy and adolescence, whereas iodine is necessary for normal growth and intellectual development. Iron deficiency is associated with loss of appetite, higher morbidity and growth retardation.

Iron deficient children tend to be shorter and lighter, but growth improved after iron supplementation.

The mechanism for improved growth may be improved appetite and food intake, or improved cellular immunity and decreased morbidity. Iron-deficient children also have poor cognitive function and educational achievement and are less attentive and playful. The mechanism for these may be associated with the role of iron in nerve myelination or on the level of brain neurotransmitters.

Zinc plays a role in growth, via protein synthesis processes. Short stature is associated with zinc deficiency and an increase in height and food intake occurs after zinc supplementation. The mechanism for these is probably an increase in insulin-like growth factor-1 after zinc supplementation. Children have high calcium requirements during growth spurt periods. About 25% of peak bone mass depends on calcium intake and physical activity during childhood, which decreases risk of osteoporosis later in life.

Lower calcium intakes are due to exclusion of milk, for example in fad diets. The teenage period is associated with its growth spurt and high demand for calcium. Milk in the diet is associated with higher calcium intakes and higher levels of insulin-like growth factor (10F-l). High milk intakes have no detrimental effect on iron status. The intake of low-fat milk products is recommend for dieting teenagers.

Children from iodine sufficient regions have higher IQ scores than children from iodine poor regions.

Children born more than 3.5 years after implementation of aniodin C? supplementation programme had significantly higher IQ scores (12-t 7 IQ points) than children born before the implementation of the programme. Iodine status plays a crucial role in the intellectual development of children. In SA iodine has been added to table salt since 1995.

High calcium intakes may interfere with iron absorption. In a supplementation trial 1500mg Ca/day was still associated with favourable serum ferritin and haemoglobin levels. High zinc intakes may interfere with iron absorption, but such interactions are only likely to be important at levels of intake achieved by me use of supplements. The recommendation is to take supplements between meals.

Key vitamins for child development include vitamin A for normal growth. Eyesight and immunity, and folate for growth and development of new cells. B-vitamins are involved in behavioural and cognitive outcomes. Vitamin A is essential for growth, eyesight bone development immunity and healthy epithelial tissue. The mechanism for' growth regulation is through regulation of nocturnal growth hormone secretion or by reduction of infection. Thereby allowing optimal growth. Folate is essential for cell division and development. There is an increased demand during the growth spurt periods. Folate deficiency is associated with megaloblastic anaemia. An increased risk of cardiovascular disease and an increased risk of babies born with neural tube defects. Other 8-vitamins are linked to a variety of behavioural and cognitive outcomes. Vitamin 86 plays a role in neurotransmitter systems of learning and memory. Most results are &01'1'1 observational studies, with no definite proof of cause and effect.

Breastfeeding; alcohol and smoking Studies in low-birth-weight infants show an advantage of breastfeeding in cognitive function measured by IQ points. These studies are difficult to interpret, because socioeconomic factors confound the association between breastfeeding and cognitive function. Breastmilk has higher concentrations of certain fatty acids than cow's milk, especially docosahexaenoic acid (DHA). Low intakes of omega-3 fatty acids during early child development lead to changes in visual acuity in human infants. Results of studies indicate that overall nutritional status (measured as head circumference) and educational status of the mother have a stronger association with childhood intellectual development than breastfeeding only. Maternal smoking was negatively associated with IQ.

The Western Cape farm areas has the highest reported. Rate of fetal alcohol syndrome (FAS) in the world (65-74 per 1000 children). FA5 is associated with poor growth and development and lower intellectual functioning and negative behaviour outcomes. Stunted children had significantly lower intelligence and academic achievement scores than children of normal height.

Eating habits of children

Childhood offers a unique opportunity to positively influence the adoption of healthful eating and physical activity patterns. Adolescents as a group have poor eating habits that do not meet dietary recommendations. Concerns include unhealthy dieting, skipping meals, high intakes of fast foods and cold drinks, low intake of m ilk, fruit and vegetables. These are due to social and environmental changes, including growing independence, eating away from home, peer pressure and concern with physical appearance.

The environment changed over the past decades, with more tasty, energy-dense foods generally available and more sedentary lifestyles. Children's eating habits changed: they eat more high fat foods and drink more cold drinks. The additional kJ intake provided by cold drinks is about 800kJ extra /day, up to an additional 4000kJ/day. Milk consumption among adolescents decreased dramatically. Cold drinks replaced milk in the diet. An increasing body of literature suggests that dairy calcium may play a role in maintaining stable body weight. Overweight children had an increased risk factors, such as increased blood pressure and total serum cholesterol. Long-term low intakes of milk were associated with shorter stature, with more body fat and poor bone health. SA studies showed that children had low intakes of milk, fruit and vegetables and thus low intakes of calcium, vitamin A and C.

Recommendations

Recommendations are to match nutrition intervention strategies with factors that motivate children to select a certain diet and lifestyle. More research is necessary to determine the motivational factors that affect children's food and activity choices. School and community based programmes that promote regular physical activity and healthy eating among children could be the most effective strategy for reducing the burden of chronic diseases associated with sedentary lifestyles and unhealthy eating patterns. Schools can be an environment where healthy lifestyle is reinforced, by encouraging policy to restrict the sale of soft drinks and foods high in fat and sugar in the school environment. Nutrition information can be displayed in school tuck-shops and pricing in tuck-shops can have a strong effect on food choices. Department of Education, teachers, school governing boards and children's representatives should work together to create a more healthy school environment that fosters good eating and physical activity habits. Interventions to improve the mineral and vitamin nutritional status of children have a positive impact on growth and health of children, educational outcomes, productivity as adults and eventually national economies.

Understanding How the Brain Develops

To understand how this happens, we need to understand a bit about how the brain works. The brain is comprised of many regions that perform specific functions, such as identifying what we see, processing spoken language, or assessing whether we are in danger. Within each of these brain areas are millions of neurons, or nerve cells, which send messages to each other across synapses. These trillions of nerves and synapses and the pathways they form make up the "wiring" of the brain; they allow all of the various areas to communicate and function together in a coordinated way. The number and organization of connections in the brain influence everything from the ability to recognize letters of the alphabet to facility at managing complex social relationships.

In most regions of the brain, no new neurons are formed after birth. Instead, brain development consists of an ongoing process of wiring and re-wiring the connections among neurons. New synapses between cells are constantly being formed, while others are broken or pruned away. This happens throughout life. However, in early childhood the brain is genetically programmed to produce more synapses than it will ultimately use. Indeed, by 8 months of age a baby may have an astounding 1,000 trillion synapses in his brain! This blooming of synapses happens at different times in different areas of the brain. Development then proceeds by keeping the synapses that are used and pruning away those that aren't. The pruning of synapses happens over the childhood years as the different areas of the brain develop.

Pruning allows the brain to keep the connections that have a purpose, while eliminating those that aren't doing anything. In short, pruning increases the efficiency with which the brain can do what it needs to do. But, because the brain operates on the "use it or lose it" rule, an "over-pruning" of these connections can occur when a child is deprived of normally expected experiences in the early years. This leaves the child struggling to do what would have come more naturally otherwise.

Some areas of the brain, such as those which help us see clearly, become less "plastic" or changeable when the pruning is over. This has led to tremendous concern about providing what the brain needs to prune and organize itself correctly before the "windows of opportunity" close. For example, surgeons now remove congenital cataracts as early in infancy as possible, because they know that if they wait until the child is older, the neural connections between his eyes and his brain will fail to develop properly, and he will never be able to see. Brain scientists are also working diligently to unlock the secrets of how the brain turns on and off its ability to change itself. There is real hope that if we can understand the ways this happens, we can create therapies, both those that use drugs and those that use carefully structured experiences and training exercises, that can open up windows and re-wire brains that were deprived of normally expected experiences early in life or those that get damaged later in life.

The Power of Early Experiences

Our brains shape and reshape themselves in ways that depend on what we use them for throughout our lives.

Learning language is a nice example of how experiences contribute to each person's unique pattern of brain development. The ability to speak and to understand other's speech requires only the minimal opportunity to communicate that almost all children experience. However, *which* language a child learns to speak depends on the language he experiences, and his brain will adapt to this specific language. When an infant is 3 months old. his brain can distinguish several hundred different spoken sounds, many more than are present in his native language. Over the next several months, however, his brain will organize itself more efficiently so that it only recognizes those spoken sounds that are part of the language that he regularly hears. For example, a one-year-old Japanese baby will not recognize that "la" is different from "ra," because the former sound is never used in his language. During early childhood, the brain retains the ability to re-learn sounds it has discarded, so young children typically learn new languages easily and without an accent. After about age 10, however, plasticity for this function is greatly diminished; therefore, most people find it difficult to learn to speak a foreign language as well as a native speaker if they only begin to learn it in adolescence or adulthood.

More importantly, early experiences can determine how proficient a child becomes in his or her native language.

Researchers found that when mothers frequently spoke to their infants, their children learned almost 300 more words by age 2 than did their peers whose mothers rarely spoke to them. Furthermore, studies have suggested that mere exposure to language such as listening to the television or to adults talking amongst themselves provides little benefit. Rather infants need to interact directly with other human beings, to hear people talking about what they are seeing and experiencing, in order for them to develop optimal language skills. Unfortunately, many parents are under the mistaken impression that talking to babies is not very important because they are too young to understand what is being said.

A new consensus is emerging about the importance of intervening with families of disadvantaged children in the first months and years of life to ensure they provide the kinds of experiences that support optimal development.

Psychologists have long known that children of poorly educated, low-income parents often don't reach the same intellectual levels as children of well-educated, wealthy parents. The recent developments in brain research have provided new insights into why this is so. Parents who are preoccupied with a daily struggle to ensure that their children have enough to eat and are safe from harm may not have the resources, information, or time they need to provide the stimulating experiences that foster optimal brain development. Infants and children who are rarely spoken to, who are exposed to few toys, and who have little opportunity to explore and experiment with their environment may fail to fully develop the neural connections and pathways that facilitate later learning.

Despite their normal genetic endowment, these children are at a significant intellectual disadvantage and are likely to require costly special education or other remedial services when they enter school. Fortunately, intervention programs that start working with children and their families at birth or even prenatally can help prevent this tragic loss of potential.

Brain Development and Developmental Disabilities

Children and adults with developmental (intellectual) and learning difficulties may exhibit delayed cognitive development. Some may suffer from profound delays, while others may show minor difficulties in learning. We know, from our current state of knowledge that the functional organisation of the brain, as it develops, may be disrupted at various stages, starting from when the foetal brain is in its early stages of development to post birth, until adolescence. Various genetic and environmental factors may cause such disruption in the regulation of the orderly development of the brain.

It is, therefore, of interest to briefly look at some of the developmental stages in the foetal brain and also look at how a normal brain develops after birth. This gives us a frame of reference for understanding many of the syndromes that unfortunately represent maldevelopment of the brain.

Initial Stages in Brain Development

About the 18th day of gestation, the nervous system begins as a plate of tissue. The edges of this plate fold to form a tube, much as one may fold a rolled sheet of dough. The two ends of the tube then close by the 26th day. This closed tube eventually develops into the brain and spinal cord. Disturbances to this process result in errors in the neural tube closure.

The following are some examples:

Anencephaly: In this condition, the head end of the tube has not closed, resulting in the absence of major parts of the skull, brain and brain stem. These foetuses do not survive.

Myelomeningocele: The tail end of the neural tube fails to develop appropriately, resulting in deficiency in the axial skeleton. These infants survive but have major deficits.

Middle Stages of Development

During this stage, intense growth of the neural tube takes place resulting in the formation of the face and forebrain. The most intense activity takes place during the 5th and 6th weeks: Much of the nerve tracts associated with the eye and nose develop, as well as the cranial nerves, basal ganglia (inner parts of the brain) and the two cerebral hemispheres. In the 2nd and 3rd months, other structures such as the hypothalamic plate (the centre that controls endocrines, temperature and appetite) develop. Most important, the bridge between the hemisphere called the corpus callosum develops, to be completed by 20 weeks of gestation.

Understandably, disruptions at this stage may cause profound damage; however, some damage may not even be detected during life.

Agenesis of Corpus Callosum: In this condition, the bridge between the two brain hemispheres is defective, resulting in problems in the communication between the two parts of the brain. Depending on the extent of the damage, the brain may compensate for these defects and the individual may be able to function, albeit with some difficulties.

Later Stages of Development

From between two and four months, the basic structure of the brain starts growing. Nerve cells, receptors and the supporting structures start proliferating. Disorders at this stage may result in small brains called micrencephaly or excessive deranged proliferation called macrencephaly. Various degrees of cognitive difficulties result from this.

Apart from growth during this stage, millions of nerve cells move to various specific regions of the brain and settle down. This migration is at its peak around the 5th month. Disturbances can result in serious malformations of the brain to patches of nerve cells found in abnormal places. Seizures are frequent clinical events. Carbon monoxide poisoning at around 22 weeks of gestation may cause some types of migrational problems.

From about the 5th month to several years after birth, the brain goes through an organisational phase. During this stage, the nerve cells and receptors grow in numbers initially but after two years of age are gradually pruned until adolescence to nearly 50% of the original number. This process is very important and enables the infant to adapt to living in the world with all its various demands. This process enables appropriate connections to develop in the circuitry in the brain. The organisation of the brain is dependent on a certain structure within the brain called the subplate. This structure provides a docking site for the connections that flow from the rest of the brain to the future cortex. These neurones also wait in the subplate, like passengers in a railway station, and in the process, mature and get ready for an onward journey. Eventually, they travel to a specific layer of the cortex (the outer brain) which is now differentiating into a six layered structure. If the subplate neurones are damaged during the 2nd and 3rd trimesters of pregnancy, the subsequent organisation of the neural network in the brain is severely disrupted. These networks are the basic wiring needed for cognitive development.

The growth of the brain continues, as alluded to above, even after birth. However, after birth, it is more a process of pruning the excessive wiring, and the development of extensive connections between the neurones and synapses. This process of dendritic connections (dendrites are wiring that sprout from the head of the nerve cell) is most active during and after adolescence. At the same time, the density of receptors in layer II and III of the cortex increases. These are the layers that are involved in information processing. Localised disruption to this process will only become evident clinically after several years, around adolescence. This explains why in some children cognitive abilities decline in mid or later childhood. Disorders of the organisation of neural connections, as described above, are associated with mental retardation with or without seizures; Down's syndrome, Angelman syndrome, infantile autism, Duchene's muscular dystrophy, etc.

Another important development is myelination. Myelin is a sheath that wraps around the neuronal wiring to insulate and facilitate faster transmission of electrical potentials. This process begins prior to birth and continues until adulthood in an orderly fashion. For example, sensory pathways are myelinated first and motor pathways after. The rear lobe (occipital) that is concerned with vision is myelinated first and the frontal lobe (the executive brain) later. This explains why in children sensory efficiency develops before motor efficiency and why complex problem solving and such cognitive abilities develop much later. Disorders of myelination lead to conditions such as cerebral white matter hypoplasia, amino and organic acidopathies, congenital hypothyroidism, periventricular leukomalacia.

6

Emotional Development

A child's development includes both physical and emotional stages. We frequently concentrate on the stages of our child's physical development and have little insight or understanding about the importance of our child's emotional development. Understanding the stages of your child's emotional development will help you to make sense of your child's behaviour. It will help you to think about and acknowledge how your child might be feeling at a particular time and enable you to help him/her to work through what has been experienced. It is important to remember that each child develops in his/her own unique way depending on personality and at different rates from each other.

The following are guidelines for the emotional developmental stages of children:

Babies (0 – 1 Months);

- Baby is adjusting to life outside the womb
- Crying is a normal
- Needs to feel calm, safe and have a routine .

2-3 Months;

- Showing a wide variety of feelings and expresses emotions through smiles frowns, body movements, gurgling and cooing
- Comforted by being fed and cuddled
- More settled – beginning to settle into a more regular routine and happy to be changed
- Recognises familiar people and likes to smile at them .

4 – 6 Months;

- Beginning to show fear around unknown people
- Able to laugh and make happy sounds
- Calmed when picked up and on hearing familiar voice.

6 – 12 Months;

- Strong reaction to strangers and clings to parent.
- May start to resist when not happy to do something
- Enjoys attention
- May soothe him/herself with familiar toy or thumb sucking
- Emotional expressions are increased to include fear and sadness.

12 – 18 Months;

- Beginning to show negative emotions and may resist naps, refuse some foods and may have tantrums
- Begins to understand turn taking games
- Needs comfort and reassurance from parents/carers
- Afraid of being apart from carer and cry when they see carer leave.

Two Years;

- Shows extreme behaviour-dependent/interdependent, very aggressive/calm, and helpful/stubborn.
- Gets angry when stopped doing something that is unsafe
- Temper tantrums are common and tends to cry, scream, kick, bite and can be rough with other children
- Needs parent/teacher/carer to tell him what is right and wrong
- Easily distracted because of short attention span
- Has little concept of sharing – plays alone alongside other children
- Likes routine and any changes are upsetting
- Beginning to show feelings of sympathy, pity and pride and aware of praise and smile
- Becoming more independent
- Afraid of noises, trains, thunder and flushing toilets. Separation from parent, especially at bedtime is still frightening

- May be able to hold picture of loved one in mind which will help child to cope with separation from main carer (18 months – 3 years)
- Fear of strangers decreasing.

Three Years;

- Play is the main activity of this stage and is important in the development of identity and confidence
- Demonstrates a balance of happiness and contentment
- Continues to be self-centred and may feel responsible for everything that happens
- Vivid imagination and can have imaginary friends
- Ability to bargain but not to reason
- Distraction techniques still work
- Less frustrated and angry
- Fear of dark remains and may have fear of moving objects and fear of being abandoned by parent.

Four Years;

- Enjoys jokes and silly games and loves showing off
- Play still very important
- Can still demonstrate stubbornness, aggression, kicking, biting and blaming others for their naughtiness especially older siblings
- A sense of past/future developing
- Fear of dark continues
- May compete with parent of same sex for attention of parent of opposite sex
- Needs parent for support and reassurance.

Five Years;

- Becoming more independent and can be serious and realistic at times
- Demonstrates anger by slamming doors and stamping of feet and verbally by saying 'I hate you '.
- Friendly & talkative to strangers
- May worry that something might happen to a parent while the child is not there and parents will not be available to them when needed

- Protective and kind towards parents, younger child or pet
- Becoming less frustrated and less angry.

Fighting Between Siblings

Fighting between siblings is normal child behaviour. Some Infants fight more than others but they will all fight on occasions. While they are fighting they are learning conflict management and how to get along with each other in a safe way. They are learning valuable social skills for the future. While this is normal parents can help to keep the fighting from outright war by some careful planning.

- Be fair and try not to take sides. There are several ways of perfecting this art. If the Infants are fighting over a toy and it is getting out of hand it is a good idea to remain calm, confiscate the toy and tell them in a calm voice that they can have it back as soon as they decide what they are going to do about sharing it. Some parents use a timer once the agreement is reached and that usually works well.
- Another way of reducing fighting with older pre school children and improve problem solving is to sit down with both children and give the following list of questions to them one at a time. Where did it happen, what happened, what did you do, what did the Infants do, how did you feel, how did the sibling feel. Then ask them to come up with some suggestions for the next time this happens. You will have to adapt this idea to suit their level but many parents find that having this structure in their head helps them to keep calm and prevents them from accusing one or other and getting it wrong.
- Give your children the respect they deserve by listening to them and talking things out with them. Try not to criticize and compare them to Infants or other children. Apply discipline through consequences and not smacking.
- Acknowledge their feelings and that its ok to be angry but not ok to kick or hit their sibling and that it is best to talk things out rather than acting them out.

- Pay less attention to the fighting and don't rush in immediately to sort things out. They may find their own way to do this if you wait. Of course you will have to intervene if there is danger
- Catch them being good and give praise, hugs and cuddles.
- Make sure you give them good examples of how to solve conflict with your partner, friends and members of your family, for further advice contact your local Health Visitor or GP.

Link Between Emotions and Behaviour

Emotions and behaviour are linked. Sometimes the link is clear but at other times it is not obvious, consistent or predictable. Examples of this are, we smile and laugh when we are happy or excited but we can also do this when we are nervous. We cry when we are upset but also when we are happy. We can tremble with excitement but we can also tremble with fear. An example of a clear link is when you refuse to buy the toy or clothes your child wants and because of this she has a tantrum.

A less obvious link could be when your son becomes disinterested about school and you eventually discover that he has had a fight with his best friend.

The most important thing to remember is that a change in your child's behaviour represents a change in your child's emotions. When changes in behaviour are positive we tend to be happy about them and rarely think about the reasons for the change. However when the change is a negative one it merits close attention and it is worth taking time to think about it first before reacting, especially thinking about the possible emotions that are driving the change.

For example:

- Could your child be experiencing stress?
- Has your child behaved like this before and if so what caused the change last time?
- Is he aware of his behaviour and has he given you any explanation for it?

'Understanding alone is 70% of the solution and sometimes the only solution needed' *Michael Quinn Family Caring Trust 2003.*

Once you have understood and established the link between the behaviour and the emotions, try to decide how you can bring about a positive change.

The following suggestions may help:

- Set clear behavioural boundaries
- Encourage regular chats with your child about the things in his life and his feelings about his life in general
- Try not to expect too much from him because he is unlikely to be aware of the full range of emotions that influence his behaviour. Try naming his feelings e.g. 'you are feeling sad or you are angry about that', this will help him to understand the links between his emotions and behaviour over time.
- Before jumping to conclusions too quickly think about the simplest explanation first.

  Also give consideration to all aspects of his life e.g. home life, school and his friendships.
- Remember developmental stages bring about changes in behaviour. One example of this is just before starting primary school some children become more assertive in their behaviour which can take parents by surprise.

Emotional Development and the Infant Brain

One of the most fundamental tasks an infant undertakes is determining whether and how he can get his needs met in the world in which he lives.

He is constantly assessing whether his cries for food and comfort are ignored or lovingly answered, whether he is powerless or can influence what adults do. If the adults in his life respond predictably to his cries and provide for his needs, the infant will be more likely to use these adults as sources of safety and security. With his safety taken care of, he then can focus his attention on exploring, allowing his brain to take in all the wonders of the world around him. If, however, his needs are met only sporadically and pleas for comfort are usually ignored or met with harsh words and rough handling, the infant will focus his energies on ensuring that his needs are met. He will have more and more difficulty interacting with people and objects in his environment, and his brain will shut out the stimulation it needs to develop healthy cognitive and social skills.

Children who receive sensitive, responsive care from their parents and other caregivers in the first years of life enjoy an important head start toward success in their lives. The secure relationships they develop with the important adults in their lives lay the foundation for emotional development and help protect them from the many stresses they may face as they grow. Researchers who have examined the life histories of children who have succeeded despite many challenges in their lives consistently found that these people have had at least one stable, supportive relationship with an adult (usually a parent, relative, or teacher) beginning early in life.

The Effects of Trauma and Chronic Stress

Negative early experiences can also profoundly affect the development of the brain. Unfortunately, child abuse and neglect are pervasive social problems. Each year in the United States there are more than a million substantiated cases – and many more than that probably never come to light. Maltreatment increases a child's risk of developing depression, self-destructive behaviour, eating disorders, attention deficit disorders, drug and alcohol problems, sexual promiscuity, and delinquency. Many researchers believe that these effects can be partly explained by understanding how chaotic, stressful, and traumatic experiences affect brain development.

However, this is a new area of study, with much more that we need to learn.

At the moment, we know the most about how traumatic experiences affect the brains of children who develop Post-Traumatic Stress Disorder (PTSD). Similar to adults with PTSD, these children have trouble sleeping, can't control their memories of the trauma, and seem to be on constant alert. Estimates vary from as low as 30% to as high as 90% for the likelihood of developing PTSD for some period following sexual and physical abuse in childhood – and it can have long-lasting effects (Fletcher, 1996). While experiencing the symptoms of PTSD, children have difficulty learning and maintaining positive relationships with family and peers. Although the ability of the brain to put abused children on constant alert may help them to survive in traumatic environments (for example, the battered child may be able to better avoid the abusive father when he is in a bad mood) it exacts a cost, for the child and for society.

It is important that we not assume that a poorly parented or traumatized child is incapable of healthy functioning later in childhood or adolescence. Research on the developing brain suggests continuing opportunity for change into adulthood and provides no evidence that there is some age beyond which intervention will fail to make a difference. In fact, this research provides exciting new clues as to what kinds of therapy might be most helpful for children who have experienced difficult lives. Clearly, however, the costs (in human suffering, loss of potential, and real money) of trying to repair, remediate, or heal these children is far greater than the costs of preventing these problems by promoting healthy development of the brain during the first few years of life.

Helping Families Support Healthy Brain Development

It is now clear that what a child experiences in the first years of life profoundly influences how his brain will develop and how he will interact with the world throughout his life. Parents play the most important role in providing the nurturing and stimulation that children require, but they need information and support to develop good parenting skills. In the past, extended family members were often close by, offering good advice and acting as role models for inexperienced parents. Young families today often live far away from grandparents and other family and rely more on community resources for information and support in parenting. There is much that communities can do to help families promote their children's healthy brain development. Educate parents about the importance of early experiences for their children's development.

Often parents don't know about the many little things they can do to foster their children's healthy cognitive and emotional development, like talking to the children beginning in infancy, reading to them from a very early age, and helping them play simple games. Parents, especially new or young parents, may also need help learning to recognize their children's cues that they are hungry for stimulation or have had enough.

In some cases written materials or a few sessions of parenting education classes may be all that a parent needs to learn how to provide his or her child with appropriate stimulation. However, parenting styles and beliefs that have evolved over generations—such as rarely talking to babies—can be difficult for parents to change. Many parents benefit from community-based programs in which a parent group leader or a home visitor acts as a role model and coach, supporting parents in their relationships with their children. Programs that work with parents over several years can be very successful in helping them become effective "first teachers" of their children (Olds et al, 1993).

Prevent abuse and Neglect

Children who are abused or severely neglected are at extremely high risk of developing emotional, behavioural, social, and intellectual disabilities. By the time a child is identified as having been neglected or abused, these problems have already begun to develop. Greater attention must be given to preventing maltreatment before it starts. High-quality home visiting programs that start working with families as soon as the child is born have proven to be effective in preventing abuse and neglect. The key to these programs' success is that they help parents manage the stresses of raising children before unhealthy patterns develop and things get out of control.

Provide Accessible, Quality Mental Health Services for Parents

Research has shown that parents suffering from untreated depression often fail to respond sensitively to their children's cries and bids for attention, and that they are unlikely to provide the child with the kind of cognitive stimulation that promotes healthy brain development (Field, 1995). Other mental illnesses, such as schizophrenia, can also dramatically affect a parent's ability to interact appropriately with his or her child.

Proper mental health treatment for these parents can make a real difference in their ability to raise a competent, well-adjusted child.

Ensure adequate nutrition prenatally and in the first years after birth.

Numerous studies have shown the devastating effects on intelligence and brain development of a lack of basic nutrients in the prenatal period, in infancy and in early childhood. Programs such as the Special Supplemental Program for Women, Infants, and Children (WIC) can be effective in ensuring that babies receive the kinds of foods they need to thrive. Educational and outreach campaigns to alert women to the importance of nutrition in the first trimester of pregnancy would also be helpful in preventing problems that can arise in this critical period when brain cells begin to form.

7

Sexual Development

Your five-year-old daughter is playing in her room with a couple of friends.

You hear a lot of giggling and squealing.

When you open the door to check on the kids, you find them sitting on the floor with their panties off, pointing at and touching each other's genitals.

What do you do?

Every day, parents around the world are faced with situations like this. Being caught off-guard by young children's self-exploration and curiosity about body parts and sexual issues is one of the uncomfortable realities of parenting, and can raise a host of troubling questions, such as, "Is my child normal?" "Should I be worried?" "What should I say?"

Although talking with children about bodily changes and sexual matters may feel awkward, providing children with accurate, age-appropriate information is one of the most important things parents can do to make sure children grow up safe, healthy, and secure in their bodies.

Sexual Development and Behaviour in Young Children: The Basics

Like all forms of human development, sexual development begins at birth. Sexual development includes not only the physical changes that occur as children grow, but also the sexual knowledge and beliefs they come to learn and the behaviours they show. Any given child's sexual knowledge and behaviour is strongly influenced by:

The child's age (1-3).

What the child observes (including the sexual behaviours of family and friends).

What the child is taught (including cultural and religious beliefs concerning sexuality and physical boundaries).

Very young and preschool-aged children (four or younger) are naturally immodest, and may display open—and occasionally startling—curiosity about other people's bodies and bodily functions, such as touching women's breasts, or wanting to watch when grownups go to the bathroom. Wanting to be naked (even if others are not) and showing or touching private parts while in public are also common in young children. They are curious about their own bodies and may quickly discover that touching certain body parts feels nice.

As children age and interact more with other children (approximately ages 4–6), they become more aware of the differences between boys and girls, and more social in their exploration. In addition to exploring their own bodies through touching or rubbing their private parts (masturbation), they may begin "playing doctor" and copying adult behaviours such as kissing and holding hands. As children become increasingly aware of the social rules governing sexual behaviour and language (such as the importance of modesty or which words are considered "naughty"), they may try to test these rules by using naughty words. They may also ask more questions about sexual matters, such as where babies come from, and why boys and girls are physically different.

Age	Uncommon/Problematic Behaviours
Preschool children (less than 4 years)	Exploring and touching private parts, in public and in private Rubbing private parts (with hand or against objects) Showing private parts to others Trying to touch mother's or other women's breasts Removing clothes and wanting to be naked Attempting to see other people when they are naked or undressing (such as in the bathroom) Asking questions about their own—and others'—bodies and bodily functions Talking to children their own age about bodily functions such as "poop" and "pee"

Young Children (approximately 4-6 years)	Purposefully touching private parts (masturbation), occasionally in the presence of others Attempting to see other people when they are naked or undressing Mimicking dating behaviour (such as kissing, or holding hands) Talking about private parts and using "naughty" words, even when they don't understand the meaning Exploring private parts with children their own age (such as "playing doctor", "I'll show you mine if you show me yours," etc.)
School-Aged Children (approximately 7-12 years)	Purposefully touching private parts (masturbation), usually in private Playing games with children their own age that involve sexual behaviour (such as "truth or dare", "playing family," or "boyfriend/ girlfriend") Attempting to see other people naked or undressing Looking at pictures of naked or partially naked people Viewing/ listening to sexual content in media (television, movies, games, the Internet, music, etc.) Wanting more privacy (for example, not wanting to undress in front of other people) and being reluctant to talk to adults about sexual issues Beginnings of sexual attraction to/interest in peers.

Once children enter grade school (approximately ages 7–12), their awareness of social rules increases and they become more modest and want more privacy, particularly around adults. Although self touch (masturbation) and sexual play continue, children at this age are likely to hide these activities from adults. Curiosity about adult sexual behaviour increases—particularly as puberty approaches—and children may begin to seek out sexual content in television, movies, and printed material. Telling jokes and "dirty" stories is common. Children approaching puberty are likely to start displaying romantic and sexual interest in their peers.

Although parents often become concerned when a child shows sexual behaviour, such as touching another child's private parts, these behaviours are not uncommon in developing children. Most sexual play is an expression of children's natural curiosity and should not be a cause for concern or alarm. In general, "typical" childhood sexual play and exploration:

* Occurs between children who play together regularly and know each other well
* Occurs between children of the same general age and physical size
* Is spontaneous and unplanned
* Is infrequent
* Is voluntary (the children agreed to the behaviour, none of the involved children seem uncomfortable or upset)
* Is easily diverted when parents tell children to stop and explain privacy rules.

Some childhood sexual behaviours indicate more than harmless curiosity, and are considered sexual behaviour problems. Sexual behaviour problems may pose a risk to the safety and well-being of the child and other children.

Sexual behaviour problems include any act that:

* Is clearly beyond the child's developmental stage (for example, a three-year-old attempting to kiss an adult's genitals)
* Involves threats, force, or aggression
* Involves children of widely different ages or abilities (such as a 12-year-old "playing doctor" with a four-year-old)
* Provokes strong emotional reactions in the child—such as anger or anxiety.

Responding to Sexual Behaviours

Situations like the one described at the beginning of this handout can be unsettling for parents.

However, these situations also offer excellent opportunities to assess how much children understand and to teach important information about sexual matters.

The first step is to try to figure out what actually happened. To do this, it's important to stay calm.

Staying calm will allow you to make clear decisions about what you say and/or do, rather than acting on strong emotions. To remain composed, try taking a long, deep breath, counting to ten, or even closing the door and stepping away for a couple of minutes before saying anything. In the case described above, a parent might calmly tell the children that it's time to get dressed and then ask each child to go to a different room in the house. After taking a few moments to collect his or her thoughts—and to consult with a spouse or partner if feeling very unsettled— the parent could then talk to each child one-on-one.

When talking to children about sexual behaviours, it's important to maintain a calm and even tone of voice and to ask open-ended questions as much as possible, so the children can tell what happened in their own words, rather than just answering yes or no. So, in this case, a parent might ask each child:

* What were you doing?
* How did you get the idea?
* How did you learn about this?
* How did you feel about doing it?

In the opening scenario, all of the children involved were about the same age, had been playmates for some time, and seemed to be enjoying their game. So, it's likely the children were just curious and playing around and that no one was upset about what happened. If you encounter a situation where the children are a little embarrassed but otherwise not distressed, this can present an ideal opportunity for teaching the children about healthy boundaries and rules about sexual behaviour.

Educating Children about Sexual Issues

Just because a behaviour is typical doesn't mean the behaviour should be ignored. Often, when children participate in sexual behaviour it indicates that they need to learn something. Teach what the child needs to know, given the situation. In this case, for example, the parent might teach the children that it's okay to be curious about other people's bodies, but that private parts should be kept private, even with friends.

Although children usually respond well when parents take the time to give them correct information and answer their questions, it is important to provide information that is appropriate to the child's age and developmental level. Keep in mind that you do not need to bombard children with information all at once. Let the situation—and the child's questions—guide the lessons you share. The important thing is to let children know that you are ready to listen and to answer whatever questions they may have.

Too often, children get the majority of their sexual education from other children and from media sources such as television shows, songs, movies, and video games. Not only is this information often wrong, it may have very little to do with sexual values that parents want to convey. Explicit adult sexual activities are sometimes found during "family time" television shows, in commercials, and on cartoon/children's channels, and can have an influence on children's behaviours.

Controlling media exposure and providing appropriate alternatives is an important part of teaching children about sexual issues. Get to know the rating systems of games, movies, and television shows and make use of the parental controls available through many internet, cable, and satellite providers.

However, don't assume that just by activating those controls you will be taking care of the situation.

It's very important for you to be aware of what your children are watching on television and online, and make time to watch television with them. When appropriate, you can use this time as a springboard to talk about sexual or relationship issues, and to help children develop the skills to make healthy decisions about their behaviour and relationships.

Preschool Children (Less than 4 Years)

Basic Information

- Boys and girls are different
- Accurate names for body parts of boys and girls
- Babies come from mommies
- Rules about personal boundaries (for example, keeping private parts covered, not touching other children's private parts)
- Give simple answers to all questions about the body and bodily functions.

Safety Information

- The difference between "okay" touches (which are comforting, pleasant, and welcome) and "not okay" touches (which are intrusive, uncomfortable, unwanted, or painful)
- Your body belongs to you % % Everyone has the right to say "no" to being touched, even by grownups
- No one—child or adult—has the right to touch your private parts
- It's okay to say "no" when grownups ask you to do things that are wrong, such as touching private parts or keeping secrets from mommy or daddy
- There is a difference between a "surprise"—which is something that will be revealed sometime soon, like a present—and a "secret," which is something you're never supposed to tell.

Moral and Aesthetic Development

Giftedness denotes extraordinary brainpower, or a collection of extra abilities that seem to vary endlessly in unique and subtle combinations, all of them treasured in our society. Developmentally, it is an age-stage concept in the sense that children are "gifted" only in comparison with other children, as are adults in relation to adult standards. Psychometrically, it is a relative concept in the sense that

it deviates from age norms in *degree,* rather than in *kind.* To the extent, then, that relative mental strength can be measured at all in children of various ages, it is possible to recognize signs, or at least hints, of individual excellence among them. This applies in the earliest years of life as well, even though the aptitudes assessed at that age level are unlike those of older children.

Individual differences between infants as early as immediately following birth have focused on perceptual skills, responsiveness, alertness, rate of activity, intensity, and other psychomotor variables. Scientists seem to compete in the race to find new, yet unknown, capacities of infants, or to demonstrate how early infants are capable of perceiving and responding differentially to various stimuli.

Research on intellective attributes of the very young gifted is still rare, and whatever evidence exists deals primarily with children over age 3. The frequently quoted studies on younger subjects are Brown's two case studies (1964, 1970). However, the most extensive research has been conducted on older children, the prime example being Terman's longitudinal studies of high-IQ, elementary school samples (Oden, 1968). Since early Haley measures of young gifted children were not predictive of later tested intelligence, the use of other measures, specifically attention, memory, and language development, was recommended for the identification of very young gifted children. However, no longitudinal studies designed to test the Willerman-Fiedler hypothesis have yet been reported. As early as in 1954, Hofstaetter suggested that independent variables change in predicting tested intelligence from infancy onward. He reported that sensorimotor alertness accounts for most of the variance in children's intelligence test performance up to the age of 20 months; from 20 to 40 months the dominant source of intelligence test variance is persistence; and beginning at 48 months most of the variance is accounted for by the factor he labelled "manipulation of symbols."

A striking feature of intellectually gifted children is their ability to acquire relatively large amounts of knowledge and varieties of skills far more rapidly than do most age-mates. Gifted youngsters seem to learn easily, efficiently, and willingly, and they retain what they learn for a long time. The brighter the child, the more he or she seems able to extract ideas from the environment (Freeman, 1985).

In fact, the unusual cognitive and non-intellective traits of some children alert us to the possibility of their being gifted. For example, Feldman (1982) reported that gifted children have a near-photographic memory, a large vocabulary, a vivid imagination, lots of hobbies and collections, and an insatiable curiosity. One additional characteristic associated with their verbal precocity is the high frequency in which they formulate questions to satisfy their curiosity. Some signs of these traits can be found in children long before they are of an age to enter school.

The objective of the focus on aesthetics and art was to enrich the child's channels of expression, and to enable him or her to differentiate and enjoy the aesthetic qualities of the environment. The mediators highlighted and raised the children's awareness of objects that are aesthetically pleasing, giving reasons for and describing their aesthetic qualities.

According to developmental theory, learning occurs when individuals interact with their environments (which include people and how they behave, objects and phenomena encountered in the world) and then reflect on that interaction. The learner actively constructs understanding from processing her/his experience, making meaning of every new opportunity or bit of information.

In other words, for learning to occur, an individual does something, experiences and thinks about the results of the action (including verbal "actions"), and decides what these results mean to her/him—whether it is a child eliciting sounds from a rattle, a teenager learning to drive, or an adult trying to master a foreign language.

The Role of the Environment in Development

Human cognitive development is highly dependent on the environment to which an individual is exposed. As a child grows, and as her interactions with the environment expand and diversify, she receives stimulation for further development of meaning-making strategies by encountering new problems that call for finding new solutions.

The speed of a child's development varies widely, given different environments. Developmentally-appropriate stimulation and exposure can support and even accelerate development. For example, giving a child who has outgrown a tricycle a two-wheeler with training wheels can accelerate the speed with which s/he learns to balance and pedal the more difficult vehicle while minimizing the possibility of failure and harm.

The opposite is also true: the absence of stimulation can slow down or weaken the developmental process—so, for example, not talking to a child—naming the foods he eats, colors he wears, things he encounters, and describing actions, feelings, and so forth—may result in late and/or inadequate language development.

What is Moral Development?

As children develop their general thinking skills, they're expected to start to conform to the morality rules that society dictates. Psychological theories of moral development, differ immensely in their opinions on how moral development occurs. Freud claims that the quality of relationship the child has with his/her parent/s greatly affects the way the child develops morally. Whereas, the Social Learning theory states that children initially learn how to behave morally through modelling (imitating appropriate adult behaviour. Cognitive-developmental theories claim that a child's ability to reason morally depend on his/her general thinking abilities. All of the theories, although somewhat different from each other, help us in our plight to understand moral development.

Theories of Moral Development

Cognitive developmental theorists claim that a child's ability to reason morally depend on his/her level of general thinking abilities.

Piaget investigated moral development in two ways:

- He proposed moral issues to children and analysed their responses
- He observed the way in which children used rules in game playing.

Piaget claimed that children develop an outlook on rules in different stages.

- Preschoolers play for enjoyment and disregard rules
- Six year olds consider rules to be sacred and inflexible
- Ten year olds realise that rules can be manipulated.

Piaget claims that children differ in response to moral dilemmas depending what stage of moral development they are in.

- Children younger than ten are at the stage of development called moral realism. They determine whether an act was good or bad depending on how much damage occurred regardless of the intentions behind the act
- Next, children move onto a stage of moral reasoning called moral relativism. Moral relativism takes motives

into account and doesn't believe that every wrong action should necessarily be punished. For example, if a girl broke her sister's porcelain doll she should only be punished if she intentionally broke the doll

Kohlberg asked boys, between the ages of ten and sixteen, moral dilemmas (for example, "should a man steal an overpriced drug that he can't afford, to save his wife from cancer?") in order to analyse moral development. Through analysing the results, Kohlberg determined that there were three distinct levels of moral reasoning.

- The first level, called the preconventional level, is when the child's actions are primarily motivated in order to gain a reward or to avoid punishment
- At the second level, the conventional level, children's moral decisions are greatly influenced by society. The child wants to be an upstanding citizen and therefore wants to obey the rules and laws of society.
- Finally, at the postconventional level, the child is more civic minded. They are able to determine which rules can be bent, but the child also considers some values such as human dignity to be sacred.

Chronology of Child Moral Development

Understanding moral and pro-social development:1-2 years Helps others when they are upset by offering physical comfort: 2-3 years Starts to show guilt for bad behaviour: 3-6 years Actions are motivated in order to gain a reward or to avoid punishment : 7-10 years Children's actions are primarily motivated by what other people in society will think: 10-16 years Judges moral dilemmas according to the intentions of the perpetrator: 16+ years.

Reasons on the Basis of Internal Principles

Factors Affecting Child Development

Gender : Carol Gilligan (1982) is well known for criticising Kohlberg's stages of moral development as being biased against females. Gilligan claims that females view moral dilemmas differently than males do. She argues that women tend to be more concerned with the relationships involved in a moral dilemma, whereas men are more concerned with the rights of others. Gilligan knows that not all men deal with moral issues in the same way. She's also aware that some men deal with moral issues in the same way that women do, and vice-versa. But, Gilligan still claims that Kohlberg's stages of moral development inadequately represent how women deal with moral dilemmas. However, (Walker, 1984) discovers that in most morality studies, men and women receive similar results. Walker finds that in studies where males ranked higher in moral reasoning skills, it was because the males were usually more educated than their female counterparts. Walker claims that even though women often view moral dilemmas somewhat differently than men, that women aren't penalised for their different views on Kohlberg's moral scoring system. Therefore, Kohlberg's different stages of moral reasoning seem to be unbiased in terms of gender.

Culture : Kolberg's stages of moral development are not suited to certain cultures. Research reveals that people from developed cultures pass through Kolberg's stages of moral development quicker than people from undeveloped cultures. In fact, people from undeveloped cultures rarely reach stage 4 or above. Stages 4 and above require an understanding of laws and government institutions. People in different cultures have quite different moral beliefs. For example, people in India believe that calling a parent by their first name, is regarded more serious than domestic violence. On the other hand, people in Australia condemn domestic violence, but believe that calling a parent by their first name is acceptable.

Television and Video Games

Violence

- 82% of television programs broadcast in the USA contain at least some violence
- In children's programs there are 32 acts of violence per hour (higher than adult programming)
- Cartoons are the most violent
- Young children are more susceptible to violence because they do not fully understand the link between actions and consequences

- Young children also find it difficult to separate real life from television, unless extreme violations of reality occur.
- Researchers agree that exposure to television violence results in more frequent aggressive acts by children. This is evident in long term studies as well as short term studies.
- The more violent television a child watches, the more violent he/she becomes, and the more violent television they want to watch. Children hence become accustomed to violence, and begin to view the world as a scary place.
- 80% of Nintendo and Sega genesis games surveyed contained aggression or violence as the strategy for winning (Dietz 1998)
- Dietz (1998) found that 27% was socially acceptable violence, 50% was directed at others and 21% was towards women.

Temperament

- Recent research suggests that child temperament is a valid variable which affects child development. This has implications for discipline strategies.
- Aurbach and Sharon (1997) suggests that child temperament and parental discipline directly correlate with child social competence.
- House (1997) found that positive attention and communication practices between parents decreases the likelihood of child aggression towards peers. Also harsh punishment and criticism from parents result in increased aggression.
- To assist early child moral development, it is suggested (Kochanska 1995) that parents should adapt their strategies of child rearing to fit their children.

Temperamentally inhibited children respond to gentle reasoning because this develops their conscience. Fearless impulsive children require a strong attachment bond with the care-giver.

8

Social Development

A child, as young as a few months old shows a distinct social behaviour. Most children who receive a loving and caring upbringing show a very healthy social development. The process of social development in children is gradual and stretches over many years. During this period, the parents, teachers and other close family members play a crucial role. The social development continues even when the child steps into adolescence, then youth and eventually adulthood.

What is Social Development in Children?

Social development in children can be simply defined as a child's interaction with others. During the initial stages, the child depends greatly on her parents and other caregivers. Hence, in this phase, the child's interaction is mainly limited to these people. Eventually, the child begins interacting with other kids and adults.

A child dwells a lot upon the love, security and care provided by her parents and caregivers. Eventually, the child also learns to impart love and care and shows signs of empathetic behaviour. This is an indication of sound social development of the child.

Childhood friendships provide kids with much more than just people to play with. Learning to make friends as well as learning to be a good friend are important parts of a child's social development skills that will help them to find success in both their personal and professional lives.

First Friends

For their first few years, most children are exposed largely to family members and close family friends. Being on the receiving end of the unconditional love and acceptance that family provides gives children a solid base of confidence and self-esteem from which they are able to build further social attachments. Often, a child's very first friends are the children that they meet at preschool.

Learning Through Play

Most of the learning that young children do is through play, and building social competence is no different. Typically, 2-3 year olds will initially play side-by-side, rather than directly with one another, but as they observe each other and become comfortable, the little ones will begin to interact and share toys. By preschool, kids become even more interactive, engaging each other in simple conversation. They will talk about the things that they did after school or on the weekend and respond positively to the stories of their friends. This give-and-take is a great step in social development as they work from being self-focused to other-focused.

Looking out for One Another

As friendships develop, kids become increasingly aware of the feelings of other people, expressing happiness when their friends are happy and showing empathy for a friend's hurt feelings. They will also seek out their similarities, instinctively knowing that sharing common bonds is important to maintaining friendships. They'll focus on favourite colours, foods, or games, and delight in the fact that they are alike in many ways. Another common development as friendship capacity develops is a child's desire to protect their friends. Friends stick together, and that lesson comes to most children during their school years as one friend goes through a difficulty and another's instinct is to stand up for their troubled friend. Further bonded by their common experience, their loyalty to the friendship deepens.

Stages of Social Development in Children

Eric Erikson, an educationalist and psychiatrist proposed a theory of the eight-staged social development, known as

Erikson's psychological stages of development. The process begins in infancy and stretches over into adulthood. The eight stages of social development as proposed by Erikson are as follows.

Basic Trust Versus Basic Mistrust

This is the first stage of a child's social behaviour that begins in infancy and ends by the time the child is 1-2 years old. A child who is well taken care of develops security, trust and a general feeling of optimism towards her surroundings, whereas a badly parented child develops feelings of insecurity and becomes mistrustful.

Autonomy Versus Shame

This is the second phase of the child's social development which extends up to 4 years of age. During this period the child becomes confident and takes liberty in exploring the world around her. She becomes increasingly aware of her independence and doesn't mind breaking away from her parents in familiar surroundings. The child also shows an understandable anxiety towards strangers. The child may also throw occasional temper tantrums.

Initiative Versus Guilt

During this stage the child becomes more interactive towards other kids. She learns to cooperate with others. She also indulges in group plays and other activities. The child learns to lead as well as to follow. The emotional and physical dependence on parents is still there as the child is being introduced to new emotions such as fear, guilt etc.

Industry Versus Inferiority

The child gets acquainted with the rules of the world. Since, children of this age begin formal education, they become accustomed to fixed schedules and certain rules and regulations that we are supposed to abide by. Their play also becomes more rule-oriented as they now shift from individual games to team games, which follow a framework of rules. Normal children grow up to become quite industrious by this time. However, children who are not well taken care of, often develop a mistrust for their future or develop an inferiority complex.

Identity Versus Identity Diffusion

This is the phase where the child enters adolescence. She becomes conscious of her own identity and seeks an answer to the question 'who am I?' A slightly rebellious behaviour is normal during this stage, as the child experiences a flood of myriad emotions. The child becomes aware of her sexual identity during the later stages of adolescence.

Intimacy Versus Isolation

The child (now an adult) becomes capable of establishing lasting relationships, such as marriage or friendship. For the first time in her life the child experiences a feeling of true intimacy.

Generativity Versus Self-Absorption

The person begins to fulfil various responsibilities on the personal as well as professional front. She is usually at the peak of her career and also experiences joys of parenthood.

Integrity Versus Despair

Person feels a sense of accomplishment and pride about her life. She attains a worldly wisdom and develops a general feeling of gratification. A person who failed to achieve normal social development state at any of the above stages may experience a feeling of despair in her life.

Thus, the importance of social development in children cannot be undermined as it lays the foundation for a physically and emotionally healthy adulthood. As parents, it is your responsibility to create a conducive environment for your child's sound social development.

Social Development, Ages 2-3

From the ages of two to three, social development in toddlers tends to be very self-centred. Despite this, toddlers are willing to conform and will imitate the behaviour of those around them. They will imitate their parents, so the example parents are setting at this point in time is so important. If toddlers see fighting, they will exhibit fighting. If they see kindness, they will generally exhibit kindness. With support, they have the ability to recognize others' rights and will wait briefly for their own turn. This age is very important because it forms the child's attitude towards others, towards authority, and towards their parents. Toddlers generally want to help and please. Additionally, their nervous system is sensitive to overstimulation and by noise and confusion, so in this type of situation, you will see possible frustration, leading to crying, kicking, biting, or temper tantrums. Temper tantrums are sometimes caused by the inability to express their feelings or emotions or by stress. Emotionally, toddlers are very curious and ask a lot of questions, but also learn by observing and exploring.

Social Development, Ages 4-5

From ages four to five, children love to imitate adults. Little girls love to play with dolls with a mommy and babies, while boys like to imitate action figures or cartoon stars. At times, four to five year olds begin to show leadership and begin to become bossy, both with peers and with younger siblings. They begin to understand the concept of fairness and will often complain that things are unfair. Four to five year olds do have the social development to share with peers or with siblings, at least to a higher degree than a two to three year old. At four to five years old, children become aware of how others perceive them and are concerned about peer relationships. They want to be liked by others. They love to be praised at this age. Their imaginations are developing, and this is evident in their role playing.

Social Development, Ages 6 to 8

From the ages of six to eight years old, children are increasingly concerned about how they are viewed by their peers, and friendship is extremely important. Competition becomes a part of life, and many children want to be the best or to be the winner. Many children are starting competitive sports, and this adds to the pressure to be a winner and to be good at something. Children become very protective of their younger siblings at this age. Children begin to show confidence in the things they are good at, but can also show frustration at things that are difficult. For example, some children find learning to read an easy process, while others find it to be very difficult, so self-esteem begins to be at stake during these years of social development. Children at this age are very literal or concrete and are increasing their vocabulary quickly, so they are better able to express their feelings. This leads to more maturity in actions and less frustration and temper tantrums.

Social Development, Ages 9-12

From ages nine to twelve, children's dominant or submissive personalities begin to emerge in their peer relationships. They have the ability to sacrifice their own interests for the interests of the group. They have particular interests and know what their interests are. They are sensitive to their strengths and weaknesses and can analyse these. They have the ability to make changes. They like a challenge and most enjoy competing. Nine to twelve year olds have a code of rules of fairness that they apply. They can begin to move beyond the concrete stage and begin to learn abstract concepts. Social peer groups have formed and bullying exists. Bullying for boys tends to include more physical fighting, teasing, and picking on weaker children, where bullying among girls tends to include teasing and social isolation.

Instincts and their Transformation

Freud talks about the three forces of the psychical apparatus: the id, the ego and the superego. The id has the quality of being unconscious and contains everything that is inherited, everything that is present at birth, and the instincts. The ego has the quality of being conscious and is responsible for controlling the demands of the id and of the instincts, becoming aware of stimuli, and serving as a link between the id and the external world. In addition, the ego responds to stimulation by either adoption or flight, regulates activity, and strives to achieve pleasure and avoid unpleasure. Finally, the superego, whose demands are managed by the id, is responsible for the limitation of satisfactions and represents the influence of others, such as parents, teachers, and role models, as well as the impact of racial, social and cultural traditions.

Freud states that the instincts are the ultimate cause of all behaviour. The two basic instincts are Eros (love) and the destructive or death instinct. The purpose of Eros is to establish and preserve unity through relationships. On the other hand, the purpose of death instinct is to undo connections and unity via destruction. The two instincts can either operate against each other through repulsion or combine with each other through attraction.

Freud contends that sexual life begins with manifestations that present themselves soon after birth. The four main phases in sexual development are the oral phase, the sadistic-anal phase, the phallic phase and the genital phase, and each phase is characterized by specific occurrences.

Freud defines the qualities of the psychical process as being either conscious, preconscious, or unconscious. The unconscious is the psychical quality that one has no direct access to. The properties that originate in the unconscious are usually repressed. One can only access the unconscious through indirect interpretations, such as dreams. The preconscious is the psychical quality that one does have access to. While the elements in the preconscious are not present in one's immediate consciousness, these elements can easily be recovered if necessary. The conscious is the psychical quality that deals with a person's immediate state of mind. It is composed of what one is thinking and acting right at that moment.

Freud talks about the three forces of the psychical apparatus: the id, the ego and the superego. The id has the quality of being unconscious and contains everything that is inherited, everything that is present at birth, and the instincts. The ego has the quality of being conscious and is responsible for controlling the demands of the id and of the instincts, becoming aware of stimuli, and serving as a link between the id and the external world. In addition, the ego responds to stimulation by either adoption or flight, regulates activity, and strives to achieve pleasure and avoid unpleasure. Finally, the superego, whose demands are managed by the id, is responsible for the limitation of satisfactions and represents the influence of others, such as parents, teachers, and role models, as well as the impact of racial, social and cultural traditions.

Freud states that the instincts are the ultimate cause of all behaviour. The two basic instincts are Eros (love) and the destructive or death instinct. The purpose of Eros is to establish and preserve unity through relationships. On the other hand, the purpose of death instinct is to undo connections and unity via destruction. The two instincts can either operate against each other through repulsion or combine with each other through attraction.

Freud contends that sexual life begins with manifestations that present themselves soon after birth. The four main phases in sexual development are the oral phase, the sadistic-anal phase, the phallic phase and the genital phase, and each phase is characterized by specific occurrences.

Freud defines the qualities of the psychical process as being either conscious, preconscious, or unconscious. The unconscious is the psychical quality that one has no direct access to. The properties that originate in the unconscious are usually repressed. One can only access the unconscious through indirect interpretations, such as dreams. The preconscious is the psychical quality that one does have access to. While the elements in the preconscious are not present in one's immediate consciousness, these elements can easily be recovered if necessary. The conscious is the psychical quality that deals with a person's immediate state of mind. It is composed of what one is thinking and acting right at that moment.

General Tendencies : Suggestion, Imitation and Sympathy

Suggestion is the psychological process by which one person guides the thoughts, feelings, or behaviour of another. Nineteenth century writers on psychology such as William James used the words "suggest" and "suggestion" in senses close to those they have in common speech—one idea was said to *suggest* another when it brought that other idea to mind. Early scientific studies of hypnosis by Clark Leonard Hull and others extended the meaning of these words in a special and technical sense (Hull, 1933). The original neuro-psychological theory of hypnotic suggestion was based upon the ideo-motor reflex response of William B. Carpenter and James Braid.

Imitation

Imitation is an advanced behaviour whereby an individual observes and replicates another's. It's an inevitable fact about children-they like to imitate what others do. This is something you can't stop, and you should not try either. Imitation is an important part of children's early learning skills. It's actually another "humans see, humans do" thing.

You see, human beings are hard-wired to learn through imitation. It is written in your biological make-up, in your brains. You have the so-called "mirror neurons" that ensure you learn by observing alone. This is yet another equipment for survival that you are born with. As thus, you don't have to teach your child to imitate, for he is born to do so.

So how does learning through imitation contribute to a person's survival? Imitation is found to play a crucial role in the process by which you learn to tie your shoelace, to feed yourself, or to follow complex dance steps. The mirror neurons that are behind the process of imitation are also responsible for an important human emotion — empathy. It is through this natural human emotion that people learn to care for each other and to survive as a civilization.

More so, nature uses this type of learning to convey culture. Imitation contributes to the natural bequeathal of the tradition of music and sports from one generation to another.

But as crucial and necessary a learning tool as it is, it can also be gravely dangerous. You must ensure that your child, in his vulnerable state, is not exposed to undesirable models to imitate. You may already have noticed how children like 'pretend play', which is yet another manifestation of the process of imitation.

Learning Through Imitation

The imitative nature of the baby and young child is so obvious and so all-pervasive that we tend to be blind to it, unaware of its implications for parenting. Your child learns everything through imitation-walking, talking, toilet training, tying shoes, endless tasks. Imitation also manifests in expressions and gestures, as when we see and hear ourselves in our children's play.

The little child, up to the age of seven, up to the change of teeth, is essentially imitative. He learns by doing what he sees being done around him. Fundamentally, all activities of the child's early years are imitations." How does this affect the young child-what does he or she imitate? *Everything.* Every action, every sight, sound, or other sense impression, every emotion from those around the child is taken in and absorbed right into the child's inner being. Even when not obviously imitated or reproduced in the child's actions, these impressions become indelibly etched in the child's nervous system and can affect the development of the whole organism. Young children do not have the buffers and filters that adults have to block out impressions. Indeed, all that babies can do to stop the flow of impressions is go to sleep.

The awareness that the French obstetrician Fredrick Leboyer brought to our understanding of the newborn's sensory experiences was explained by Steiner 50 years earlier. He said, "In the first part of life, before the change of teeth, the child is, so to say, altogether a sense organ.

This we have to take very literally. What is the characteristic action of a sense organ? It is receptive to impressions from the environment. If something striking occurs near him-for example, a burst of anger-then the reflection thereof goes right through the child. It will affect even his blood circulation and digestive system."

A baby and young child will benefit from a calm and loving environment, especially one in which attention is placed on rhythm and repetition, and not on overwhelming the baby with sense impressions. Americans are enthusiastically taught to stimulate their babies for early development. This seems to grow out of a misinterpretation of studies which showed that babies in orphanages failed to thrive for lack of a primary caregiver and lack of stimulation. What is needed is the attention of loving parents who hold, cuddle, and are responsive to the child-not flash cards, activity boards, or plastic mobiles.

Babies need the loving attention of their parents *and* they need to be shielded from over-stimulation. While baby carriers increase contact between mother and baby, they also become a means of transporting babies to places where the quality of the sights and sounds are so invasive that the children would frequently be better off at home. I took my first child to a large discount department store when he was 10 days old, something I would not do again! Most parents are initially aware of the openness of the senses of the newborn, but they lose this awareness as the uniqueness of the birth slips into the "everydayness" of life.

Protecting the Senses

The senses of the newborn remain wide open long after birth. Because of this, some parents like to put colored silk over the baby's basket to soften the light during the first few months. Similarly, parents can attend to the quality of the sounds their baby hears. No one is advocating tiptoeing around a baby; the baby needs to become accustomed to the sounds of your household. But it is worthwhile to ask about the quality of the sounds, "Are they connected to life?" Mechanical sounds from radio, television, tapes, or stereo not only have a different vibrational quality, but they also lack a living force behind them. Steiner explained how such mechanical sounds could have a detrimental effect on the developing discriminatory function of the hearing apparatus as well as on other organs. Taped lullabies and television programs, which take the place of singing to our babies or interacting with our children, also produce sound having a mechanical quality that is best avoided until after the age of seven.

In a similar way, images on television, movies, or computer screens are two-dimensional and composed of dots and emissions that can affect the developing organs and vitality of the child, regardless of the educational content of the programs. For this reason, and because television keeps young children passive and immobile when their nature is to be in movement, parents and teachers working out of the indications of Rudolf Steiner recommend that children under seven not watch television or play video games. It is helpful to realize that the effect of television on an older child is very different from its effect on a young child. The task of the first seven years, according to Steiner, is the determination of the health and vitality of the body's organs, which is directly influenced by all that the child takes in. Anthroposophical medicine, which Steiner developed and which is well recognized in Europe, details the relationship between various illnesses in later life and the interaction of sensory impressions on the hereditary predisposition received from the parents.

With regard to the sense of touch, most parents realize the value of skin-to-skin contact with their newborn. And an increasing number of parents are using natural fibers, because they "breathe" and can help to prevent newborn rashes. Fibers from living sources such as wool, silk, and cotton have subtle qualities, which Steiner described as enhancing (rather than depleting) the body's energy—important considerations for children and adults of all ages. Hospitals have substantiated this by reporting that premature babies gain weight faster when placed on wool sheets.

Clothing also relates to the sense of warmth, which is especially important in the young child since it helps to determine how connected the consciousness of the child is with his or her body. Remember how sitting in an overheated room could put you to sleep, while a crisp autumn day could make you feel invigorated and ready for action? Young children need evenness of temperature, and slightly on the warm side because they are dreamier and not yet as fully "on the earth" as adults. They are usually unable to accurately report when they are cold because they do not yet have much awareness in their limbs. Keeping young children adequately clothed is an adult's task, even if the children assure you that they are warm enough.

Many nurseries are now putting stockinette caps on babies to prevent heat loss. Actually, continuing to cover the head in the first year is valuable because it will protect the baby's fontanels. These soft spots, with brain tissue just underneath the skin, can take up to a year and a half to close. A hat protects the central nervous system and the infant's sensitive energy centre in the top of the head (the crown chakra), which remains wide open until the fontanels close.

Keeping the head covered is also an important way of protecting the baby and young child from direct sunlight, which has an extremely powerful effect. This fact is well known in other countries, where often only North American visitors let their babies run around in just a diaper. Waldorf preschool teachers attest to the beneficial effect of hats, for they have found that when the children wear sun hats in May and June, they tend to be less wild and "out of themselves" when they come in from outside play.

Imitation and Discipline

A baby's consciousness is dreamy and diffused, connected with the body but also surrounding it. Have you ever walked into a newborn's room and wondered how such a small baby could somehow fill the entire room? Because of this quality of consciousness, it is impossible to spoil a baby; babies are not yet sufficiently aware of themselves as separate beings to be able to learn manipulative behaviour. Rather, meeting a baby's needs teaches him or her that the world is a trustworthy place.

Discipline in the early years can only be understood in terms of guidance. To discipline a young child is to provide an example of how things are done. If we remember that children learn by imitation, then we can correct them through our own example, and with positive statements rather than commands. For example, you might say, "We eat with a spoon" while you demonstrate this for the child, rather than saying "Stop eating with your fingers" or losing your temper.

Just as taking control of the body is a gradual process which proceeds from the head downward, so the awakening of consciousness of the "I" is also a gradual process. We could say that the child "grows down and wakes up." A contraction of consciousness occurs from the diffused, undifferentiated consciousness of the baby to the more focused, concentrated, and self-centred awareness of the two year old. This first dawning of self-awareness during the third year is repeated again at ages 9 and 13 with even greater power.

The "Terrible Twos" seem more terrible because of our perception that the child begins to be "wilful," to misbehave "on purpose." This is true in the sense that suddenly we are aware of a new "doer" being present, of someone who can consciously oppose our will with his or her own. But the young child still has no memory or moral sense of right and wrong (which, Steiner says, begins to develop at age five). Knowing about this inpouring of the child's sense of self can help parents to stay calm and accept it as a necessary stage of development.

The most effective way to correct behaviour in the young child is to provide an example in movement rather than to reason it out. In these times when many women are questioning patriarchy and authoritarianism, some mothers feel ambivalent about getting their child to obey and may engage in endless disputes as a result. You correct your child by virtue of the "natural authority" you have as his or her parent, teacher, and guide into the adult world that your child will one day join. Instinctively, the child accepts your authority along with your love and care.

It is confusing to the child to be treated as your "equal" in this respect, and to be provided with countless reasons, threats, promises, or options. In fact, reasoning with your child is not very appropriate before the age of nine. Instead, out of your inner conviction that creating good habit patterns in early childhood is beneficial, you might say with absolute conviction, "We stay at the table until we're finished," as you remain seated while your child eats.

Or, "It's time to put the toys away," while you hand your child a truck and put a horse away yourself. Children find it almost impossible to resist movement—imitation is part of their nature. However, if you start reasoning with your child to get him or her to do what you want, your child will imitate *that* and become a five year old who can talk *you* into doing things with great success.

Rhythm, example, and consistency go a long way toward preventing discipline problems. If naptime occurs every day at the same time, it becomes a part of life, not something that invites resistance. Or, if bedtime occurs every night with the same kind of ritual (pajamas, brushing teeth, lighting a candle, story, song, and prayers, for example), then going to bed will not raise questions or problems.

Avoiding problems and correcting your child without any sense that he or she should have "remembered to do it right" can help you to keep your perspective. Scolding or shouting is not effective; it simply forms part of the impression that the child takes so deeply into himself or herself. Remember, no one is perfect, and our own inner efforts and work on ourselves are the best things we can do for our young children. Striving to be models *worthy* of imitation (with renewed resolve rather than guilt) is the hardest and the most valuable work of parents, and it has the most benefit for our children. To help frazzled parents replenish their energy, Steiner suggests: sleep, meditation, and artistic activity.

Walking: The Task of the First Year

The earliest learning tasks of the child involve gaining control of the physical body—crawling, walking, talking, using the toilet. Children have a desire to be "big" and an innate capacity to walk upright and use language, but they first must encounter models to imitate in order for these skills to develop. For example, in rare cases where children have been raised by animals in the jungle, they never achieved an upright posture; similarly, children must be exposed to speech in order for language to develop.

The age at which a child walks, talks, or reaches other developmental milestones unfolds naturally, according to that child's inner timetable. Comparisons with siblings or neighbours' children will usually only create anxiety. Nature knows best what your child needs, and developmental stages should not be hurried or skipped. It is like fussing over a seed and digging it up to see if it is growing, when all it needs is sun, water, soil, and to be left undisturbed to grow naturally. Parents, having provided a healthy environment in which their child can grow, must then remain comfortable with the wide range of normal. (Be sure to seek answers to your questions, and either relax with reassurance or else enlist professional help in the rare cases where it is necessary.) The current "Superbaby Syndrome" can sometimes accelerate early achievement, but Steiner would say that it does so at the price of later physical health and well-being.

Gaining control of the body and learning to walk are the basic tasks of the first year. We can notice how control spreads from the head downward: starting first with the eyes, then the neck, then the trunk in learning to roll over, and finally the legs in learning to creep, crawl, and walk.

Developmental therapists now tell us that children who bypass the crawling stage often have coordination and learning disabilities in later life. Movement helps to stimulate and pattern the brain, and no phase should be skipped or hurried. For this reason, there is a twofold value to the baby in being horizontal until he or she can sit and stand independently. The first is that the time of crawling is not foreshortened, as it is with the use of baby walkers. The second is that the weight of the head and brain are not placed on the central nervous system before the baby can support them. Thus, baby walkers and other devices that set the child prematurely upright do the baby a disservice. Our plastic baby carriers also contain this design flaw, whereas in many other cultures where the young baby is carried in a sling or shawl, he or she remains horizontal much longer.

Baby gymnastics are fine for the adult companionship they provide for mothers, but they are not needed for a baby's physical development. Children need to be allowed to unfold, with parents present to share in their unflagging attempts at mastery and their pride of accomplishment.

Talking: The Task of the Second Year

It is most common for walking to develop before talking, because speech sounds are related to body movements. For example, Steiner states that the forming of words has a certain parallel with the way in which the child can bend the fingers or keep them straight. Once a toddler is able to walk, speech usually develops rapidly.

In addition to being able to move, the child must also be exposed to speech in order for language to develop. Naturally, talking to your baby in clear, adult sentences provides a better model to imitate than does speaking in "baby talk."

Speech is, at first, an expression of the child's feelings, not thinking. First words express pure desire or wish. "Mama!" "Cookie!" or "Hurry!" convey whole sentences. The next phase involves naming things, which is a uniquely human act and shows the developing ability to form concepts about the world outside of oneself.

Thinking: The Task of the Third Year

Through imitation, simple speech and naming develop into full sentences and talking, so that the two year old usually has a fair command of language. Language provides the mold out of which thinking develops as the two year old becomes more aware of himself or herself as being separate from the world.

The young child is the centre of his or her universe, unaware of distinctions between inner and outer, self and other. Before the third year, children usually refer to themselves by what they hear, such as "Mary do it" or "Joey's car." Their first spoken "I" corresponds to what popular psychology has called "The Terrible Twos." This stage can better be understood (and weathered) as a time encompassing a first experience of self or individuality.

For thinking to unfold, the child must first have developed speech and also memory, which holds together sequences of experiences that the "I" gradually forms into concepts and ideas. By the age of three, the child has developed localized or "place memory," and is starting to develop rhythmic or "time memory" and concept memory. But the child is still unable to form pictures or to call up memories at will without sensory reminders. This ability does not develop until about the age of six.

The Three Year Old

The development of thinking, memory, and the sense of self all involve separating oneself from the world. The next phase involves the three-year-old child's reuniting with the world through creative play, as fantasy makes its first appearance. In play, we see the young child imitate all aspects of the surrounding world in an ever-changing way.

Sympathy

Sympathy is a social affinity in which one person stands with another person, closely understanding his or her feelings. Also known as empathic concern, it is the feeling of compassion or concern for another, the wish to see them better off or happier. Although empathy and sympathy are often used interchangeably, a subtle variation in ordinary usage can be detected. To empathize is to respond to another's perceived emotional state by experiencing feelings of a similar sort. Sympathy not only includes empathizing, but also entails having a positive regard or a non-fleeting concern for the other person.

In common usage, sympathy is usually making known one's understanding of another's unhappiness or suffering, especially when it is grief. Sympathy can also refer to being aware of other (positive) emotions as well.

What forms do empathy and sympathy take as children develop?

Although signs of empathy and sympathy in children will be small at first, teaching these skills from the start leads to big differences in attitudes as children get older.

Infants

Many infants become distressed when those around them are upset. This is because an infant cannot tell himself apart from anybody or anything else. A young baby will experience another's distress as his own, which is why one infant cries in response to another's tears.

Toddlers

Beginning around 12 months of age, children begin to realize that someone else's discomfort or distress is different from their own, but they still notice and react to it. In toddlers, empathy and sympathy might take the form of trying to comfort others. A toddler might bring a friend who is crying a toy or blanket, or he might offer a hug to someone who seems upset.

Early Preschool

During the early preschool years, children not only are able to recognize distress in others, but they have the vocabulary and ability to understand why someone else is upset or sad. They can name the emotion, suggest a cause, and try to help.

Elementary School

During the elementary school years (starting around 6 years of age), children can see things from someone else's perspective, not just their own. As their language skills increase overall, they are better able to describe others' feelings and to respond to them. Your child may say, "Kenny was sad, so I asked him to play with me on the playground," or "Grandma was happy when I gave her my picture."

Late Childhood

In late childhood (10 to 12 years of age) children can feel empathy and sympathy for people beyond their immediate radius of friends and family. For example, your child may express sympathy for strangers who are less fortunate and feel motivated to help them in some way.

Signs of Growing Empathy and Sympathy

As you nurture your child, you should see signs that your child is beginning to understand his own and other people's emotions. Some signs of growing empathy and sympathy include:

- showing sensitivity to the needs and feelings of others.
- correctly reading others' nonverbal cues, such as gestures, body language, facial expressions, and tone of voice
- recognizing when someone is distressed and responding appropriately
- tearing up or looking upset when someone else is distressed
- acting concerned when someone is treated unfairly or unkindly
- willing to understand someone else's point of view
- verbally identifying someone else's feelings.

Play

Play refers to a range of voluntary, intrinsically motivated activities that are normally associated with pleasure and enjoyment. Play may consist of amusing, pretend or imaginary interpersonal and intrapersonal interactions or "interplay". The rites of play are evident throughout nature and are perceived in people and animals, particularly in the cognitive development and socialization of those engaged in developmental processes and the young. Play often entertains props, tools, animals, or toys in the context of learning and recreation. Some play has clearly defined goals and when structured with rules is entitled a game. Whereas, some play exhibits no such goals nor rules and is considered to be "unstructured" in the literature.

Concerted endeavour has been made to identify the qualities of play, but this task is not without its ambiguities. For example, play is commonly perceived as a frivolous and non-serious activity; yet when watching children at play, one can observe the transfixed seriousness and entrancing absorption with which they engage in it. Other criteria of play include a relaxed pace and freedom versus compulsion. Yet play seems to have its intrinsic constraints, as in, "You're not playing fair."

When play is structured and goal-orientated it is often presented as a game. Play can also be seen as the activity of rehearsing life events, e.g. young animals play fighting. Play may also serve as a pretext, allowing people to explore reactions of others by engaging in playful interaction. Flirting is an example of such behaviour. These and other concepts or rhetorics of play are discussed at length by Brian Sutton-Smith in the book *The Ambiguity of Play*. Sometimes play is dangerous, such as in extreme sports. This type of play could be considered stunt play, whether engaging in play frighting, sky-diving, or riding a device at high speed in an unusual manner.

Childhood and Play

Play is freely chosen, intrinsically motivated and personally directed. Playing has been long recognized as a critical aspect of childhood and child development. Some of the earliest studies of play started in the 1890s with G. Stanley Hall, the father of the child study movement that sparked an interest in the developmental, mental and behavioural world of babies and children. The American Academy of Pediatrics (AAP) published a study in 2006 entitled: "The Importance of Play in Promoting Healthy Child Development and Maintaining Strong Parent-Child Bonds". The report states: "free and unstructured play is healthy and – in fact – essential for helping children reach important social, emotional, and cognitive developmental milestones as well as helping them manage stress and become resilient".

Many of the most prominent researchers in the field of psychology (including Jean Piaget, William James, Sigmund Freud, Carl Jung and Lev Vygotsky) have viewed play as endemic to the human species; indeed, the attributions projected upon an imaginary friend by children are key to understanding the construction of human spirituality and it pantheon(s) of deification (and demonization).

Play is explicitly recognized in Article 31 of The Convention on the Rights of the Child (adopted by the General Assembly of the United Nations, November 29, 1989). which states:

1. Parties recognize the right of the child to rest and leisure, to engage in play and recreational activities

appropriate to the age of the child and to participate freely in cultural life and the arts.

2. Parties shall respect and promote the right of the child to participate fully in cultural and artistic life and shall encourage the provision of appropriate and equal opportunities for cultural, artistic, recreational and leisure activities.

Childhood "play" is also seen by Sally Jenkinson (author of *The Genius of Play*) to be an intimate and integral part of childhood development. "In giving primacy to adult knowledge, to our 'grown-up' ways of seeing the world, have we forgotten how to value other kinds of wisdom? Do we still care about the small secret corners of children's wisdom?"

Modern research in the field of "affective neuroscience" has uncovered important links between role playing and neurogenesis in the brain. Sociologist Roger Caillois coined the word *ilinx* to describe the momentary disruption of perception that comes from forms of physical play that disorient the senses, especially balance.

In addition, evolutionary psychologists have begun to expound the phylogenetic relationship between higher intelligence in humans and its relationship to play.

Stevanne Auerbach mentions the role of play therapy in treating children suffering from traumas, emotional issues, and other problems. She also emphasizes the importance of toys with high play value for child development and the role of the parent in evaluating toys and being the child's *play guide*.

Sudbury model of democratic education schools assert that play is a big part of life at their schools where it is seen as a serious business. They maintain that play is always serious for kids, as well as for adults who haven't forgotten how to play, and much of the learning going on at these schools is done through play.

So they don't interfere with it. Hence play flourishes at all ages, and the graduates who leave these schools go out into the world knowing how to give their all to whatever they're doing, and still remembering how to laugh and enjoy life as it comes.

Behavioural Cusp

A behavioural cusp is any behaviour change that brings an organism's behaviour into contact with new contingencies that have far-reaching consequences. A behavioural cusp is a special type of behaviour change because it provides the learner with opportunities to access (1) new reinforcers, (2) new contingencies (3) new environments, (4) new related behaviours (generativeness), (5) competition with archaic or problem behaviours, and it (6) impacts the people around the learner, and (7) these people agree to the behaviour change and support its development after the intervention is removed.

The concept has far reaching implication for every individual, and for the field of developmental psychology, because it provides a behavioural alternative to the concept of maturation and change due to the simple passage of time, such as developmental milestones. The cusp is a behaviour change that presents special features when compared to other behaviour changes.

The concept was first proposed by Sidney W. Bijou, an American developmental psychologist. The idea of the cusp was to link behavioural principles to rapid spurts in development.

A behavioural cusp as conceptualized by Jesus Rosales-Ruiz & Donald Baer in 1997 is an important behaviour change that has an impact on future behaviour changes. The behavioural cusp, like the reinforcer, is apprehended by its effects. Whereas a reinforcer acts on a single response or a group of related responses, the effects of a behavioural cusp regulate a large number of responses in a more distant future.

The concept has been compared to a developmental milestone, however, all cusps are not milestones. For example, learning to play soccer is not a milestone, but it was life-changing for Pelé.

As a result of learning to kick grapefruits (the initial important change or cusp), Pelé accessed (1) new environments, (2) new reinforcers, (3) new soccer moves, (4) dropped competing behaviours (smoking), and (5) gained international acclaims for his skill. Soccer is not a developmental milestone because is not a necessary skill in most environments.

Properties of a Behavioural Cusp

The following properties are special features of a behavioural change that lead to more change, and an increased likelihood of social adaptation, independence, and cultural fitness.

New Reinforcers

New reinforcers are accessible and enrich the perspective of the learner. Additionally these reinforcers may lead to an increase in the variety of behaviours. If the reinforcers are promoting health and social behaviours, they will lead to an improved quality of life.

Case Example

A child who learns to open a door may access the swing for the first time and learns to use the swing.. Here, the new skill (swinging motion is the reinforcer) may lead to more complex and social activities such as (1) turn taking, (2) asking someone to share the swing, (3) taking turn pushing someone, which in turn (4) may provide more social opportunities to speak and (5) interact with the play partners, etc.

Case Non-example

A child learns to open a door and walks outside. He finds some ants behind a shrubbery and watches the ants. His parents are looking for him, they get worried and are calling him. The child is usually mesmerized by columns of ants on the ground and does not hear the calls. His parents find him shortly after, but they are frantic from their 5 minute search and accidentally scare him from going outside. In this non-example, learning to open doors that lead outside resulted in consequences that did not directly benefit the child and maybe decrease important skills related to exploration and search.. In this case, no new reinforcers were contacted and learning to open the backyard door (that has a special latch) was effectively a waste of time because the child's parents don't usually approve being alone in the backyard.

New Contingencies of Reinforcement

New contingencies are responsible for the selection of novel and more adaptive behaviours while decreasing problematic or archaic behaviours. Contingencies of reinforcement produce and maintain each and every learned behaviour. New contingencies establish the control of new stimuli over our behaviours, and therefore make us more sensitive and aware of our surrounding.

New Environments

New environments are geographical and/or virtual areas of potential change (receiving environments). New environments regulate, maintain, and set the micro-cultural boundaries for reinforcers, (and punishers), and their antecedents. They include tools and stakeholders controlling the pace and content of instruction and, as a result, they regulate boundary of what the learner learns (e.g., school curriculum). New environments must contain some of the stakeholders' preferences and reinforcers to create lasting positive reinforcement practices for the learner.

Generativeness

Generativeness describes the ability of the receiving environment to regulate novel responses, functions, values or response products derived from the original cusp response. For a behaviour, it is the ability to recombine or merge into more complex units, or the ability to contact environments.

Case Example

A child learns phonetic reading and can recombine the 50 or so English phonemes into 50.000 words by recombining the individual sounds he has learned to read. The generative index for this act of learning the basic English phonemes is approximately 10.000 (where one new behaviour results in a potential 10.000 applications).

Case Non-example

A child learns sight reading for 50 words. When a new word is presented the child learns by listening to a teacher and memorizes the words rather than using what he has previously learned (reading 50 words). Additionally, he is now dependent on a someone for learning each new vocabulary word.

Competition with Archaic Behaviours

Behaviour competition is the ability of cusp behaviours

(killer app) to displace previously established behaviours on a continuum of intensity and rate, across repertoires, and environments. Competing archaic behaviours occur on a corresponding continuum of severity.

Impact on Stakeholders

Impact on others comes from the learner's behaviour impacting the stakeholders who control reinforcers and punishers in a specific environments. It is important to identify these stakeholders' motivations and reinforcers in selecting potential cusps. Impact refers to the changes in values & behaviours of the stakeholder resulting from a cusp in the learner. The initial and gradually more complex behaviours that constituted the entry point for an important behaviour change that, once initiated, so profoundly alters, displaces, or transforms one's behavioural repertoire that it renders preexisting behavioural repertoires obsolete. A behavioural cusp is an important behaviour change that alters the probability of the learner's future repertoires and interactions with stakeholders repertoires.

Social Validity

Social validity is an indicator of social acceptability of a behaviour and its consequences for the stakeholders representing the communities which the learner is accessing or will access. Some seemingly insignificant changes in a stakeholder may dramatically impact the learner. All stakeholders (e.g., government officials, teachers, parents, and other interventionists) should agree to the goals, methods, and tools for the intervention and the norms from the local community suggest the boundaries of what should be learned.

Applications

Life Span/Development Guidelines

The behavioural cusp has implications for the selection and sequencing of skills during the life span. While milestones are mainly concerned with the chronology of behaviours, the concept of behavioural cusp is concerned with the fitness of the behaviour within a context or a receiving environment. As Rosales-Ruiz and Baer (1997) stated, "One child's cusp may be another child's waste of time." Thus, there is a great need for empirically based guidelines in making decisions related to the initial selection of skills.

Importance of Play in Child Development

Play is universal throughout the animal kingdom — whether it's a puppy chasing its tail, or young birds swooping through the air. The importance of play to youngsters should not be underestimated. Play is an essential part of growing up and researchers believe it's critical to ensure children reach their full potential in life.

Research in animals show that brain connections develop during periods of play, and there's no reason to suppose the same is not true of young humans.

Parents don't always understand the importance of play however, and in today's competitive world, the temptation is to stop your children "wasting time" and to put the time to what they believe is more constructive use.

For a child, however, there is no more constructive activity than play. When analysing the importance of play, particularly if you're tempted to introduce a more "worthwhile" activity such as flash cards, educational computer games or dancing lessons, you should take into account the following points:

Play allows a young child to be "in charge." Think about this — in their everyday lives, they're small and powerless, always being told what to do, and how to do it. Without an adult around, they're running the show!

Play helps children learn about the world in which they live. They can investigate and discover, test their theories, spatial relationships, explore cause and effect, societal roles and family values. Such is the importance of play, that there's virtually no area of life about which it can't teach a child something.

Play builds self-esteem. Children will often play at something they know they can do well, at which they can be successful.

Play builds social skills. Children will begin playing with inanimate and non-threatening objects, like cuddly toys, bricks etc., so practising their interactive skills. Later, playing with other children will build on this foundation as they learn to share, take turns, assert themselves and begin to empathise with others.

Play with parents shouldn't be underestimated either, as research shows that children whose parents play with them ultimately develop superior social skills.

Play also provides the opportunity for children to work out their feelings. The importance of dealing with difficult or unpleasant emotions is immense. A child who's worried about going to the dentist, for example, may deal with the anxiety by setting up a clinic for dolls with toothache.

Play helps with language development. Think of the vast number of words a toddler uses during play, many of them repeatedly, enhancing their language skills. Play allows children to grow beyond their years. They can pretend to be all sorts of things in play-a doctor, a surgeon, a civil engineer even!

Finally, don't forget to consider the importance of stimulating your child's creativity and imagination-making a castle in the sand, or a car garage out of a shoe box, taking an order in their own (imaginary) restaurant or dressing up as a king or queen-these all allow children to stretch the limits of their world and experience the fun in make-believe.

Sports and Child-physiological Considerations

The sports physical is an annual rite for many students who have to get a check-up to participate in school athletics — but it's also a great opportunity to track your child's health and educate him or her on proper diet and fitness techniques.

Every year more than seven million high school students participate in interscholastic athletics. Almost all of these athletes are required to undergo a physical evaluation prior to starting practice.

For the vast majority of students, these physicals serve as their only contact with the health care system, and should not be considered as an annual inconvenience.

The purpose of the sports physical is to:

- Identify medical or musculoskeletal conditions that might make participation in a particular sport unsafe

- Screen for any previously undetected health problem
- Assure that any previous injuries have been adequately rehabilitated so that the athlete is not at risk for further injury.

But these visits can also provide an opportunity to educate athletes and parents about injury prevention, conditioning, and training appropriate for level of physical maturity, as well as healthy nutritional approaches to sport participation.

Many youth are seen in mass screenings in high schools or sports medicine clinics; such physicals should not replace an annual evaluation by the student's primary care provider.

However, at an annual evaluation a pediatrician can incorporate the essential elements of the pre-sports physical into a yearly checkup. With access to the medical record, including growth charts and previous blood pressures, chances of identifying medical problems are significantly increased.

In addition, referrals to specialists for additional evaluation are more easily coordinated by the primary care provider.

When to Go

Timing for the sports physical is very important. Ideally, the sports physical should be at least six to eight weeks prior to start of practice. Too often parents forget how quickly the year has gone, and end up scheduling a visit in urgent fashion — "She needs this form filled out today because tryouts are tomorrow."

This does not allow sufficient time for any further evaluation of a newly found medical condition or rehabilitation of an injury. Unfortunately, this may keep an athlete from trying out for a sport.

Medical History is Key

Studies show that the vast majority of significant medical conditions identified at pre-participation evaluations are picked up through a detailed history.

Although many schools use limited, outdated sports physical forms, pediatricians have access through the American Academy of Pediatrics to a more complete, standardized form endorsed by the majority of sports medicine organizations in the US.

Parents and athletes should jointly complete the history portion of any sports form prior to arriving at the office to assure accurate responses. Family history is especially important. Premature death or significant disability from cardiovascular disease in a close relative under 50 years of age or specific knowledge of close relatives with certain cardiovascular conditions such as hypertrophic cardiomyopathy, long QT syndrome, or Marfan's syndrome, all require further evaluation and, in many cases, clearance by a cardiologist before participation in sports.

Dietary Concerns

A complete nutritional history, including use of supplements, is also important. The sports physical provides an early opportunity to identify athletes with disordered eating patterns, and those at risk for a true eating disorder.

This is where a growth chart covering several years is essential. In addition to dietary intake information (servings of dairy, fruits, vegetables, meat, soda), information should be obtained about the athlete's highest and lowest weight over the past 12 months, as well as the athlete's perceived ideal weight.

Your pediatrician should ask about use of any pathogenic weight control behaviours, such as self-induced vomiting, use of laxatives or diet pills, or excessive exercise. If an athlete is developing disordered eating patterns, careful follow-up and early intervention is critical in preventing a potential life-threatening condition.

Best Diet for Performance

Many athletes are interested in the best diet for athletic performance or to gain weight. For endurance athletes, like cross country runners or soccer players, it is important that at least 55 percent of their total calories come from carbohydrates like breads and pasta. This saturates their muscles with glycogen, the optimum energy source for working muscles.

Non-athletic adolescents age 15 to 18 need only 0.8 gram of protein per kilogram (2.2 pounds) of body weight each day. Some adolescent athletes who are training intensively and trying to put on muscle mass may need as much as 1.5 gm of protein per kilogram body weight per day.

For many American children, their standard diet already fulfills this need; rarely are expensive protein supplements needed — or helpful. Vegetarian athletes need to pay special attention to both their protein and iron intake.

Proper Hydration

During the school year, most adolescents exist in a state of relative dehydration — they just don't drink enough throughout the day.

In addition to the recommended eight to 10 glasses of liquid as baseline, athletes with fluid losses in sweat may require as additional 1 to 3 liters of fluid per day. Attention to hydration is important both to maximize athletic performance as well as decrease susceptibility to heat illness.

Guidelines for fluid intake are:

- Drink 16 ounces of water 30 to 60 minutes before activity
- Drink 4 to 8 ounces water every 15 to 30 minutes during activity
- Drink 16 ounces (1 pint) water for every pound of weight lost after activity.

Signs and symptoms of heat illness should be reviewed. Any athlete exercising in the heat who experiences muscle cramps, dizziness, nausea, severe headache, or unusual muscle weakness should stop exercising, get in as cool a place as possible and start drinking cool water.

Many sports programs are now willing to reschedule or cancel practices when conditions of extreme heat and humidity occur.

Weight Loss Guidelines

Many athletes who want or need to lose weight (body fat) do not have the luxury of consultation with a dietitian.

These athletes can follow some basic guidelines:

- Aerobic activity (walking, running, biking) can be increased by 30 minutes a day
- Consume more fruits and vegetables
- Water should be the primary fluid source; Drink less soda, juice, and sports drinks

- Use reduced-fat or fat-free dairy
- Limit use of butter, margarine, mayonnaise, and dressings. Mustard can be used on sandwiches and salsa on salads and baked potatoes
- Portion sizes of meat can be decreased, and only served at one meal a day
- Never try to lose more than two pounds per week

Weight Training

Weight training can play an important role in preventing athletic injuries as well as improving athletic performance. Weight training can serve to balance the strength in muscle groups around specific joints and reduce the risk of injury; consultation with an athletic trainer, physical therapist or sports medicine physician may help design such programs. As the adolescent grows and develops, the design and goal of a weight training program changes. For the pre-teen, a program using lighter weights with 12 to 15 repetitions per set and a maximum of two sets per exercise will improve muscle strength by causing more of the muscle fibers to respond to nerve stimulation; a significant increase in muscle bulk will not occur until after the athlete stops growing taller. It is important that proper technique be used by the athletes, and that careful stretching is done before and after lifting to maintain or improve flexibility.

Off-Season Workouts

It is important for the one-season athlete to maintain fitness throughout the year by engaging in at least 30 minutes of moderately vigorous activity five days a week.

In anticipation of the start of the season, slowly advance training loads to reduce the risk of stress fractures. Workouts should be increased by no more than 10 percent per week.

This means that fall sport athletes need to begin their conditioning program early in the summer to be ready when school practices officially begin.

For Female Athletes

Finally, for the female athlete, attention should be paid to menstrual function.

An athlete who hasn't begun menstruation by age 16 or misses more than three consecutive cycles after regular monthly cycles are established should be evaluated for nutritional adequacies as well as other hormonal abnormalities that can affect menstrual function. Missing repetitive periods is not normal for an athlete.

A history of stress fractures should prompt evaluation for the "female athlete triad": eating disorder, menstrual abnormalities, and osteoporosis.

9

Learning, Maturation and Manual Skill

Learning is acquiring new knowledge, behaviours, skills, values, preferences or understanding, and may involve synthesizing different types of information. The ability to learn is possessed by humans, animals and some machines. Progress over time tends to follow learning curves.

Human learning may occur as part of education, personal development, or training. It may be goal-oriented and may be aided by motivation. The study of how learning occurs is part of neuropsychology, educational psychology, learning theory, and pedagogy.

Learning may occur as a result of habituation or classical conditioning, seen in many animal species, or as a result of more complex activities such as play, seen only in relatively intelligent animals. Learning may occur consciously or without conscious awareness.

There is evidence for human behavioural learning prenatally, in which habituation has been observed as early as 32 weeks into gestation, indicating that the central nervous system is sufficiently developed and primed for learning and memory to occur very early on in development.

Play has been approached by several theorists as the first form of learning. Children play, experiment with the world, learn the rules, and learn to interact. Vygotsky agrees that play is pivotal for children's development, since they make meaning of their environment through play.

Types of Learning

Simple Non-associative Learning

Habituation : In psychology, habituation is an example of non-associative learning in which there is a progressive diminution of behavioural response probability with repetition stimulus. An animal first responds to a stimulus, but if it is neither rewarding nor harmful the animal reduces subsequent responses. One example of this can be seen in small song birds—if a stuffed owl (or similar predator) is put into the cage, the birds initially react to it as though it were a real predator. Soon the birds react less, showing habituation. If another stuffed owl is introduced (or the same one removed and re-introduced), the birds react to it again as though it were a predator, demonstrating that it is only a very specific stimulus that is habituated to (namely, one particular unmoving owl in one place). Habituation has been shown in essentially every species of animal, including the large protozoan *Stentor coeruleus*.

Sensitization : Sensitization is an example of non-associative learning in which the progressive amplification of a response follows repeated administrations of a stimulus (Bell et al., 1995). An everyday example of this mechanism is the repeated tonic stimulation of peripheral nerves that will occur if a person rubs his arm continuously. After a while, this stimulation will create a warm sensation that will eventually turn painful. The pain is the result of the progressively amplified synaptic response of the peripheral nerves warning the person that the stimulation is harmful. Sensitization is thought to underlie both adaptive as well as maladaptive learning processes in the organism.

Associative learning : Associative learning is the process by which an element is taught through association with a separate, pre-occurring element. It is also referred to as classical conditioning.

Operant conditioning is the use of consequences to modify the occurrence and form of behaviour. *Operant conditioning* is distinguished from *Pavlovian conditioning* in that operant conditioning uses reinforcement/punishment to alter a behaviour. Behaviourism is a psychological movement that seeks to alter behaviour by arranging the environment to elicit successful changes and to arrange consequences to maintain or diminish a behaviour. Behaviourists study behaviours that can be measured and changed by the environment. However, they do not eliminate that there are thought processes that interact with those behaviours.

Delayed discounting is the process of devaluing rewards based on the delay of time they are presented. This process is thought to be tied to impulsivity. Impulsivity is a core process for many behaviours (e.g., substance abuse, problematic gambling, OCD). Making decisions is an important part of everyday functioning. How we make those decisions is based on what we perceive to be the most valuable or worthwhile actions. This is determined by what we find to be the most reinforcing stimuli. So when teaching an individual a response, you need to find the most potent reinforcer for that person. This may be a larger reinforcer at a later time or a smaller immediate reinforcer.

Classical Conditioning

The typical paradigm for classical conditioning involves repeatedly pairing an unconditioned stimulus (which unfailingly evokes a reflexive response) with another previously neutral stimulus (which does not normally evoke the response). Following conditioning, the response occurs both to the unconditioned stimulus and to the other, unrelated stimulus (now referred to as the "conditioned stimulus").

The response to the conditioned stimulus is termed a *conditioned response*. The classic example is Pavlov and his dogs. Meat powder naturally will make a dog salivate when it is put into a dog's mouth; salivating is a reflexive response to the meat powder. Meat powder is the unconditioned stimulus (US) and the salivation is the unconditioned response (UR). Then Pavlov rang a bell before presenting the meat powder. The first time Pavlov rang the bell, the neutral stimulus, the dogs did not salivate, but once he put the meat powder in their mouths they began to salivate. After numerous pairings of the bell, and then food the dogs learned that the bell was a signal that the food was about to come and began to salivate just when the bell was rang. Once this occurs the bell becomes the conditioned stimulus (CS) and the salivation to the bell is the conditioned response (CR). Another influential person in the world of Classical Conditioning is John B. Watson. Watson's work was very influential and paved the way for B. F. Skinner's radical behaviourism. Watson's behaviourism (and philosophy of science) stood in direct contrast to Freud. Watson's view was that Freud's introspective method was too subjective, and that we should limit the study of human development to directly observable behaviours. In 1913, Watson published the article "Psychology as the Behaviourist Views," in which he argued that laboratory studies should serve psychology best as a science. Watson's most famous, and controversial, experiment, "Little Albert," where he demonstrated how psychologists can account for the learning of emotion through classical conditioning principles.

Imprinting

Imprinting is the term used in psychology and ethology to describe any kind of phase-sensitive learning (learning occurring at a particular age or a particular life stage) that is rapid and apparently independent of the consequences of behaviour. It was first used to describe situations in which an animal or person learns the characteristics of some stimulus, which is therefore said to be "imprinted" onto the subject.

Observational Learning

The learning process most characteristic of humans is imitation; one's personal repetition of an observed behaviour, such as a dance. Humans can copy three types of information simultaneously: the demonstrator's goals, actions and environmental outcomes. Through copying these types of information, (most) infants will tune into their surrounding culture.

Play

Play generally describes behaviour which has no particular end in itself, but improves performance in similar situations in the future. This is seen in a wide variety of vertebrates besides humans, but is mostly limited to mammals and birds. Cats are known to play with a ball of string when young, which gives them experience with catching prey. Besides inanimate objects, animals may play with other members of their own species or other animals, such as orcas playing with seals they have caught. Play involves a significant cost to animals, such as increased vulnerability to predators and the risk of injury and possibly infection. It also consumes energy, so there must be significant benefits associated with play for it to have evolved. Play is generally seen in younger animals, suggesting a link with learning. However, it may also have other benefits not associated directly with learning, for example improving physical fitness.

Enculturation

Enculturation is the process by which a person learns the requirements of their native culture by which he or she is surrounded, and acquires values and behaviours that are appropriate or necessary in that culture. The influences which as part of this process limit, direct or shape the individual, whether deliberately or not, include parents, other adults, and peers. If successful, enculturation results in competence in the language, values and rituals of the culture. (compare acculturation, where a person is within a culture different to their normal culture, and learns the requirements of this different culture).

Multimedia Learning

Multimedia learning is where a person uses both auditory and visual stimuli to learn information (Mayer 2001). This type of learning relies on dual-coding theory (Paivio 1971).

E-learning and Augmented Learning

Electronic learning or e-learning is a general term used to refer to Internet-based networked computer-enhanced learning. A specific and always more diffused e-learning is mobile learning (m-learning), which uses different mobile telecommunication equipment, such as cellular phones.

When a learner interacts with the e-learning environment, it's called augmented learning. By adapting to the needs of individuals, the context-driven instruction can be dynamically tailored to the learner's natural environment. Augmented digital content may include text, images, video, audio (music and voice). By personalizing instruction, augmented learning has been shown to improve learning performance for a lifetime.

Rote Learning

Rote learning is a technique which avoids understanding the inner complexities and inferences of the subject that is being learned and instead focuses on memorizing the material so that it can be recalled by the learner exactly the way it was read or heard. The major practice involved in rote learning techniques is *learning by repetition*, based on the idea that one will be able to quickly recall the meaning of the material the more it is repeated. Rote learning is used in diverse areas, from mathematics to music to religion. Although it has been criticized by some schools of thought, rote learning is a necessity in many situations.

Informal Learning

Informal learning occurs through the experience of day-to-day situations (for example, one would learn to look ahead while walking because of the danger inherent in not paying attention to where one is going). It is learning from life, during a meal at table with parents, play, exploring, etc.

Formal Learning

Formal learning is learning that takes place within a teacher-student relationship, such as in a school system.

Nonformal Learning

Nonformal learning is organized learning outside the formal learning system. For example: learning by coming together with people with similar interests and exchanging viewpoints, in clubs or in (international) youth organizations, workshops.

Nonformal Learning and Combined Approaches

The educational system may use a combination of formal, informal, and nonformal learning methods. The UN and EU recognize these different forms of learning. In some schools students can get points that count in the formal-learning systems if they get work done in informal-learning circuits. They may be given time to assist international youth workshops and training courses, on the condition they prepare, contribute, share and can proof this offered valuable new insight, helped to acquire new skills, a place to get experience in organizing, teaching, etc.

In order to learn a skill, such as solving a Rubik's cube quickly, several factors come into play at once:

- Directions help one learn the patterns of solving a Rubik's cube.
- Practicing the moves repeatedly and for extended time helps with "muscle memory" and therefore speed.
- Thinking critically about moves helps find shortcuts, which in turn helps to speed up future attempts.
- The Rubik's cube's six colors help anchor solving it within the head.
- Occasionally revisiting the cube helps prevent negative learning or loss of skill.

Tangential Learning

Tangential learning is the process by which some portion of people will self-educate if a topic is exposed to them in something that they already enjoy such as playing a musical instrument.

Dialogic Learning

Dialogic learning is a type of learning based on dialogue.

Domains of Learning

Benjamin Bloom has suggested three domains of learning:

- Cognitive – To recall, calculate, discuss, analyse, problem solve, etc.
- Psychomotor – To dance, swim, ski, dive, drive a car, ride a bike, etc.
- Affective – To like something or someone, love, appreciate, fear, hate, worship, etc.

These domains are not mutually exclusive. For example, in learning to play chess, the person will have to learn the rules of the game (cognitive domain); but he also has to learn how to set up the chess pieces on the chessboard and also how to properly hold and move a chess piece (psychomotor). Furthermore, later in the game the person may even learn to love the game itself, value its applications in life, and appreciate its history (affective domain).Memory and Association In psychology, memory is an organism's ability to store, retain, and recall information and experiences. Traditional studies of memory began in the fields of philosophy, including techniques of artificially enhancing memory. The late nineteenth and early twentieth century put memory within the paradigms of cognitive psychology. In recent decades, it has become one of the principal pillars of a branch of science called cognitive neuroscience, an interdisciplinary link between cognitive psychology and neuroscience.

How does our Memory Work?

We remember things by association. Every piece of information in our memory is connected to other pieces in some way or another. For example, if you are given the word "apple", what do you think of? Perhaps something like this:

APPLE: red, round, sweet, teacher, tree, fruit.

But it's unlikely that we might see "apple" and think of "dog" (unless you remember some funny incident in which your dog investigated an apple). And what if you were asked what the 7th letter of the alphabet was? Chances are, you wouldn't know that "G = 7," but you could easily think to yourself, "A B C D E F G," and then say "G". You used association to get to the letter G, because you knew A was the first letter, then you kept choosing the next letter in the sequence until you got to the right one.

Why do most of us have a bad Memory?

Most of us don't. Most of us have a really good memory, but we just don't have practice in using it efficiently.

If the above is true, then why is it so hard for me to remember things?

As stated before, our memory works by association. If there is no obvious association between things, it's very difficult to remember them. For example, suppose you needed to remember that your plane takes off at 2 P.M. There is nothing about the plane that would suggest the number 2 more than it would any other number (at least at first glance). Therefore, 2 is easily forgotten. Likewise, how does your best friend relate to his phone number, an arbitrary string of digits? Or how does a new word, like "hypothalamus," relate to what it represents?

How can we Learn to Remember Things Better?

Simple. If memory works by association, we actively work to create an association between two bits of information. For example, for the plane that we need to catch at 2 P.M., we can imagine the plane in our mind, and notice that it has 2 wings. Two wings, 2 P.M. There's an association. We are now ten times more likely to remember the take-off time long after it has faded from our short-term memory.

Sometimes an association comes very easily. For example, suppose you are introduced to a Mr. Hill who lives on a hill at the end of town. Mr. Hill on a hill. Pretty easy, huh? Or what if you're trying to remember the classroom number for a Chemistry class, and it just so turns out that it's the same as your dorm room number. Another natural association! Do you think you'll have a problem remembering it?

When pieces of information are not obviously related in any way, however, we have to be a bit more creative in linking things together. But it isn't as hard as it seems. Most of us learned rhymes and acronyms in school that helped us remember things. Do any of the following look familiar to you?

- i before e except after c, or when sounded like a as in neighbor and weigh (rule for remembering ei or ie)
- ROY G. BIV (colors of the rainbow)
- All cows eat grass; Every good boy does fine (notes of musical scale)
- Never eat sour watermelons (directions on a compass).

Why do they work? Because they form an easy-to-remember and clever association between themselves and the information that is to be remembered.

The idea is to be creative and clever. You don't have to invent a rhyme or a poem every time you want to remember something, though — just think of a picture in your mind that links pieces of information together, preferably something unusual or silly so it is more memorable. For example, suppose you want to remember that the football field is on Maple Street. You might imagine in your mind a burly football player eating a football for breakfast... he pours some maple syrup on the football, cuts off a chunk and eats it!

To demonstrate how effectively this works, look at the following list of words, and try to come up with an association between the left word and the right word of each row. Some will be easy; others may be harder. As an example, for the first pair, you might want to imagine a mouse that has a long, wavy tail that is in the shape of the letter S.

mouse	S
fur	R
train	bridge
moat	boat
popcorn	chair
elephant	pancake
toothbrush	canal
umbrella	triangle

After you have formed the associations (if you had trouble on one or two of them, that's okay; just skip them for now), cover up the right side of the list and then try to name the word associated with each word on the left. If you formed vivid, clear associations, you may be surprised at how quickly and easily you were able to remember everything!

Processes

From an information processing perspective there are three main stages in the formation and retrieval of memory:

- *Encoding* or registration (receiving, processing and combining of received information)
- *Storage* (creation of a permanent record of the encoded information)
- *Retrieval*, *recall* or *recollection* (calling back the stored information in response to some cue for use in a process or activity)

Sensory Memory

Sensory memory corresponds approximately to the initial 200–500 milliseconds after an item is perceived. The ability to look at an item, and remember what it looked like with just a second of observation, or memorisation, is an example of sensory memory. With very short presentations, participants often report that they seem to "see" more than they can actually report. The first experiments exploring this form of sensory memory were conducted by George Sperling (1960) using the "partial report paradigm". Subjects were presented with a grid of 12 letters, arranged into three rows of four. After a brief presentation, subjects were then played either a high, medium or low tone, cuing them which of the rows to report. Based on these partial report experiments, Sperling was able to show that the capacity of sensory memory was approximately 12 items, but that it degraded very quickly (within a few hundred milliseconds). Because this form of memory degrades so quickly, participants would see the display, but be unable to report all of the items (12 in the "whole report" procedure) before they decayed. This type of memory cannot be prolonged via rehearsal.

Short-term

Short-term memory allows recall for a period of several seconds to a minute without rehearsal. Its capacity is also very limited: George A. Miller (1956), when working at Bell Laboratories, conducted experiments showing that the store of short-term memory was 7±2 items (the title of his famous paper, "The magical number 7±2"). Modern estimates of the capacity of short-term memory are lower, typically on the order of 4–5 items, however, memory capacity can be increased through a process called chunking. For example, in recalling a ten-digit telephone number, a person could chunk the digits into three groups: first, the area code (such as 215), then a three-digit chunk (123) and lastly a four-digit chunk (4567). This method of remembering telephone numbers is far more effective than attempting to remember a string of 10 digits; this is because we are able to chunk the information into meaningful groups of numbers. Herbert Simon showed that the ideal size for chunking letters and numbers, meaningful or not, was three. This may be reflected in some countries in the tendency to remember telephone numbers as several chunks of three numbers with the final four-number groups, generally broken down into two groups of two.

Short-term memory is believed to rely mostly on an acoustic code for storing information, and to a lesser extent a visual code. Conrad (1964) found that test subjects had more difficulty recalling collections of words that were acoustically similar.

However, some individuals have been reported to be able to remember large amounts of information, quickly, and be able to recall that information in seconds.

Long-term

The storage in sensory memory and short-term memory generally have a strictly limited capacity and duration, which means that information is available only for a certain period of time, but is not retained indefinitely. By contrast, long-term memory can store much larger quantities of information for potentially unlimited duration (sometimes a whole life span). Its capacity is immeasurably large. For example, given a random seven-digit number we may remember it for only a few seconds before forgetting, suggesting it was stored in our short-term memory. On the other hand, we can remember telephone numbers for many years through repetition; this information is said to be stored in long-term memory.

While short-term memory encodes information acoustically, long-term memory encodes it semantically: Baddeley (1966) discovered that after 20 minutes, test subjects had the most difficulty recalling a collection of words that had similar meanings.

Short-term memory is supported by transient patterns of neuronal communication, dependent on regions of the frontal lobe (especially dorsolateral prefrontal cortex) and the parietal lobe. Long-term memories, on the other hand, are maintained by more stable and permanent changes in neural connections widely spread throughout the brain. The hippocampus is essential (for learning new information) to the consolidation of information from short-term to long-term memory, although it does not seem to store information itself. Without the hippocampus, new memories are unable to be stored into long-term memory, and there will be a very short attention span. Furthermore, it may be involved in changing neural connections for a period of three months or more after the initial learning. One of the primary functions of sleep is thought to be improving consolidation of information, as several studies have demonstrated that memory depends on getting sufficient sleep between training and test. Additionally, data obtained from neuroimaging studies have shown activation patterns in the sleeping brain which mirror those recorded during the learning of tasks from the previous day, suggesting that new memories may be solidified through such rehearsal.

Models

Models of memory provide abstract representations of how memory is believed to work. Below are several models proposed over the years by various psychologists. Note that there is some controversy as to whether there are several memory structures, for example, Tarnow (2005) finds that it is likely that there is only one memory structure between 6 and 600 seconds.

Atkinson-Shiffrin Model

The multi-store model (also known as Atkinson-Shiffrin memory model) was first recognised in 1968 by Atkinson and Shiffrin.

The multi-store model has been criticised for being too simplistic. For instance, long-term memory is believed to be actually made up of multiple subcomponents, such as episodic and procedural memory. It also proposes that rehearsal is the only mechanism by which information eventually reaches long-term storage, but evidence shows us capable of remembering things without rehearsal.

The model also shows all the memory stores as being a single unit whereas research into this shows differently. For example, short-term memory can be broken up into different units such as visual information and acoustic information. Patient KF proves this. Patient KF was brain damaged and had problems with his short term memory. He had problems with things such as spoken numbers, letters and words and with significant sounds (such as doorbells and cats meowing). Other parts of short term memory were unaffected, such as visual (pictures).

It also shows the sensory store as a single unit whilst we know that the sensory store is split up into several different parts such as taste, vision, and hearing.

Working Memory

In 1974 Baddeley and Hitch proposed a working memory model which replaced the concept of general short term memory with specific, active components. In this model, working memory consists of three basic stores: the central executive, the phonological loop and the visuo-spatial sketchpad. In 2000 this model was expanded with the multimodal episodic buffer.

The central executive essentially acts as attention. It channels information to the three component processes: the phonological loop, the visuo-spatial sketchpad, and the episodic buffer.

The phonological loop stores auditory information by silently rehearsing sounds or words in a continuous loop: the articulatory process (for example the repetition of a telephone number over and over again). Then, a short list of data is easier to remember.

The visuospatial sketchpad stores visual and spatial information. It is engaged when performing spatial tasks (such as judging distances) or visual ones.

The episodic buffer is dedicated to linking information across domains to form integrated units of visual, spatial, and verbal information and chronological ordering (e.g., the memory of a story or a movie scene). The episodic buffer is also assumed to have links to long-term memory and semantical meaning.

The working memory model explains many practical observations, such as why it is easier to do two different tasks (one verbal and one visual) than two similar tasks (e.g., two visual), and the aforementioned word-length effect. However, the concept of a central executive as noted here has been criticised as inadequate and vague.

Levels of Processing

Craik and Lockhart (1972) proposed that it is the method and depth of processing that affects how an experience is stored in memory, rather than rehearsal.

- Organization-Mandler (1967) gave participants a pack of word cards and asked them to sort them into any number of piles using any system of categorisation they liked. When they were later asked to recall as many of the words as they could, those who used more categories remembered more words. This study suggested that the act of organising information makes it more memorable.

- Distinctiveness-Eysenck and Eysenck (1980) asked participants to say words in a distinctive way, e.g. spell the words out loud. Such participants recalled the words better than those who simply read them off a list.
- Effort-Tyler *et al.* (1979) had participants solve a series of anagrams, some easy (FAHTER) and some difficult (HREFAT). The participants recalled the difficult anagrams better, presumably because they put more effort into them.
- Elaboration-Palmere *et al.* (1983) gave participants descriptive paragraphs of a fictitious African nation. There were some short paragraphs and some with extra sentences elaborating the main idea. Recall was higher for the ideas in the elaborated paragraphs.

Classification by Information Type

Anderson (1976) divides long-term memory into *declarative (explicit)* and *procedural (implicit)* memories.

Declarative memory requires conscious recall, in that some conscious process must call back the information. It is sometimes called *explicit memory*, since it consists of information that is explicitly stored and retrieved.

Declarative memory can be further sub-divided into semantic memory, which concerns facts taken independent of context; and episodic memory, which concerns information specific to a particular context, such as a time and place. Semantic memory allows the encoding of abstract knowledge about the world, such as "Paris is the capital of France". Episodic memory, on the other hand, is used for more personal memories, such as the sensations, emotions, and personal associations of a particular place or time.

Autobiographical memory-memory for particular events within one's own life-is generally viewed as either equivalent to, or a subset of, episodic memory. Visual memory is part of memory preserving some characteristics of our senses pertaining to visual experience. One is able to place in memory information that resembles objects, places, animals or people in sort of a mental image. Visual memory can result in priming and it is assumed some kind of perceptual representational system underlies this phenomenon.

In contrast, procedural memory (or *implicit memory*) is not based on the conscious recall of information, but on implicit learning. Procedural memory is primarily employed in learning motor skills and should be considered a subset of implicit memory. It is revealed when one does better in a given task due only to repetition-no new explicit memories have been formed, but one is unconsciously accessing aspects of those previous experiences. Procedural memory involved in motor learning depends on the cerebellum and basal ganglia.

Topographic memory is the ability to orient oneself in space, to recognize and follow an itinerary, or to recognize familiar places. Getting lost when travelling alone is an example of the failure of topographic memory. This is often reported among elderly patients who are evaluated for dementia. The disorder could be caused by multiple impairments, including difficulties with perception, orientation, and memory.

Classification by Temporal Direction

A further major way to distinguish different memory functions is whether the content to be remembered is in the past, retrospective memory, or whether the content is to be remembered in the future, prospective memory. Thus, retrospective memory as a category includes semantic, episodic and autobiographical memory. In contrast, prospective memory is memory for future intentions, or *remembering to remember* (Winograd, 1988). Prospective memory can be further broken down into event-and time-based prospective remembering. Time-based prospective memories are triggered by a time-cue, such as going to the doctor (action) at 4pm (cue). Event-based prospective memories are intentions triggered by cues, such as remembering to post a letter (action) after seeing a mailbox (cue). Cues do not need to be related to the action (as the mailbox example is), and lists, sticky-notes, knotted handkerchiefs, or string around the finger are all examples of cues that are produced by people as a strategy to enhance prospective memory.

Physiology

Brain areas involved in the neuroanatomy of memory such as the hippocampus, the amygdala, the striatum, or the mammillary bodies are thought to be involved in specific types of memory. For example, the hippocampus is believed to be involved in spatial learning and declarative learning, while the amygdala is thought to be involved in emotional memory. Damage to certain areas in patients and animal models and subsequent memory deficits is a primary source of information. However, rather than implicating a specific area, it could be that damage to adjacent areas, or to a pathway travelling through the area is actually responsible for the observed deficit. Further, it is not sufficient to describe memory, and its counterpart, learning, as solely dependent on specific brain regions. Learning and memory are attributed to changes in neuronal synapses, thought to be mediated by long-term potentiation and long-term depression.

Hebb distinguished between short-term and long-term memory. He postulated that any memory that stayed in short-term storage for a long enough time would be consolidated into a long-term memory. Later research showed this to be false. Research has shown that direct injections of cortisol or epinephrine help the storage of recent experiences. This is also true for stimulation of the amygdala. This proves that excitement enhances memory by the stimulation of hormones that affect the amygdala. Excessive or prolonged stress (with prolonged cortisol) may hurt memory storage. Patients with amygdalar damage are no more likely to remember emotionally charged words than nonemotionally charged ones. The hippocampus is important for explicit memory. The hippocampus is also important for memory consolidation. The hippocampus receives input from different parts of the cortex and sends its output out to different parts of the brain also. The input comes from secondary and tertiary sensory areas that have processed the information a lot already. Hippocampal damage may also cause memory loss and problems with memory storage.

Genetics

Study of the genetics of human memory is in its infancy. A notable initial success was the association of APOE with memory dysfunction in Alzheimer's Disease. The search for genes associated with normally-varying memory continues. One of the first candidates for normal variation in memory is the gene *KIBRA*, which appears to be associated with the rate at which material is forgotten over a delay period.

Disorders

Much of the current knowledge of memory has come from studying *memory disorders*. Loss of memory is known as amnesia. There are many sorts of amnesia, and by studying their different forms, it has become possible to observe apparent defects in individual sub-systems of the brain's memory systems, and thus hypothesize their function in the normally working brain. Other neurological disorders such as Alzheimer's disease can also affect memory and cognition.

Hyperthymesia, or hyperthymesic syndrome, is a disorder which affects an individual's autobiographical memory, essentially meaning that they cannot forget small details that otherwise would not be stored. Korsakoff's syndrome, also known as Korsakoff's psychosis, amnesic-confabulatory syndrome, is an organic brain disease that adversely affects memory.

While not a disorder, a common *temporary* failure of word retrieval from memory is the tip-of-the-tongue phenomenon. Sufferers of Nominal Aphasia (also called Anomia), however, do experience the tip-of-the-tongue phenomenon on an ongoing basis due to damage to the frontal and parietal lobes of the brain.

Methods

Methods to Optimize Memorization

Memorization is a method of learning that allows an individual to recall information verbatim. Rote learning is the method most often used. Methods of memorizing things have been the subject of much discussion over the years with some writers, such as Cosmos Rossellius using visual alphabets.

The spacing effect shows that an individual is more likely to remember a list of items when rehearsal is spaced over an extended period of time. In contrast to this is cramming which is intensive memorisation in a short period of time. Also relevant is the Zeigarnik effect which states that people remember uncompleted or interrupted tasks better than completed ones.

Interference from Previous Knowledge

At the Centre for Cognitive Science at Ohio State University, researchers have found that memory accuracy of adults is hurt by the fact that they know more than children and tend to apply this knowledge when learning new information. The findings appeared in the August 2004 edition of the journal Psychological Science. Interference can hamper memorisation and retrieval. There is retroactive interference when learning new information causes forgetting of old information, and proactive interference where learning one piece of information makes it harder to learn similar new information.

Influence of Odors and Emotions

In March 2007 German researchers found they could use odors to re-activate new memories in the brains of people while they slept and the volunteers remembered better later. Emotion can have a powerful impact on memory. Numerous studies have shown that the most vivid autobiographical memories tend to be of emotional events, which are likely to be recalled more often and with more clarity and detail than neutral events.

Memory and Aging

One of the key concerns of older adults is the experience of memory loss, especially as it is one of the hallmark symptoms of Alzheimer's disease. However, memory loss is qualitatively different in normal aging from the kind of memory loss associated with a diagnosis of Alzheimer's.

Improving Memory

A UCLA research study published in the June 2006 issue of the American Journal of Geriatric Psychiatry found that people can improve cognitive function and brain efficiency through simple lifestyle changes such as incorporating memory exercises, healthy eating, physical fitness and stress reduction into their daily lives. There are a loosely associated group of mnemonic principles and techniques that can be used to vastly improve memory known as the Art of memory.

The International Longevity Centre released in 2001 a report which includes in pages 14–16 recommendations for keeping the mind in good functionality until advanced age.

Some of the recommendations are to stay intellectually active through learning, training or reading, to keep physically active so to promote blood circulation to the brain, to socialize, to reduce stress, to keep sleep time regular, to avoid depression or emotional instability and to observe good nutrition.

Memory Tasks

- Paired associate learning-when one learns to associate one specific word with another. For example when given a word such as "safe" one must learn to say another specific word, such as "green". This is stimulus and response.
- Free recall-during this task a subject would be asked to study a list of words and then sometime later they will be asked to recall or write down as many words that they can remember.
- Recognition-subjects are asked to remember a list of words or pictures, after which point they are asked to identify the previously presented words or pictures from among a list of alternatives that were not presented in the original list.

Learning and Motivation

Motivation is the activation of goal-oriented behaviour. Motivation is said to be intrinsic or extrinsic. The term is generally used for humans but, theoretically, it can also be used to describe the causes for animal behaviour as well. This article refers to human motivation. According to various theories, motivation may be rooted in the basic need to minimize physical pain and maximize pleasure, or it may include specific needs such as eating and resting, or a desired object, goal, state of being, ideal, or it may be attributed to less-apparent reasons such as altruism, selfishness, morality, or avoiding mortality. Conceptually, motivation should not be confused with either volition or optimism. Motivation is related to, but distinct from, emotion.

Motivation Concepts

Intrinsic motivation refers to motivation that is driven by an interest or enjoyment in the task itself, and exists within the individual rather than relying on any external pressure. Intrinsic motivation has been studied by social and educational psychologists since the early 1970s. Research has found that it is usually associated with high educational achievement and enjoyment by students. Explanations of intrinsic motivation have been given in the context of Fritz Heider's attribution theory, Bandura's work on self-efficacy, and Deci and Ryan's cognitive evaluation theory. Students are likely to be intrinsically motivated if they:

- attribute their educational results to internal factors that they can control (e.g. the amount of effort they put in),
- believe they can be effective agents in reaching desired goals (i.e. the results are not determined by luck),
- are interested in mastering a topic, rather than just rote-learning to achieve good grades.

Extrinsic motivation comes from outside of the individual. Common extrinsic motivations are rewards like money and grades, coercion and threat of punishment. Competition is in general extrinsic because it encourages the performer to win and beat others, not to enjoy the intrinsic rewards of the activity. A crowd cheering on the individual and trophies are also extrinsic incentives. Social psychological research has indicated that extrinsic rewards can lead to overjustification and a subsequent reduction in intrinsic motivation. In one study demonstrating this effect, children who expected to be (and were) rewarded with a ribbon and a gold star for drawing pictures spent less time playing with the drawing materials in subsequent observations than children who were assigned to an unexpected reward condition and to children who received no extrinsic reward. Self-determination theory proposes that extrinsic motivation can be internalised by the individual if the task fits with their values and beliefs and therefore helps to fulfil their basic psychological needs. Internalised extrinsic motivation has been shown to lead to more positive outcomes, such as wellbeing, increased productivity and task satisfaction.

Self-control

The self-control of motivation is increasingly understood as a subset of emotional intelligence; a person may be highly intelligent according to a more conservative definition (as measured by many intelligence tests), yet unmotivated to dedicate this intelligence to certain tasks. Yale School of Management professor Victor Vroom's "expectancy theory" provides an account of when people will decide whether to exert self control to pursue a particular goal.

Drives and desires can be described as *a deficiency or need that activates behaviour that is aimed at a goal or an incentive.* These are thought to originate within the individual and may not require external stimuli to encourage the behaviour. Basic drives could be sparked by deficiencies such as hunger, which motivates a person to seek food; whereas more subtle drives might be the desire for praise and approval, which motivates a person to behave in a manner pleasing to others.

By contrast, the role of extrinsic rewards and stimuli can be seen in the example of training animals by giving them treats when they perform a trick correctly. The treat motivates the animals to perform the trick consistently, even later when the treat is removed from the process.

Motivational Theories

Incentive Theory

A reward, tangible or intangible, is presented after the occurrence of an action (i.e. behaviour) with the intent to cause the behaviour to occur again. This is done by associating positive meaning to the behaviour. Studies show that if the person receives the reward immediately, the effect would be greater, and decreases as duration lengthens. Repetitive action-reward combination can cause the action to become habit. Motivation comes from two sources: oneself, and other people. These two sources are called intrinsic motivation and extrinsic motivation, respectively.

Applying proper motivational techniques can be much harder than it seems. Steven Kerr notes that when creating a reward system, it can be easy to reward A, while hoping for B, and in the process, reap harmful effects that can jeopardize your goals.

A reinforcer is different from reward, in that reinforcement is intended to create a measured increase in the rate of a desirable behaviour following the addition of something to the environment.

Incentive theory in psychology, treats motivation and behaviour of the individual, as they are influenced by beliefs, such as engaging in activities that are expected to be profitable. Incentive theory is promoted by behavioural psychologists, such as B.F. Skinner and literalized, by behaviourists, especially by Skinner in his philosophy of Radical behaviourism, to mean that a person's actions always have social ramifications: and if actions are positively received people are more likely to act in this manner, or if negatively received people are less likely to act in this manner. Incentive theorists tend to distinguish between wanting and liking, where *liking* is a passive function evaluating a stimulus, but *wanting* adds an active process "attracting" the person towards the stimulus.

Incentive theory distinguishes itself from other motivation theories, such as drive theory, in the direction of the motivation. In incentive theory, stimuli "attract", to use the term above, a person towards them. As opposed to the body seeking to reestablish homeostasis pushing it towards the stimulus. In terms of behaviourism, *incentive theory* involves positive reinforcement: the stimulus has been conditioned to make the person happier. For instance, a person knows that eating food, drinking water, or gaining social capital will make them happier. As opposed to in *drive theory*, which involves negative reinforcement: a stimulus has been associated with the removal of the punishment— the lack of homeostasis in the body. For example, a person has come to know that if they eat when hungry, it will eliminate that negative feeling of hunger, or if they drink when thirsty, it will eliminate that negative feeling of thirst.

Drive-reduction Theories

There are a number of drive theories. The Drive Reduction Theory grows out of the concept that we have certain biological drives, such as hunger. As time passes the strength of the drive increases if it is not satisfied (in this case by eating). Upon satisfying a drive the drive's strength is reduced. The theory is based on diverse ideas from the theories of Freud to the ideas of feedback control systems, such as a thermostat.

Drive theory has some intuitive or folk validity. For instance when preparing food, the drive model appears to be compatible with sensations of rising hunger as the food is prepared, and, after the food has been consumed, a decrease in subjective hunger. There are several problems, however, that leave the validity of drive reduction open for debate. The first problem is that it does not explain how secondary reinforcers reduce drive. For example, money satisfies no biological or psychological needs, but a pay check appears to reduce drive through second-order conditioning. Secondly, a drive, such as hunger, is viewed as having a "desire" to eat, making the drive a homuncular being—a feature criticized as simply moving the fundamental problem behind this "small man" and his desires.

In addition, it is clear that drive reduction theory cannot be a complete theory of behaviour, or a hungry human could not prepare a meal without eating the food before he finished cooking it. The ability of drive theory to cope with all kinds of behaviour, from not satisfying a drive (by adding on other traits such as restraint), or adding additional drives for "tasty" food, which combine with drives for "food" in order to explain cooking render it hard to test.

Cognitive Dissonance Theory

Cognitive dissonance is an uncomfortable feeling caused by holding conflicting ideas simultaneously. The theory of cognitive dissonance proposes that people have a motivational drive to reduce dissonance. They do this by changing their attitudes, beliefs, and actions. Dissonance is also reduced by justifying, blaming, and denying. It is one of the most influential and extensively studied theories in social psychology.

Experience can clash with expectations, as, for example, with buyer's remorse following the purchase of a new car. In a state of dissonance, people may feel surprise, dread, guilt, anger, or embarrassment. People are biased to think of their choices as correct, despite any contrary evidence. This bias gives dissonance theory its predictive power, shedding light on otherwise puzzling irrational and destructive behaviour.

A classical example of this idea (and the origin of the expression "sour grapes") is expressed in the fable *The Fox and the Grapes* by Aesop (ca. 620–564 BCE). In the story, a fox sees some high-hanging grapes and wishes to eat them. When the fox is unable to think of a way to reach them, he surmises that the grapes are probably not worth eating, as they must not be ripe or that they are sour. This example follows a pattern: one desires something, finds it unattainable, and reduces one's dissonance by criticizing it. Jon Elster calls this pattern "adaptive preference formation."

A powerful cause of dissonance is an idea in conflict with a fundamental element of the self-concept, such as "I am a good person" or "I made the right decision." The anxiety that comes with the possibility of having made a bad decision can lead to rationalization, the tendency to create additional reasons or justifications to support one's choices. A person who just spent too much money on a new car might decide that the new vehicle is much less likely to break down than his or her old car. This belief may or may not be true, but it would reduce dissonance and make the person feel better. Dissonance can also lead to confirmation bias, the denial of disconfirming evidence, and other ego defence mechanisms.

Examples

The most famous case in the early study of cognitive dissonance was described by Leon Festinger and others in the book *When Prophecy Fails*. The authors infiltrated a group that was expecting the imminent end of the world on a certain date. When that prediction failed, the movement did not disintegrate, but grew instead. By sharing cult beliefs with others, they gained acceptance and thus reduced their own dissonance.

Another famous example of cognitive dissonance is the Ben Franklin effect. Franklin won over a political opponent by asking him a favor and he relates thus:

I did not... aim at gaining his favour by paying any servile respect to him but, after some time, took this other method. Having heard that he had in his library a certain very scarce and curious book, I wrote a note to him, expressing my desire of perusing that book, and requesting he would do me the favour of lending it to me for a few days. He sent it immediately, and I return'd it in about a week with another note, expressing strongly my sense of the favour. When we next met in the House, he spoke to me (which he had never done before), and with great civility; and he ever after manifested a readiness to serve me on all occasions, so that we became great friends, and our friendship continued to his death. This is another instance of the truth of an old maxim I had learned, which says, *"He that has once done you a kindness will be more ready to do you another, than he whom you yourself have obliged."*

This perception of Franklin has led to what has become known as the Ben Franklin effect. After lending Franklin the book, the opponent had to resolve the dissonance of his attitude towards Franklin, whom he also had just done a favor. He justified doing the favor by telling himself that he actually liked Franklin, and, as a result, he treated him with respect instead of rudeness from then on.

Smoking is often postulated as an example of cognitive dissonance because it is widely accepted that cigarettes can cause lung cancer, yet virtually everyone wants to live a long and healthy life. In terms of the theory, the desire to live a long life is dissonant with the activity of doing something that will most likely shorten one's life. The tension produced by these contradictory ideas can be reduced by quitting smoking, denying the evidence of lung cancer, or justifying one's smoking. For example, smokers could rationalize their behaviour by concluding that only a few smokers become ill, that it only happens to very heavy smokers, or that if smoking does not kill them, something else will. While chemical addiction may operate in addition to cognitive dissonance for existing smokers, new smokers may exhibit a simpler case of the latter.

This case of dissonance could also be interpreted in terms of a threat to the self-concept. The thought, "I am increasing my risk of lung cancer" is dissonant with the self-related belief, "I am a smart, reasonable person who makes good decisions." Because it is often easier to make excuses than it is to change behaviour, dissonance theory leads to the conclusion that humans are rationalizing and not always rational beings.

Variants

There are two main forms of dissonance: hedonistic dissonance and moral dissonance.

- *Hedonistic dissonance* is elicited when people act in a way which results in negative consequences for themselves. For instance, a person is late for a meeting because of traffic but could have been on time had he taken the subway.

- *Moral dissonance* is aroused when people act in a way that causes negative consequence for others. For instance, cheating and lying.

Theory and Research

Most of the research on cognitive dissonance takes the form of one of four major paradigms. Important research generated by the theory has been concerned with the consequences of exposure to information inconsistent with a prior belief, what happens after individuals act in ways that are inconsistent with their prior attitudes, what happens after individuals make decisions, and the effects of effort expenditure.

The Belief Disconfirmation Paradigm

Dissonance is aroused when people are confronted with information that is inconsistent with their beliefs. If the dissonance is not reduced by changing one's belief, the dissonance can result in misperception or rejection or refutation of the information, seeking support from others who share the beliefs, and attempting to persuade others to restore consonance.

An early version of cognitive dissonance theory appeared in Leon Festinger's 1956 book, *When Prophecy Fails*. This book gave an inside account of the increasing belief which sometimes follows the failure of a cult's prophecy. The believers met at a pre-determined place and time, believing they alone would survive the earth's destruction. The appointed time came and passed without incident. They faced acute cognitive dissonance: had they been the victim of a hoax? Had they donated their worldly possessions in vain? Most members chose to believe something less dissonant: the aliens had given earth a second chance, and the group was now empowered to spread the word: earth-spoiling must stop. The group dramatically increased their proselytism despite the failed prophecy.

The Induced-Compliance Paradigm

In Festinger and Carlsmith's classic 1959 experiment, students were asked to spend an hour on boring and tedious tasks (e.g., turning pegs a quarter turn, over and over again). The tasks were designed to generate a strong, negative attitude. Once the subjects had done this, the experimenters asked some of them to do a simple favor. They were asked to talk to another subject (actually an actor) and persuade them that the tasks were interesting and engaging. Some participants were paid $20 (inflation adjusted to 2010, this equates to $150) for this favor, another group was paid $1 (or $7.50 in "2010 dollars"), and a control group was not asked to perform the favor.

When asked to rate the boring tasks at the conclusion of the study (not in the presence of the other "subject"), those in the $1 group rated them more positively than those in the $20 and control groups. This was explained by Festinger and Carlsmith as evidence for cognitive dissonance. The researchers theorized that people experienced dissonance between the conflicting cognitions, "I told someone that the task was interesting", and "I actually found it boring." When paid only $1, students were forced to internalize the attitude they were induced to express, because they had no other justification. Those in the $20 condition, however, had an obvious external justification for their behaviour, and thus experienced less dissonance.

In subsequent experiments, an alternative method of inducing dissonance has become common. In this research, experimenters use counter-attitudinal essay-writing, in which people are paid varying amounts of money (e.g. $1 or $10) for writing essays expressing opinions contrary to their own. People paid only a small amount of money have less justification for their inconsistency and tend to experience more dissonance.

A variant of the induced-compliance paradigm is the forbidden toy paradigm. An experiment by Aronson and Carlsmith in 1963 examined self-justification in children. In this experiment, children were left in a room with a variety of toys, including a highly desirable toy steam-shovel (or other toy). Upon leaving the room, the experimenter told half the children that there would be a severe punishment if they played with that particular toy and told the other half that there would be a mild punishment. All of the children in the study refrained from playing with the toy. Later, when the children were told that they could freely play with whatever toy they wanted, the ones in the mild punishment condition were less likely to play with the toy, even though the threat had been removed. The children who were only mildly threatened had to justify to themselves why they did not play with the toy. The degree of punishment by itself was not strong enough, so the children had to convince themselves that the toy was not worth playing with in order to resolve their dissonance.

The Free-Choice Paradigm

In a different type of experiment conducted by Jack Brehm, 225 female students rated a series of common appliances and were then allowed to choose one of two appliances to take home as a gift. A second round of ratings showed that the participants increased their ratings of the item they chose, and lowered their ratings of the rejected item. This can be explained in terms of cognitive dissonance. When making a difficult decision, there are always aspects of the rejected choice that one finds appealing and these features are dissonant with choosing something else. In other words, the cognition, "I chose X" is dissonant with the cognition, "There are some things I like about Y." More recent research has found similar results in four-year-old children and capuchin monkeys.

The Effort-Justification Paradigm

Dissonance is aroused whenever individuals voluntarily engage in an unpleasant activity to achieve some desired goal. Dissonance can be reduced by exaggerating the desirability of the goal. Aronson & Mills had individuals undergo a severe or mild "initiation" in order to become a member of a group. In the severe-initiation condition, the individuals engaged in an embarrassing activity. The group turned out to be very dull and boring. The individuals in the severe-initiation condition evaluated the group as more interesting than the individuals in the mild-initiation condition. All of the above paradigms continue to be used in fruitful research.

Washing one's hands has been shown to eliminate post-decisional dissonance, presumably because the dissonance is often caused by moral disgust (with oneself) which is related to disgust from unsanitary conditions.

Challenges and Qualifications

Daryl Bem was an early critic of cognitive dissonance theory. He proposed self-perception theory as a more parsimonious alternative explanation of the experimental results. According to Bem, people do not think much about their attitudes, let alone whether they are in conflict. Bem interpreted people in the Festinger and Carlsmith study or the induced-compliance paradigm as inferring their attitudes from their behaviour. Thus, when asked "Did you find the task interesting?" they decided that they must have found it interesting because that is what they told someone. Bem suggested that people paid $20 had a salient, external incentive for their behaviour and were likely to perceive the money as their reason for saying the task was interesting, rather than concluding that they actually found it interesting.

In many experimental situations, Bem's theory and Festinger's dissonance theory make identical predictions, but only dissonance theory predicts the presence of unpleasant tension or arousal. Lab experiments have verified the presence of arousal in dissonance situations. This provides support for cognitive dissonance theory and makes it unlikely that self-perception by itself can account for all the laboratory findings.

In 1969, Elliot Aronson reformulated the basic theory by linking it to the self-concept. According to this new interpretation, cognitive dissonance does not arise because people experience dissonance between conflicting cognitions. Instead, it occurs when people see their actions as conflicting with their normally positive view of themselves. Thus, about the original Festinger and Carlsmith study using the induced-compliance paradigm, Aronson stated that the dissonance was between the cognition, "I am an honest person" and the cognition, "I lied to someone about finding the task interesting." Other psychologists have argued that maintaining cognitive consistency is a way to protect public self-image, rather than private self-concept. However, a recent result seems to rule out such an explanation by showing revaluation of items following a choice even when people have forgotten their choices.

During the 1980s, Cooper and Fazio argued that dissonance was caused by aversive consequences, rather than inconsistency.

According to this interpretation, the fact that lying is wrong and hurtful, not the inconsistency between cognitions, is what makes people feel bad. Subsequent research, however, found that people experience dissonance even when they feel they have not done anything wrong. For example, Aronson and his students showed that people experience dissonance even when the consequences of their statements are beneficial—as when they convince sexually active students to use condoms, when they, themselves are not using condoms.

Chen and colleagues have criticized the free-choice paradigm and have suggested that the "Rank, choice, rank" method of studying dissonance is invalid. They argue that research design relies on the assumption that, if the subject rates options differently in the second survey, then the subject's attitudes towards the options have therefore changed. They show that there are other reasons one might get different rankings in the second survey—perhaps the subjects were largely indifferent between choices. However, some follow-up research has provided contradictory evidence to this account.

Modelling in Neural Networks

Neural network models of cognition have provided the necessary framework to integrate the empirical research done on cognitive dissonance and attitudes into one model of explanation of attitude formation and change.

Various neural network models have been developed to predict how cognitive dissonance will influence an individual's attitude and behaviour. These include:

- Parallel Constraint Satisfaction Processes
- The Meta-Cognitive Model (MCM) of attitudes
- Adaptive connectionist model of cognitive dissonance
- Attitudes as constraint satisfaction model.

Cognitive Dissonance in the Brain

Using fMRI, Van Veen and colleagues investigated the neural basis of cognitive dissonance in a modified version of the classic induced compliance paradigm. While in the scanner, participants "argued" that the uncomfortable MRI environment was nevertheless a pleasant experience. The researchers replicated the basic induced compliance findings; participants in an experimental group enjoyed the scanner more than participants in a control group who simply were paid to make their argument. Importantly, responding counter-attitudinally activated the dorsal anterior cingulate cortex and the anterior insular cortex; furthermore, the degree to which these regions were activated predicted individual participants' degree of attitude change. Van Veen and colleagues argue that these findings support the original dissonance theory by Festinger, and support the "conflict theory" of anterior cingulate functioning.

Using the free choice paradigm, Sharot and colleagues have shown that after making a choice, activity in the striatum changes to reflect the new evaluation of the choice object, increasing if the object was chosen and decreasing if it was rejected.

Need Theories

Need Hierarchy Theory

Abraham Maslow's theory is one of the most widely discussed theories of motivation.

The theory can be summarized as follows:

- Human beings have wants and desires which influence their behaviour. Only unsatisfied needs influence behaviour, satisfied needs do not.
- Since needs are many, they are arranged in order of importance, from the basic to the complex.
- The person advances to the next level of needs only after the lower level need is at least minimally satisfied.
- The further the progress up the hierarchy, the more individuality, humanness and psychological health a person will show.

The needs, listed from basic (lowest-earliest) to most complex (highest-latest) are as follows:

- Physiology (hunger, thirst, sleep, etc.)
- Safety/Security/Shelter/Health
- Belongingness/Love/Friendship

- Self-esteem/Recognition/Achievement
- Self actualization.

Herzberg's Two-factor Theory

Frederick Herzberg's two-factor theory, a.k.a. intrinsic/extrinsic motivation, concludes that certain factors in the workplace result in job satisfaction, but if absent, they don't lead to dissatisfaction but no satisfaction.

The factors that motivate people can change over their lifetime, but "respect for me as a person" is one of the top motivating factors at any stage of life.

He distinguished between:

- Motivators; (e.g. challenging work, recognition, responsibility) which give positive satisfaction, *and*
- Hygiene factors; (e.g. status, job security, salary and fringe benefits) that do not motivate if present, but, if absent, result in demotivation.

The name Hygiene factors is used because, like hygiene, the presence will not make you healthier, but absence can cause health deterioration.

The theory is sometimes called the "Motivator-Hygiene Theory" and/or "The Dual Structure Theory."

Herzberg's theory has found application in such occupational fields as information systems and in studies of user satisfaction

Alderfer's ERG Theory

Alderfer, expanding on Maslow's hierarchy of needs, created the ERG theory (existence, relatedness and growth). Physiological and safety, the lower order needs, are placed in the existence category, while love and self esteem needs are placed in the relatedness category. The growth category contains our self-actualization and self-esteem needs. Alderfer argues that there are three groups of core needs — existence, relatedness, and growth hence the label: ERG theory. The existence group is concerned with providing our basic material existence requirements. They include the items that Maslow considered to be physiological and safety needs. The second group of needs are those of relatedness-the desire we have for maintaining important interpersonal relationships. These social and status desires require interaction with others if they are to be satisfied, and they align with Maslow's social need and the external component of Maslow's esteem classification. Finally, Alderfer isolates growth needs' an intrinsic desire for personal development. These include the intrinsic component from Maslow's esteem category and the characteristics included under self-actualization.

Self-determination Theory

Self-determination theory (SDT) is a macro theory of human motivation and personality, concerning peoples' inherent growth tendencies and their innate psychological needs. It is concerned with the motivation behind the choices that people make without any external influence and interference. SDT focuses on the degree to which an individual's behaviour is self-motivated and self-determined.

In the 1970s, research on SDT evolved from studies comparing the intrinsic and extrinsic motives, and the dominant role extrinsic motivation played in an individual's behaviour but it was not until mid 1980s that SDT was formally introduced and accepted as a sound empirical theory. Research applying SDT to different areas in social psychology has increased considerably since the 2000's.

Key studies that led to emergence of SDT included research on intrinsic motivation. Intrinsic motivation refers to initiating an activity for its own sake because it is interesting and satisfying in itself, as opposed to doing an activity to obtain an external goal (extrinsic motivation). Different types of motivations have been described based on the degree they have been internalised. Internalisation refers to the active attempt to transform an extrinsic motive into personally endorsed values and thus assimilate behavioural regulations that were originally external (Ryan, 1995).

Deci and Ryan (1991, 1995) later expanded on the early work differentiating between intrinsic and extrinsic motivation and proposed three main intrinsic needs involved in self-determination. According to Deci and Ryan, the three psychological needs motivate the self to initiate behaviour and specify nutriments that are essential for psychological health and well-being of an individual. These needs are said to be universal, innate and psychological and include the need for competence, autonomy, and relatedness.

Basic Theory

SDT is centred on the belief that human nature shows persistent positive features, that it repeatedly shows effort, agency and commitment in their lives that the theory calls "inherent growth tendencies." People also have innate psychological needs that are the basis for self-motivation and personality integration.

SDT identifies three innate needs that, if satisfied, allow optimal function and growth:

- Competence
- Relatedness
- Autonomy.

These needs are seen as universal necessities that are innate not learned and seen in humanity across time, gender and culture.

Deci and Vansteenkiste (2003) claim that there are three essential elements of the theory:

1. Humans are inherently proactive with their potential and mastering their inner forces (such as drives and emotions)
2. Humans have inherent tendency toward growth development and integrated functioning
3. Optimal development and actions are inherent in humans but they don't happen automatically

To actualise their inherent potential they need nurturing from the social environment.

If this happens there are positive consequence (e.g. well being and growth) but if not, there are negative consequences. So SDT emphasises humans' natural growth toward positive motivation, however this is thwarted if their basic needs are not fulfilled.

Needs

SDT supports three basic psychological needs that must be satisfied to foster well-being and health, these needs can be universally applied. However some may be more salient than others at certain times and will be expressed differently based on time, culture or experience.

Competence

Refers to being effective in dealing with the environment a person finds themselves in (White, 1959)

Relatedness

Is the universal want to interact, be connected to and experience caring for others – (Baumeister & Leary, 1995)

Autonomy

Is the universal urge to be causal agents of our own life and act in harmony with our integrated self. However Deci and Vansteenkiste (2004) note this doesn't mean to be independent of others.

Motivations

SDT claims to give a different approach to motivation, considering what motivates a person at any given time as opposed to seeing motivation as a unitary concept. SDT makes distinctions between different types of motivation and the consequences of them.

Intrinsic Motivation

Intrinsic motivation is the natural, inherent drive to seek out challenges and new possibilities that SDT associated with cognitive and social development.

Cognitive Evaluation Theory is a sub-theory of SDT that specifies factors explaining intrinsic motivation and variability with it and looks at how social and environmental factors help or hinder intrinsic motivations. CET focuses on the needs of competence and autonomy.

Claiming social context events like feedback on work or rewards lead to feelings of competence and so enhance intrinsic motivations. Deci (1975) found positive feedback enhanced intrinsic motivations and negative feedback diminished it. Vallerand and Reid (1984) went further and found that these effects were being mediated by perceived control.

Autonomy however must accompany competence in order for people to see their behaviours as self determined by intrinsic motivation.

For this to happen there must be immediate contextual support for both needs or inner resources based on prior development support for both needs CET and intrinsic motivation is also linked to relatedness through the hypothesis that intrinsic motivation will flourish if linked with a sense of security and relatedness. Grolnick and Ryan (1989) found lower intrinsic motivation in children who believed their teachers to be uncaring or cold and so not fulfilling their relatedness needs.

Extrinsic Motivation

Extrinsic motivation comes from external sources. Deci and Ryan (1985) developed Organismic Integration Theory (OIT), as a sub-theory of SDT, to explain the different ways in which extrinsically motivated behaviour is regulated.

OIT details the different forms of extrinsic motivation and the contexts in which they come about. It is the context of such motivation that concerns the SDT theory as these contexts affect whether the motivations are internalised and so integrated into the sense of self.

OIT describes four different types of extrinsic motivations that often vary in terms of their relative autonomy:

1. Externally regulated behaviour: Is the least autonomous, it is performed because of external demand or possible reward. Such actions can be seen to have an externally perceived locus of control
2. Introjected regulation of behaviour: describes taking on regulations to behaviour but not fully accepting said regulations as your own. Deci and Ryan (1995) claim such behaviour normally represents regulation by contingent self-esteem, citing ego involvement as a classic form of introjections. This is the kind of behaviour where people feel motivated to demonstrate ability to maintain self worth. While this is internally driven Deci and Ryan say introjected behaviour is on an externally perceived locus of control because they aren't perceived as part of self.

3. Regulation through identification: Is a more autonomy driven form of extrinsic motivation. If involves consciously valuing a goal or regulation so that said action is accepted as personally important.
4. Integrated Regulation: Is the most autonomous kind of extrinsic motivation. Occurring when regulations are fully assimilated with self so they are included in a person's self evaluations and beliefs on personal needs. Because of this integrated motivations share qualities with intrinsic motivation, but are still classified as extrinsic because the goals that are trying to be achieved are for reasons extrinsic to the self, rather than the inherent enjoyment or interest in the task.

Extrinsically motivated behaviours can be integrated into self. OIT proposes internalization is more likely to occur when there is a sense of relatedness.

Ryan, Stiller and Lynch (1994) found children will internalize school's extrinsic regulations when they felt secure and cared for by parents and teachers.

Internalisation of extrinsic motivation is also linked to competence. OIT suggests that feelings of competence in activities should facilitate internalisation of said actions.

Autonomy is particularly important when its regulations are trying to be integrated into a person's sense of self. If an external context allows a person to integrate regulations they must feel competent, related and autonomous. They must also understand in terms of their other goals the regulation in order for a sense of autonomy to be facilitated. This was supported by Deci, Eghrari, Patrick and Leone (1994) who found in laboratory settings if a person was given a meaningful reason for uninteresting behaviour along with support for their sense of autonomy and relatedness they internalized and integrated their behaviour.

Basic needs and Intrinsic Motivation

White (1959) and deCharms (1968) proposed that the need for competence and autonomy is the basis of intrinsic motivation and behaviour. This is a link between people's basic needs and their motivations.

Autonomy

Deci (1971) found that offering people extrinsic rewards for behaviour that is intrinsically motivated undermined the intrinsic motivation as they grow less interested in it. Initially intrinsically motivated behaviour becomes controlled by external rewards, which undermines their autonomy.

Further research by Amabile, DeJong and Lepper (1976) found other external factors like deadlines, which restrict and control, also decrease intrinsic motivation.

Situations that give autonomy as opposed to taking it away also have a similar link to motivation. Studies looking at choice have found that increasing a participant's options and choices increases their intrinsic motivation to said activities.

Competence

Deci (1971) found that giving people positive feedback on a task increases people's intrinsic motivation to do it, meaning that this was because the positive feedback was fulfilling people's need for competence.

Vallerand and Reid (1984) found negative feedback has the opposite effect (i.e., decreasing intrinsic motivation by taking away from people's need for competence).

Relatedness

Frodi, Bridges and Grolnick (1985) said that need for relatedness supports intrinsic motivation in a less key way.

Individual Differences

SDT argues that needs are innate but can be developed in a social context. Some people will develop stronger needs than others, creating individual differences. However individual differences within the theory focus on concepts resulting from the degree which needs have been satisfied or not satisfied.

Within SDT there are two general individual difference concepts, Causality Orientations and Life Goals.

Causality Orientations

Causality orientations are motivational orientations that refer to either the way people orient to an environment and regulate their behaviour because of this or the extent to which they are self determined in general across many settings. SDT created three orientations autonomous, controlled and impersonal.

1. Autonomous Orientations: result from satisfaction of the basic needs
2. Strong controlled orientations: Result from satisfaction of competence and relatedness needs but not of autonomy and is linked to regulation through internal and external contingences, which lead to rigid functioning and diminished well being.
3. Impersonal Orientations: Results from failing to fulfil all three needs. This is also related to poor functioning and ill being.

According to the theory people have some amount of each of the orientations, which can be used to make predictions on a persons psychological health and behavioural outcomes

Life Goals

Life goals are long term goals people use to guide their activities and they fall into two categories. Intrinsic aspirations and extrinsic aspirations;

1. Intrinsic Aspirations: Contain life goals like affiliation generativity and personal development.
2. Extrinsic Aspirations: Have life goals like wealth, fame and attractiveness.

There have been several studies on this subject that chart intrinsic goals being associated with greater health, well being and performance.

Key Studies

Deci (1971): External Rewards on Intrinsic Motivation

Deci investigated the effects of external rewards on intrinsic motivation in two laboratory and one field experiment. Based on the results from earlier animal and human studies regarding intrinsic motivation the author explored two possibilities. In the first two experiments he looked at the effect of extrinsic rewards in terms of a decrease in intrinsic motivation to perform a task. Earlier studies showed contradictory or inconclusive findings regarding decrease in performance on a task following an external reward. The third experiment was based on findings of developmental learning theorists and looked at whether a different type of reward enhances intrinsic motivation to participate in an activity.

Experiment I

This experiment tested the hypothesis that if an individual is intrinsically motivated to perform an activity, introduction of an extrinsic reward decreases the degree of intrinsic motivation to perform the task.

Twenty-four undergraduate psychology students participated in the first laboratory experiment and were assigned to experimental (n =12) and control group (n = 12). Each group participated in three sessions conducted on three different days. During the sessions the participants were engaged in working on a Soma cube puzzle which was assumed to be an activity that college students would be intrinsically motivated to do. The puzzle could be put together to form numerous different configurations. In each session, the participants were shown four different configurations drawn on a piece of paper and were asked to use the puzzle to reproduce the configurations while they were being timed.

The first and third session of the experimental condition were identical to control, but in the second session the participants in the experimental condition were given a dollar for completing each puzzle within time. During the middle of each session, the experimenter left the room for eight minutes and the participants were told that they were free to do whatever they wanted during that time, while the experimenter observed during that period. The amount of time spent working on the puzzle during the free choice period was used to measure motivation.

As Deci expected, when external reward was introduced during session two, the participants spent more time working on the puzzles during the free choice period in comparison to session 1 and when the external reward was removed in the third session, the time spent working on the puzzle dropped lower than the first session. All subjects reported finding the task interesting and enjoyable at the end of each session, providing evidence for the experimenter's assumption that the task was intrinsically motivating for the college students. The study showed some support of the experimenter's hypothesis and a trend towards decrease in intrinsic motivation was seen after money was provided to the participants as external reward.

Experiment II

The second experiment was a field experiment, similar to laboratory Experiment I, but was conducted in a natural setting.

Eight student workers were observed at a college biweekly newspaper. Four of the students served as a control group and worked on Friday. The experimental group worked on Tuesdays.

The control and experimental group students were not aware that they were being observed. The 10-week observation was divided into three time periods. The task in this study required the students to write headlines for the newspaper.

During "Time 2," The students in the experimental group were given 50 cents for each headline they wrote. At the end of Time 2, they were told that in the future the newspaper cannot pay them 50 cent for each headline anymore as the newspaper ran out of the money allocated for that and they were not paid for the headlines during Time 3.

The speed of task completion (headlines) was used as a measure of motivation in this experiment. Absences were used as a measure of attitudes.

In order to assess the stability of the observed effect, the experimenter observed the students again (Time 4) for two weeks. There was a gap of five weeks between Time 3 and Time 4. Due to absences and change in assignment etc., motivation data was not available for all students. The results of this experiment were similar to Experiment I and monetary reward was found to decrease the intrinsic motivation of the students, supporting Deci's hypothesis.

Experiment III

Experiment III was also conducted in the laboratory and was identical to Experiment I in all respects except for the kind of external reward provided to the students in experimental condition during Session 2. In this experiment, verbal praise was used as an extrinsic reward.

The experimenter hypothesized that a different type of reward, i.e. social approval in form of verbal reinforcement and positive feedback for performing the task that a person is intrinsically motivated to perform, will enhance the degree of internal motivation even after the extrinsic reward is removed.

The results of the experiment III confirmed the hypothesis and the students' performance increased significantly during the third session in comparison to session one, showing that verbal praise and positive feedback enhances performance in tasks that a person is initially intrinsically motivated to perform. This provides evidence that verbal praise as external reward increases intrinsic motivation.

The author explained differences between the two types of external rewards as having different effects on intrinsic motivation. When a person is intrinsically motivated to perform a task and money is introduced to work on the task, the individual cognitively re-evaluates the importance of the task and the intrinsic motivation to perform the task (because the individual finds it interesting) shifts to extrinsic motivation and the primary focus changes from enjoying the task to gaining financial reward. However, when verbal praise is provided in a similar situation increases intrinsic motivation as it is not evaluated to be controlled by external factors and the person sees the task as an enjoyable task that is performed autonomously. The increase in intrinsic motivation is explained by positive reinforcement and an increase in perceived locus of control to perform the task.

Pritchard, Campbell and Campbell (1975): Evaluation of Deci's Hypothesis

Pritchard, Campbell and Campbell conducted a similar study to evaluate Deci's hypothesis regarding the role of extrinsic rewards on decreasing intrinsic motivation.

Participants were randomly assigned to two groups. A chess-problem task was used in this study. Data was collected in two sessions.

Session I

Participants were asked to complete a background questionnaire that included questions on the amount of time the participant played chess during the week, the number of years that the participant has been playing chess for, amount of enjoyment the participant gets from playing the game, etc.

The participants in both groups were then told that the experimenter needed to enter the information in the computer and for the next 10 minutes the participant were free to do whatever they liked.

The experimenter left the room for 10 minutes. The room had similar chess-problem tasks on the table, some magazines as well as coffee was made available for the participants if they chose to have it.

The time spent on the chess-problem task was observed through a one way mirror by the experimenter during the 10 minutes break and was used as a measure of intrinsic motivation. After the experimenter returned, the experimental group was told that there was a monetary reward for the participant who could work on the most chess problems in the given time and that the reward is for this session only and would not be offered during the next session. The control group was not offered a monetary reward.

Session II

The second session was the same for the two groups:

After a filler task, the experimenter left the room for 10 minutes and the time participants spent on the chess-problem task was observed. The experimental group was reminded that there was no reward for the task this time.

After both sessions the participants were required to respond to questionnaires evaluating the task, i.e. to what degree did they find the task interesting. Both groups reported that they found the task interesting.

The results of the study showed that the experimental group showed a significant decrease in time spent on chess-problem task during 10 minute free time from session 1 to session 2 in comparison to the group that was not paid, thus confirming the hypothesis presented by Deci that contingent monetary reward for an activity decreases the intrinsic motivation to perform that activity. Other studies were conducted around this time focusing at other types or rewards as well as other external factors that play a role in decreasing intrinsic motivation.

Sook Ning Chua and Richard Koestner (2008)

SDT and Solitude

Sook Ning Chua and Richard Koestner (2008) explored the consequences of activities done in solitude.

They argued that relation of solitary activities to feelings of loneliness and life satisfaction depends on whether individuals feel autonomous rather than controlled about spending time alone.

Participants (N = 108) reported the percentage of waking time they spent in solitude per day and completed measures of attachment styles, motivation for solitary activities, loneliness, and well-being. The results suggest that relative autonomy is important regardless of one's decision to act or not to act. The results also emphasize the importance of autonomous social behaviour.

New Developments

Principles of SDT have been applied in many domains of life, e.g., job demands; teaching and health etc. Besides the domains mentioned above, self-determination theory research has been widely applied to the field of sports.

SDT and Exercise

Murcia, Roman, Galindo, Alonso and Gonzalez-Cutre (2008) looked at the influence of peers on enjoyment in exercise. Specifically, the researchers looked at the effect of motivational climate generated by peers on exercisers by analyzing data collected through questionnaires and rating scales. The assessment included evaluation of motivational climate, basic psychological needs satisfaction, levels of self determination and self-regulation (amotivation, external, introjected, identified and intrinsic regulation) and also the assessment of the level of satisfaction and enjoyment in exercising.

Data analysis revealed that a climate in which the peers are supportive and there is an emphasis on cooperation, effort and personal improvement, influences variables like basic psychological needs, motivation and enjoyment. The task climate positively predicted the three basic psychological needs (competence, autonomy and relatedness) and so positively predicted self-determined motivation. Task climate and the resulting self-determination were also found to positively influence level of enjoyment the exercisers experienced during the activity.

SDT and Awareness

Awareness has always been associated with autonomous functioning; however it was only recently that the SDT researchers incorporated the idea of mindfulness and its relationship with autonomous functioning and emotional wellbeing in their research.

Brown and Ryan (2003) conducted a series of five experiments to study mindfulness: They defined mindfulness as open, undivided attention to what is happening within as well as around oneself.

From their experiments, the authors concluded that when individuals act mindfully, their actions are consistent with their values and interest. Also, there is a possibility that being autonomous and performing an action because it is enjoyable to oneself increases mindful attention to one's actions.

Vitality and Self-regulation

Another area of interest for SDT researchers is the relationship between vitality and self-regulation. Ryan and Deci (2008) define vitality as energy available to the self, either directly or indirectly, from basic psychological needs. This energy allows individuals to act autonomously.

Many theorists have posited that self-regulation depletes energy but SDT researchers have proposed and demonstrated that only controlled regulation depletes energy, autonomous regulation can actually be vitalizing.

SDT and Education

A recent study by Hyungshim Jang in which the capacity of two different theoretical models of motivation were used to explain why an externally provided rationale for doing a particular assignment often helps in a student's motivation, engagement, and learning during relatively uninteresting learning activities.

Undergraduate students (N = 136; 108 women, 28 men) worked on a relatively uninteresting short lesson after either receiving or not receiving a rationale. Students who received the rationale showed greater interest, work ethic, and determination.

Structural equation modelling was used to test three alternative explanatory models to understand why the rationale produced such benefits:

1. An identified regulation model based on self-determination theory
2. An interest regulation model based on interest-enhancing strategies research
3. An additive model that integrated both models.

The data fit all three models; but only the model based on self-determination theory helped students to engage and learn. Findings show the role that externally provided rationales can play in helping students generate the motivation they need to engage in and learn from uninteresting, but personally important, material.

The importance of these findings to those in the field of education is that when teachers try to find ways to promote student's motivation during relatively uninteresting learning activities, they can successfully do so by promoting the value of the task. One way teachers can help students value what they may deem "uninteresting" is by providing a rationale that identifies the lesson's otherwise hidden value, helps students understand why the lesson is genuinely worth their effort, and communicates why the lesson can be expected to be useful to them.

An example of SDT and education are Sudbury Model schools where people decide for themselves how to spend their days. In these schools, students of all ages determine what they will do, as well as when, how, and where they will do it. This freedom is at the heart of the school; it belongs to the students as their right, not to be violated. The fundamental premises of the school are simple: that all people are curious by nature; that the most efficient, long-lasting, and profound learning takes place when started and pursued by the learner; that all people are creative if they are allowed to develop their unique talents; that age-mixing among students promotes growth in all members of the group; and that freedom is essential to the development of personal responsibility. In practice this means that students initiate all their own activities and create their own environments.

The physical plant, the staff, and the equipment are there for the students to use as the need arises. The school provides a setting in which students are independent, are trusted, and are treated as responsible people; and a community in which students are exposed to the complexities of life in the framework of a participatory democracy. Sudbury schools do not perform and do not offer evaluations, assessments, or recommendations, asserting that they do not rate people, and that school is not a judge; comparing students to each other, or to some standard that has been set is for them a violation of the student's right to privacy and to self-determination. Students decide for themselves how to measure their progress as self-starting learners as a process of self-evaluation: real life-long learning and the proper educational evaluation for the 21st century, they adduce.

Self-determination theory and Alcohol Use

According to self-determination theory, individuals who attribute their actions to external circumstances rather than internal mechanisms are far more likely to succumb to peer pressure. In contrast, individuals who consider themselves autonomous tend to be initiators of actions rather than followers. Research examining the relationship between self-determination theory and alcohol use among college students has indicated that individuals with the former criteria for decision making are associated with greater alcohol consumption and drinking as a function of social pressure. For instance, in a study conducted by Knee and Neighbours (2002), external factors in the individuals who claim to not be motivated by internal factors were found to be associated with drinking for extrinsic reasons, and with stronger perceptions of peer pressure, which in turn was related to heavier alcohol use. Given the evidence suggesting a positive association between an outward motivation and drinking, and the potential role of perceived social influence in this association, understanding the precise nature of this relationship seems important. Further, it may be hypothesized that the relationship between self-determination and drinking may be mediated to some extent by the perceived approval of others.

Self-determination Theory and Motivational Interviewing

Motivational Interviewing (MI) is a popular approach to positive behavioural change. Used initially in the area of addiction it is now used for a wider range of issues. It is a client-centred method that doesn't persuade or coerce patients to change and instead attempts to explore and resolve their ambivalent feelings, which allows them to choose themselves whether to change or not.

Markland and Ryan et al. (2005) believe that SDT provides a framework behind how and the reasons why MI works. They believe that MI provides an autonomy-supportive atmosphere, which allows clients to find their own source of motivation and achieve their own success (in terms of overcoming addiction.) Patients randomly assigned to an MI treatment group found the setting to be more autonomy supportive than those in a regular support group.

Broad Theories

The latest approach in Achievement Motivation is an integrative perspective as lined out in the "Onion-Ring-Model of Achievement Motivation" by Heinz Schuler, George C. Thornton III, Andreas Frintrup and Rose Mueller-Hanson. It is based on the premise that performance motivation results from the way broad components of personality are directed towards performance. As a result, it includes a range of dimensions that are relevant to success at work but which are not conventionally regarded as being part of performance motivation. Especially it integrates formerly separated approaches as Need for Achievement with e.g. social motives like dominance. The Achievement Motivation Inventory (AMI) is based on this theory and assesses three factors (17 separated scales) relevant to vocational and professional success.

Cognitive Theories

Goal-setting Theory

Goal-setting theory is based on the notion that individuals sometimes have a drive to reach a clearly defined end state. Often, this end state is a reward in itself. A goal's efficiency is affected by three features: proximity, difficulty and specificity. An ideal goal should present a situation where the time betweer the initiation of behaviour and the end state is close. This explains why some children are more motivated to learn how to ride a bike than mastering algebra. A goal should be moderate, not too hard or too easy to complete. In both cases, most people are not optimally motivated, as many want a challenge (which assumes some kind of insecurity of success). At the same time people want to feel that there is a substantial probability that they will succeed. Specificity concerns the description of the goal in their class. The goal should be objectively defined and intelligible for the individual. A classic example of a poorly specified goal is to get the highest possible grade. Most children have no idea how much effort they need to reach that goal.

Models of Behaviour Change

Social-cognitive models of behaviour change include the constructs of motivation and volition. Motivation is seen as a process that leads to the forming of behavioural intentions. Volition is seen as a process that leads from intention to actual behaviour. In other words, motivation and volition refer to goal setting and goal pursuit, respectively. Both processes require self-regulatory efforts. Several self-regulatory constructs are needed to operate in orchestration to attain goals. An example of such a motivational and volitional construct is perceived self-efficacy. Self-efficacy is supposed to facilitate the forming of behavioural intentions, the development of action plans, and the initiation of action. It can support the translation of intentions into action.

Unconscious Motivation

Some psychologists believe that a significant portion of human behaviour is energized and directed by unconscious motives. According to Maslow, "Psychoanalysis has often demonstrated that the relationship between a conscious desire and the ultimate unconscious aim that underlies it need not be at all direct." In other words, stated motives do not always match those inferred by skilled observers. For example, it is possible that a person can be accident-prone because he has an unconscious desire to hurt himself and not because he is careless or ignorant of the safety rules. Similarly, some overweight people are not hungry at all for food but for fighting and kissing. Eating is merely a defensive reaction to lack of attention. Some workers damage more equipment than others do because they harbor unconscious feelings of aggression toward authority figures.

Psychotherapists point out that some behaviour is so automatic that the reasons for it are not available in the individual's conscious mind. Compulsive cigarette smoking is an example. Sometimes maintaining self-esteem is so important and the motive for an activity is so threatening that it is simply not recognized and, in fact, may be disguised or repressed. Rationalization, or "explaining away", is one such disguise, or defence mechanism, as it is called. Another is projecting or attributing one's own faults to others. "I feel I am to blame", becomes "It is her fault; she is selfish". Repression of powerful but socially unacceptable motives may result in outward behaviour that is the opposite of the repressed tendencies. An example of this would be the employee who hates his boss but overworks himself on the job to show that he holds him in high regard. Unconscious motives add to the hazards of interpreting human behaviour and, to the extent that they are present, complicate the life of the administrator. On the other hand, knowledge that unconscious motives exist can lead to a more careful assessment of behavioural problems. Although few contemporary psychologists deny the existence of unconscious factors, many do believe that these are activated only in times of anxiety and stress, and that in the ordinary course of events, human behaviour—from the subject's point of view—is rationally purposeful.

Intrinsic Motivation and the 16 Basic Desires Theory

Starting from studies involving more than 6,000 people, Professor Steven Reiss has proposed a theory that find 16 basic desires that guide nearly all human behaviour. The desires are:

- Acceptance, the need for approval
- Curiosity, the need to learn
- Eating, the need for food
- Family, the need to raise children
- Honor, the need to be loyal to the traditional values of one's clan/ethnic group
- Idealism, the need for social justice
- Independence, the need for individuality
- Order, the need for organized, stable, predictable environments
- Physical activity, the need for exercise
- Power, the need for influence of will
- Romance, the need for sex
- Saving, the need to collect
- Social contact, the need for friends (peer relationships)
- Status, the need for social standing/importance
- Tranquility, the need to be safe
- Vengeance, the need to strike back/to win.

In this model, people differ in these basic desires. These basic desires represent intrinsic desires that directly motivate a person's behaviour, and not aimed at indirectly satisfying other desires. People may also be motivated by non-basic desires, but in this case this does not relate to deep motivation, or only as a means to achieve other basic desires.

Applications

Education

Motivation is of particular interest to educational psychologists because of the crucial role it plays in student learning. However, the specific kind of motivation that is studied in the specialized setting of education differs qualitatively from the more general forms of motivation studied by psychologists in other fields. Motivation in education can have several effects on how students learn and how they behave towards subject matter. It can:

1. Direct behaviour toward particular goals

2. Lead to increased effort and energy
3. Increase initiation of, and persistence in, activities
4. Enhance cognitive processing
5. Determine what consequences are reinforcing
6. Lead to improved performance.

Because students are not always internally motivated, they sometimes need *situated motivation*, which is found in environmental conditions that the teacher creates.

There are two kinds of motivation:

- Intrinsic motivation occurs when people are internally motivated to do something because it either brings them pleasure, they think it is important, or they feel that what they are learning is significant. It has been shown that intrinsic motivation for education drops from grades 3-9 though the exact cause cannot be ascertained. Also, in younger students it has been shown that contextualizing material that would otherwise be presented in an abstract manner increases the intrinsic motivation of these students.
- Extrinsic motivation comes into play when a student is compelled to do something or act a certain way because of factors external to him or her (like money or good grades).

Note also that there is already questioning and expansion about this dichotomy on motivation, e.g., Self-Determination Theory.

Motivation has been found to be a pivotal area in treating Autism Spectrum Disorders, as in Pivotal Response Therapy.

Motivation is also an important element in the concept of Andragogy (what motivates the adult learner).

Sudbury Model schools' Approach to Motivation

Sudbury Model schools adduce that the cure to the problem of procrastination, of learning in general, and particularly of scientific illiteracy is to remove once and for all what they call the underlying disease: compulsion in schools. They contend that human nature in a free society recoils from every attempt to force it into a mold; that the more requirements we pile onto children at school, the surer we are to drive them away from the material we are trying to force down their throats; that after all the drive and motivation of infants to master the world around them is legendary. They assert that schools must keep that drive alive by doing what some of them do: nurturing it on the freedom it needs to thrive.

Sudbury Model schools do not perform and do not offer evaluations, assessments, transcripts, or recommendations, asserting that they do not rate people, and that school is not a judge; comparing students to each other, or to some standard that has been set is for them a violation of the student's right to privacy and to self-determination. Students decide for themselves how to measure their progress as self-starting learners as a process of self-evaluation: real life-long learning and the proper educational evaluation for the 21st century, they adduce. According to Sudbury Model schools, this policy does not cause harm to their students as they move on to life outside the school. However, they admit it makes the process more difficult, but that such hardship is part of the students learning to make their own way, set their own standards and meet their own goals. The no-grading and no-rating policy helps to create an atmosphere free of competition among students or battles for adult approval, and encourages a positive cooperative environment amongst the student body.

Attention and Interest

Because some forms of learning are critically dependent upon attention, it is important for educators to be familiar with modern developments in this field. The most widely known definition of attention extends back to the late 1800s. The psychologist and philosopher William James (1842–1910) defined it as "the taking possession of the mind, in clear and vivid form, of one out of what seem several simultaneously possible objects or trains of thought".

This definition conveys intuitive feeling for the subject. However, it is common to break the subject down into two subdivisions: (1) arousal and (2) selection of information. The processes involved in *arousal* involve achieving and maintaining an alert state sufficient to remain in contact with environmental stimuli. This sense of attention separates the waking state from conditions such as sleep or coma. *Selective attention* refers to the processes involved in selecting information for consciousness, for immediate response, or for storing information in memory. The conscious content of selective attention is only a small subset of the information that could be available at any given moment. Thus, the ability to switch or orient one's attention is critical to the successful use of attention in any environment.

Attention can also be considered in terms of its underlying anatomy. It is useful for educators to think about attention as an organ system, not unlike the familiar organ systems of respiration and circulation. Attention has a distinct anatomy that carries out basic psychological functions and that can be influenced by specific brain injuries and states. The network involved in achieving an alert state involves midbrain centres that are the source of the chemical norepinepherine. This network appears to be asymmetric at the cortical level, with greatest involvement of the right cerebral hemisphere, particularly in the frontal regions. Two networks are involved in the process of selection of information. One of these relates to orienting to sensory information, and involves areas of the parietal lobe, frontal eye fields, and superior colliculus, which are also part of the eye movement system. A second network is related to attention to internal thoughts. This network involves areas of the frontal midline (anterior cingulate), the left and right lateral prefrontal cortex, and the underlying basal ganglia.

The Study of Attention

The study of attention has greatly expanded as new methods have become available for its study. From the early beginnings of psychology in the late 1880s, studies of attention employed simple experimental tasks that required rapid responses to single targets–or to one of a small number of targets–in an effort to study limitations in people's speed and capacity for attending to input information. A good example of the type of tasks used is the *Stroop effect.* This effect occurs when subjects are asked to respond to the colour of ink in which a conflicting word may be written (e.g., the word blue written in red ink). Performance on this task requires an act of selection to ignore the word and respond to the ink colour. Another task used to explore selection is a *visual search task.* It has been shown that attention can be efficiently summoned to any part of a natural scene in which luminance or motion clearly signal a change, but even radical changes of content that occur outside the focus of attention are not reported. This indicates that the subjective impression of being fully aware of the world around one is largely an illusion. People have very poor knowledge about things they are not currently attending to, but a very good ability to orient toward an area of change.

In the 1950s functional models of information flow in the nervous system were developed in conjunction with an interest in computer simulation of cognitive processes. In the 1970s studies using microelectrodes on alert monkeys showed that the firing rate of cells in particular brain areas were enhanced when the monkey attended to a stimulus within the cells' receptive field. In the 1980s and 1990s human neuroimaging studies allowed examination of the whole brain during tasks involving attention. These newer methods of study also improved the utility of more traditional methods, such as: (1) the kinds of experimental tasks discussed above, (2) the use of patients with lesions of particular brain areas, and (3) the use of recordings of brain waves (EEG) from scalp electrodes. The ability to trace anatomical changes over time has provided methods for validating and improving pharmacological and other forms of therapy.

Attention in Infants

Infants as young as four months old can learn to anticipate the location of an event and demonstrate this by moving their eyes to a location where the event will occur. Thus, caregivers can teach important aspects of where a child should focus, and they can also use orienting to counteract an infant's distress well before the infant begins to speak. Infants also show preferences for novel objects in the first few months of life. In early childhood, more complex forms of attentional control begin to emerge as the frontal areas undergo considerable development. These networks allow children to make selections in the face of conflicting response tendencies. Late in the first year, infants first show the ability to reach away from the line of sight, and later the developing toddler and preschooler begin to develop the ability to choose among conflicting stimuli and courses of action.

Infants come into the world with a definite set of reactions to their environment, and even siblings can be very different in their reactions to various events. These individual differences, which include individual differences in orienting and effortful control of attention, constitute *temperament.* One infant, for example, is easily frustrated, has only a brief attention span, and becomes upset with even moderate levels of stimulating play. Another may tolerate very rough play and frequently seek out exciting events, focusing on each interest so strongly that it is difficult to get the child's attention. Thus, even early in life, when attention serves mainly orienting functions, children will differ in what captures their interest–and in how this interest is maintained. These functions will continue to serve the child during the school years, where interest accounts for about 10 percent of the variability in children's achievement. However, later-developing attention systems will prove to be even more important in schooling.

Effortful Control

Later in childhood, maturation of the frontal lobe produces more reliance on executive attention, allowing increased scope for methods of socialization. The strength and effectiveness of this later developing effortful control system is also an important source of temperamental differences. Among older children, some will be able to intentionally focus and switch attention easily, to use attention to inhibit actions they have been told not to perform, and to plan for upcoming activities. Other children will be less able to control their own attention and actions. These differences reflect effortful control and have been found to play an important role in the development of higher-level systems of morality and conscience as well as being generally important in the control and programming of action and emotion.

Intelligence

Children's abilities also differ in the cognitive domain, as is shown in tests of intelligence. Differences in cognitive ability rest in part on the frontal structures related to the development of the executive attention systems. Areas of the left and right ventral prefrontal cortex become active in questions that require general intelligence. A likely reason is that these areas are important for holding information in the mind, while other brain areas retrieve related knowledge that might be important in solving problems. The ability to solve problems like those present in intelligence tests requires both specific knowledge and the ability to retrieve information in response to the prompts present on the test. High-level attentional networks involving frontal areas are very important in this process.

The learning of new skills, such as reading and arithmetic, also requires attention so that relevant input can be stored. The storage of such information rests upon structures that lie deep within the temporal lobe. Attention appears to play an important role at several stages of acquisition of reading. It is important for subjects to be able to break visual and auditory words into their constituent letters or phonemes in order to gain knowledge of the alphabetic principle that allows visual letters to be related to word sounds. The role of frontal attentional networks also plays a key role in accessing word meanings.

Teachers are usually aware that maintaining an alert state in the school environment is dependent both upon factors that are intrinsic to the child–such as adequate rest, good nutrition, and high motivation–and those that can be controlled by the teacher, such as the use of novel and involving exercises at an appropriate level to challenge the student. Capturing the child's interest is important in fostering achievement, but effortful control allows the practice of skills that can lead to new interests, and the developing goal structures of children will allow the development of interest in activities or skills that will lead them to their chosen goals.

Teachers thus need to be aware of individual differences in the development of the mechanisms of selective attention important in the storage and retrieval of information relevant to various tasks. Assessment of attentional capacities may be very useful for this purpose. Children can then be encouraged by exercises appropriate to their level to sustain the effort necessary for effective problem solving. Assessment of the school environment may also be useful in considering children's attentional capacities. The application of effortful control can be tiring, and the opportunities for skill learning and for active play may be important in supporting its activity.

Finally, attention is also important in the development of children's social skills. When teachers point out aspects of other children's experiences and focus on the welfare of others, they can train the direction of a child's interest and concern. Again, this activity will be easier with some children than with others, but it can serve the goal of encouraging empathy and discouraging aggression in a child's development.

Development of Thinking Skills

Young children possess only the beginnings of metacognitive and cognitive skills. They are able to direct their attention (the beginning of a metacognitive skill) but they lack other sophisticated skills needed to integrate higher order thought processes. In contrast, mature thinkers and strategy users possess a wide variety of higher-order, goal-specific, monitoring skills, in addition to factual and procedural knowledge to which they can apply these thinking skills. That is, in addition to having a thorough understanding of a wide range of strategies, mature learners also know when, where, and how to apply their knowledge and strategies. They develop these skills by acquiring and overlearning these strategies and using them in combination with an ever-increasing knowledge about their world. At the present time knowledge about the development of cognitive and metacognitive skills is just beginning to develop. As this knowledge expands, one result will be more effective ways to train thinking skills in classroom settings.

Metacognitive and cognitive theory is deeply rooted in constructivism, including the ideas of Piaget, and in contemporary insights from cognitive science and information processing. One reason for developmental maturity of formal operational learners is that they are more skilled than younger learners at using appropriate metacognitive skills to assimilate and accommodate information. Of course, they have acquired this higher level of metacognitive skills through a gradual process of assimilation and accommodation as they progressed from the sensorimotor stage to the stage of formal operations.

Throughout their lives, successful thinkers (including most of the readers of this book) have developed numerous thinking skills. In most cases they have accomplished this by finding important, interesting things to think about-and then thinking about them. Effective thinking skills are logically and naturally adaptive; and as long as there are no obstructions to learning, many learners are able to develop effective skills "automatically" by thinking about problems at an appropriate level of complexity. Until recently, little specific attention has been given to instruction in metacognitive or other thinking skills. However, since a large number of learners &emdash; especially those who have trouble in school &emdash; rely on ineffective strategies, a greater focus on how to teach thinking skills would seem to be productive. If learners are going to use cognitive skills and strategies effectively, they must possess the following skills (Garner, 1990):

1. *They must be able to monitor their cognitive processes.* If learners do not notice that they are not learning, for example, they are not likely to change strategies in order to learn more effectively.
2. *They must resist using primitive strategies that superficially seem to get the job done.* For example, they must know the difference between a verbatim restatement of a reading passage and a summary and be willing to engage in the more strategic process of summarizing information they wish to learn rather than merely restating it.
3. *They must have an adequate knowledge base.* That is, they must both have adequate information about the subject matters and strategies pertinent to that subject matter and adequate familiarity with the settings in which cognitive strategies will be used.
4. *They must set goals and make attributions that support the use of cognitive strategies.* For example, students with low self-esteem who attribute success and failure to something other than effort are unlikely to initiate or persist in the use of cognitive strategies.
5. *They must transfer thinking strategies to new situations in which they would be appropriate.*

Children as early as twelve months use reasoning skills to understand the environment, the sequence of events and how to follow directions. Toddlers naturally are active learners. An 18 month old who has been given the independence to feed himself may mash, break up or sort his food. He is learning through touch, taste and from the reaction of his caregiver. The actual process of mashing the food is where the toddler gains the most knowledge, not the end result. Allowing your child to be an active learner will facilitate their ability to make decisions. Reasoning skills are the foundation to understanding language, reading, writing and arithmetic. Providing opportunities for your child to experiment in their environment will develop their reasoning skills which is important for school readiness and their self confidence.

There are simple ways to foster reasoning skills in toddlers:

- Provide children the opportunity to fill cups with water or sand. Show them how to pour, empty and refill the cups.
- Establish small routines with your children. For example, every evening at 7:30 it is time to get ready for bed. Describe the routine: "It is 7:30-let's take a bath, brush our teeth, put on our pajamas, read a story and go to bed"
- At the completion of each stage you then describe the next step. This helps children understand the order of events and time frames.
- Describe the object your child is playing with in third person. "Jack is playing with a green ball"
- Describe routine events such as getting dressed. "Mommy is putting on your left sock"
- Allow your child pick the book you are going to read together.
- Teach children to follow simple directions. "Please put your shoes away"
- Encourage their imagination
- Follow their lead in conversation
- Provide a variety of clothes or old costumes for dramatic play. Provide children an option of outfits. Used Halloween costumes are great for dramatic play.

- Give plain white paper to colour instead of a coloring book. Have your child discuss the finished product.
- Allow your child to help you prepare meals by pouring, stirring and setting the timer.
- Discuss sizes, shapes and sorting with your child in different environments. This is great to do at the grocery store in the produce section!
- Allow your child to pick out their outfit for the day.
- Let your child help you sort and put away laundry.

Infancy (Birth–2)

What You Might Observe;

- Physical exploration of the environment becoming increasingly complex, flexible, and intentional
- Growing awareness of simple cause-effect relationships
- Emergence of ability to represent the world mentally (e.g., as reflected in make-believe play)

Diversity:

- Temperamental differences (e.g., the extent to which infants are adventuresome vs. more timid and anxious) influence exploratory behaviour.
- Infants and toddlers who are emotionally attached to their caregivers are more willing to venture out and explore their environment.
- In some cultures adults encourage infants to focus more on people than on the physical environment. When people rather than objects are the priority, children may be less inclined to touch and explore their physical surroundings.

Implications:

- Set up a safe, age-appropriate environment for exploration.
- Provide objects that stimulate different senses—for instance, things that babies can look at, listen to, feel, and smell.
- Suggest age-appropriate toys and activities that parents can provide at home.

Early Childhood (2–6)

What You Might Observe:

- Rapidly developing language skills
- Reasoning that is, by adult standards, illogical
- Limited perspective-taking ability
- Frequent self-talk
- Sociodramatic play
- Little understanding of how adults typically interpret events.

Diversity:

- Shyness may reduce children's willingness to talk with adults and peers and to engage in cooperative sociodramatic play.
- Adultlike logic is more common when children have accurate information about the world (e.g., about cause-effect relationships).
- Children learn to interpret events in culture-specific ways.

Implications:

- Provide numerous opportunities for children to interact with one another during play and other cooperative activities.
- Introduce children to a variety of real-world environments and situations through field trips and picture books.
- Talk with children about their experiences and possible interpretations.

Middle Childhood (6–10)

What You Might Observe:

- Conservation, class inclusion, and other forms of adultlike logic
- Limited ability to reason about abstract or hypothetical ideas
- Emergence of group games and team sports that involve coordinating multiple perspectives

- Ability to participate to some degree in many adult activities.

Diversity:

- Development of logical thinking skills is affected by the importance of those skills in a child's culture.
- Formal operational reasoning may occasionally appear for simple tasks and familiar contexts, especially in 9- and 10-year-olds.
- Physical maturation and psychomotor skills affect willingness to play some games and team sports.

Implications:

- Use concrete manipulatives and experiences to illustrate concepts and ideas.
- Supplement verbal explanations with concrete examples, pictures, and hands-on activities.
- Allow time for organized play activities.
- Introduce children to various adult professions, and provide opportunities to practice authentic adult tasks.

Early Adolescence (10–14)

What You Might Observe:

- Emerging ability to reason about abstract ideas
- Increasing scientific reasoning abilities (e.g., formulating and testing hypotheses, separating and controlling variables)
- Emerging ability to reason about mathematical proportions
- Emerging idealism about political and social issues, but often without taking real-world constraints into consideration
- Increasing ability to engage in adult tasks.

Diversity:

- Adolescents can think more abstractly when they have considerable knowledge about a topic.
- Adolescents are more likely to separate and control variables for situations with which they are familiar.

- Development of formal operational reasoning skills is affected by the importance of those skills in one's culture.
- The idealistic notions that young people espouse may reflect their religious, cultural, or socioeconomic backgrounds.

Implications:

- Present abstract concepts and principles central to various academic disciplines, but tie them to concrete examples.
- Have students engage in scientific investigations, focusing on familiar objects and phenomena.
- Assign mathematics problems that require use of simple fractions, ratios, or decimals.
- While demonstrating how to do a new task, also talk about how to effectively *think* about the task.

Late Adolescence (14–18)

What You Might Observe:

- Abstract thought and scientific reasoning skills more prevalent, especially for topics about which adolescents have considerable knowledge
- Idealistic notions tempered by more realistic considerations
- Ability to perform many tasks in an adultlike manner.

Diversity:

- Abstract thinking tends to be more common in some content areas (e.g., mathematics, science) than in others (e.g., history, geography).
- Formal operational reasoning skills are less likely to appear in cultures that don't require those skills.
- Teenagers' proficiency in particular adult tasks varies considerably from individual to individual and from task to task.

Implications:

- Study particular academic disciplines in depth; introduce complex and abstract explanations and theories.

- Encourage discussions about social, political, and ethical issues; elicit multiple perspectives regarding these issues.
- Involve adolescents in activities that are similar or identical to the things they will eventually do as adults.
- Explain how experts in a field think about the tasks they perform.

Imagination

Imagination, also called the faculty of imagining, is the ability of forming mental images, sensations and concepts, in a moment when they are not perceived through sight, hearing or other senses. Imagination is the work of the mind that helps create. Imagination helps provide meaning to experience and understanding to knowledge; it is a fundamental facility through which people make sense of the world, and it also plays a key role in the learning process. A basic training for imagination is listening to storytelling (narrative), in which the exactness of the chosen words is the fundamental factor to "evoke worlds."

Imagination is the faculty through which we encounter everything. The things that we touch, see and hear coalesce into a "picture" via our imagination.

It is accepted as the innate ability and process of inventing partial or complete personal realms within the mind from elements derived from sense perceptions of the shared world. The term is technically used in psychology for the process of reviving in the mind, percepts of objects formerly given in sense perception. Since this use of the term conflicts with that of ordinary language, some psychologists have preferred to describe this process as "imaging" or "imagery" or to speak of it as "reproductive" as opposed to "productive" or "constructive" imagination. Imagined images are seen with the "mind's eye."

Imagination can also be expressed through stories such as fairy tales or fantasies. Most famous inventions or entertainment products were created from the inspiration of someone's imagination.

One hypothesis for the evolution of human imagination is that it allowed conscious beings to solve problems (and hence increase an individual's survival fitness) by use of mental simulation. Children often use narratives or pretend play in order to exercise their imagination. When children create fantasy they play at two levels: first, they use role playing to act out what they have created with their imagination, and at the second level they play again with their make-believe situation by acting as if what they have created is an actual reality that already exists in narrative myth.

Description

The common use of the term is for the process of forming new images in the mind that have not been previously experienced, or at least only partially or in different combinations. Some typical examples follow:

- Fairy tale
- Fiction.

A form of verisimilitude often invoked in fantasy and science fiction invites readers to pretend such stories are true by referring to objects of the mind such as fictional books or years that do not exist apart from an imaginary world.

Imagination in this sense, not being limited to the acquisition of exact knowledge by the requirements of practical necessity, is, up to a certain point, free from objective restraints. The ability to imagine one's self in another person's place is very important to social relations and understanding. Albert Einstein said, "Imagination... is more important than knowledge. Knowledge is limited. Imagination encircles the world."

In various spheres, however, even imagination is in practice limited: thus a person whose imaginations do violence to the elementary laws of thought, or to the necessary principles of practical possibility, or to the reasonable probabilities of a given case is regarded as insane.

The same limitations beset imagination in the field of scientific hypothesis. Progress in scientific research is due largely to provisional explanations which are constructed by imagination, but such hypotheses must be framed in relation to previously ascertained facts and in accordance with the principles of the particular science.

Imagination is an experimental partition of the mind used to create theories and ideas based on functions. Taking objects from real perceptions, the imagination uses complex IF-functions to create new or revised ideas. This part of the mind is vital to developing better and easier ways to accomplish old and new tasks. These experimental ideas can be safely conducted inside a virtual world and then, if the idea is probable and the function is true, the idea can be actualized in reality. Imagination is the key to new development of the mind and can be shared with others, progressing collectively. Regarding the volunteer effort, imagination can be classified as:

- voluntary (the dream from the sleep, the daydream)
- involuntary (the reproductive imagination, the creative imagination, the dream of perspective).

Psychology of Imagination

Psychologists have studied imaginative thought, not only in its exotic form of creativity and artistic expression but also in its mundane form of everyday imagination. Ruth M.J. Byrne has proposed that everyday imaginative thoughts about counterfactual alternatives to reality may be based on the same cognitive processes that rational thoughts are based on. Children can engage in the creation of imaginative alternatives to reality from their very early years.

Imagination and Perception

From the work of Piaget it is known that perceptions depend on the world view of a person. The world view is the result of arranging perceptions into existing imagery by imagination. Piaget cites the example of a child saying that the moon is following her when she walks around the village at night. Like this perceptions are integrated into the world view to make sense. Imagination is needed to make sense of perceptions.

Imagination vs. Belief

Imagination differs fundamentally from belief because the subject understands that what is personally invented by the mind does not necessarily impact the course of action taken in the apparently shared world while beliefs are part of what one holds as truths about both the shared and personal worlds. The play of imagination, apart from the obvious limitations (e.g. of avoiding explicit self-contradiction), is conditioned only by the general trend of the mind at a given moment. Belief, on the other hand, is immediately related to practical activity: it is perfectly possible to imagine oneself a millionaire, but unless one believes it one does not, therefore, act as such. Belief endeavors to conform to the subject's experienced conditions or faith in the possibility of those conditions; whereas imagination as such is specifically free. The dividing line between imagination and belief varies widely in different stages of technological development. Thus in more extreme cases, someone from a primitive culture who ill frames an ideal reconstruction of the causes of his illness, and attributes it to the hostile magic of an enemy based on faith and tradition rather than science. In ignorance of the science of pathology the subject is satisfied with this explanation, and actually believes in it, sometimes to the point of death, due to what is known as the nocebo effect.

It follows that the learned distinction between imagination and belief depends in practice on religion, tradition, and culture.

Imagination as a Reality

The world as experienced is an interpretation of data arriving from the senses, as such it is perceived as real by contrast to most thoughts and imaginings. Users of hallucinogenic drugs are said to have a heightened imagination. This difference is only one of degree and can be altered by several historic causes, namely changes to brain chemistry, hypnosis or other altered states of consciousness, meditation, many hallucinogenic drugs, and electricity applied directly to specific parts of the brain.

The difference between imagined and perceived reality can be so imperceptible as to cause acute states of psychosis. Many mental illnesses can be attributed to this inability to distinguish between the sensed and the internally created worlds. Some cultures and traditions even view the apparently shared world as an illusion of the mind as with the Buddhist maya or go to the opposite extreme and accept the imagined and dreamed realms as of equal validity to the apparently shared world as the Australian Aborigines do with their concept of dreamtime.

Imagination, because of having freedom from external limitations, can often become a source of real pleasure and unnecessary suffering. Consistent with this idea, imagining pleasurable and fearful events is found to engage emotional circuits involved in emotional perception and experience.A person of vivid imagination often suffers acutely from the imagined perils besetting friends, relatives, or even strangers such as celebrities. Also crippling fear can result from taking an imagined painful future too seriously.

Imagination can also produce some symptoms of real illnesses. In some cases, they can seem so "real" that specific physical manifestations occur such as rashes and bruises appearing on the skin, as though imagination had passed into belief or the events imagined were actually in progress.

It has also been proposed that the whole of human cognition is based upon imagination. That is, nothing that is perceived is purely observation but all is a morph between sense and imagination.

Imagination Preceding Reality

When two existing perceptions (thesis and antithesis) are combined within the mind, a third perception (called synthesis) is formed. At this point, perception only exists as part of the imagination and can become the inspiration for a new invention or technique.

Importance of Imagination in Children

Children today can take part in an endless variety of activities. From computer games to piano lessons, and from soccer practice to karate, there is no shortage of skills for kids to learn. However, children also need regular playtime that is not focused on structure, skill building or electronics. While those things are all good for children, too much can crowd out the kind of play that is essential for developing one of the most amazing gifts of childhood: imagination.

According to Dorothy Singer, professor of psychology at Yale University and co-author of *The House of Make Believe: Children's Play and the Developing Imagination*, children who actively use their imagination reap a host of benefits, such as playing cooperatively and being successful in school.

Do children still have the time and initiative today to fight pretend dragons, have an imaginary friend, or dress up as a fairy tale princess? Or is plain old imagination fighting a losing battle with iPods, video games, organized sports and T.V. shows? Just what is so important about imagination?

Here are some amazing benefits that come from developing the imagination:

- Imagination helps school-age children solve problems by helping them think through different outcomes to various situations and role playing ways to cope with difficult or new circumstances.
- Imagination allows children to practice real-life skills. From shopping at a pretend grocery store to assigning roles and dialogue to dolls or puppets, children's pretend play helps them practice and apply new learning and better understand how those skills are used in the real world.
- Imagination encourages a rich vocabulary. Telling and hearing real or made-up stories, reading books and pretend play help children learn and retain new words.
- Imagination helps children grow up to be adults who are creative thinkers. Adults who were imaginative children often become problem solvers, innovators and creative thinkers.

As you can see, imagination can often be as important as math, science or reading. Despite how it sometimes looks to adults, imaginative and pretend play helps develop many important skills that boost a child's learning and success.

The Benefits of Imagination

"A child can express his real self in imagination because the imagination is unmediated by anybody else's expectations or demands," says Alan Flashman MD, a child psychiatrist. "It's not imposed on him. It comes from within his inner life. Imagination is important because it integrates a child's feelings and dreams and actions. It's a place where a child can experiment and feel control and power. But we should respect the integrity and freedom of the experience rather than trying to quantify it as a utilitarian activity."

Nonetheless, a child with an active imagination benefits because he has a way to deal with intense emotions. New

Jersey school psychologist, Beth Falk, PhD, explains: "Kids can become overwhelmed by their emotions but by using their imaginations, they can master their feelings. If a child is afraid of a monster, he can make up a story about hunting down the monster and scaring it and turning it into something else. He's found a way to transform it."

In her classes, actress and drama teacher Andrea Peskoff has seen students spontaneously act out their problems. Six-year-old Heather, an only child, was anxious because her mother was pregnant. In drama class, she crawled on the floor, becoming the baby she feared would draw her mother's attention away from her. In this way, the new baby became a less fearful proposition.

What's your Relationship with your Imagination?

We don't have to sign the kids up for drama classes in order to encourage imagination. "The capacity for living deeply within their imagination is natural to kids," says Falk. "The question is: Do we nurture this capacity by giving kids the space for imaginative play?"

Some parents may feel threatened by their child's imagination because they themselves are disconnected from their own imaginations. They may not respect imaginative activity. But if we undervalue imagination, we risk alienating our kids.

One way today's parents deny their children the opportunity to use their imaginations is by over-scheduling enrichment activities, lessons and tutors, and allowing a steady diet of TV. A return to some of the simpler activities of our own childhoods can pave the way to more imaginative freedom.

Reading stories is a wonderful way for a parent to imagine along with his kid because parents and children can respond to what they've just read. Spending unstructured time in nature can also evoke an imaginative response.

If you become involved in your child's imaginative play, be sure to let her take the lead. "One of the nice things about engaging with a child in fantasy play is that the child gets a chance to initiate, instead of following the parent's lead. But the parent has to be aware of the kid's borders. If the kid wants to share his fantasy, fine. But the parent shouldn't force an interaction," Flashman says.

Share Fantasies with your Child

So don't worry that your child is wasting time when he is staring off into space. If he invites you to, share his inner drama. "Connecting on the level of imagination creates a gentle meeting, a special kind of closeness," says Flashman.

It can also be a lot of fun. Just last night, as I was driving home, my 13-year-old son informed me that the moths flying at our windshield were having a demonstration. We decided that they were demonstrating for more woolen clothes to eat. Our imaginative fantasy continued for the whole ride. We had a great time and sharing the fantasy made us feel closer.

Next time you see your child lost in a daydream or in an imaginative game of crashing cars, sit down next to him. You might just rediscover the lost part of yourself, the authentic self who engages with the world without premeditation or pretense and disguise. The self who dwells in fantasy without thought of utility or service. The free and authentic self who is content just to be.

10

Perceptual Development

Perceptual development provides the foundation for interpreting the events of the world around us. Stimuli from the environment that evoke sensory experiences of hearing, seeing, and touching promote brain growth and development. For infants/toddlers with hearing loss, auditory input is limited or distorted; consequently, they are at risk for delays in speech and language development.

Sensory stimuli provide the medium through which babies learn about the world and its operation. Developmental progression in infants or toddlers is highly dependent on access to sensory information in the environment. Perceptual development occurs as infants explore and identify invariant features in the environment, discovering properties of and relationships between features. Language development evolves out of these sensory experiences that contribute to cognitive growth and development.

For infants who are developing typically, the brain circuits and neural pathways that form during the first year allow anticipation of mother's entry into a room upon hearing her voice or footsteps approaching while awakening from a nap. Infants' brains release endorphins during the experience of nurturing skin-to-skin touch thus soothing anxiety when tired or stressed. Every time babies experience new stimuli, their brains are fine-tuned to quickly interpret and process similar experiences.

During the first three months of life, infants' brains respond to the world of sensation with greater electrical activity in areas of the brain responsible for coding stimuli of sights, sounds, and touches. As perceptual development proceeds infants learn to associate stimuli with particular activities and anticipate events (Raymond, 2000). For example, babies learn that father's entry into the home suggests that he can anticipate touches and hugs. Such experiences provide the foundation for interpreting and making sense of the world. For infants and toddlers who are deaf/hard of hearing, the extent of hearing loss and/or amplification determines whether they rely primarily on hearing or vision, or combined input from both modalities to interpret their environment and gain understanding in the world around them.

Hearing loss can occur prelingually, prior to language acquisition, or postlingually, following language acquisition. Degrees of hearing loss are measured in decibels, the greater the decibel measure, the greater the degree of hearing loss.

For example, a person with a mild hearing loss, 15-40 DB (decibel) has difficulty hearing whispers at a close range in a quiet setting; a person with a moderate hearing loss 40-60 DB has difficulty hearing a normal voice at close range in a quiet setting; a person with a severe hearing loss cannot hear speech and can only hear loud noises such as those coming from machinery, power tools, vacuum cleaners, lawn mowers; a person with a profound hearing loss cannot hear speech and may only hear loud vibrating noises such as airplanes. Any type of hearing loss can present unique challenges and barriers in accessing environmental information.

Hearing loss influences children's preferences for gathering sensory information that support and shape cognitive linguistic development. Since varying degrees of auditory information are available for children with hearing loss, a need exists to maximize visual and kinesthetic intake of environmental information.

Knowledge of these sensory modalities supports an understanding of an infant's or toddler's ability to interpret, integrate and respond to environmental information. By exploring the contributions of auditory, visual, and kinesthetic development to perceptual development, a professional can understand the strengths that infants or toddlers "bring to the table".

Auditory Development

For infants who are typically developing, the auditory system first experiences sound in the womb at 20 weeks. When babies are born into a world full of stimuli, auditory information about the environment becomes readily available that can support acquisition of knowledge related to a particular setting and/or person. Through the exploration process, infants/toddlers learn to categorize and determine meaning for particular units of information. Auditory development involves an ability to identify discrete units of speech/sound within the experience of continuous sound input. Spoken language grows out of this experience. As infants experience sound, the auditory cortex explodes with new connections and growth. For infants/toddlers with hearing loss who are identified prior to 6 months and receive appropriate early intervention services, language development can proceed similarly to peers. Language development commensurate with non-verbal development can be a reality for infants with hearing loss whose families receive early intervention services. Therefore, an understanding of typical auditory milestones and development is critical in supporting an infant/toddler's prelinguistic communication and developmental progression. Infants/toddlers who have mild to severe hearing loss develop significantly more auditory skills than children with profound hearing loss.

Auditory development for infants who are typically developing proceeds in predictable fashion according to age. From birth to 4 months, there is limited auditory responsiveness, however the startle response (eyes blink or widen) to loud noise is common. Infants at this age vary in their response to soft sounds. Eyes may widen in response to soft sounds. Infants grow in their awareness of sound and attention. Infants learn that they can make sounds to communicate needs (i.e., crying to indicate need for food or express discomfort) and that sounds can be associated with meaningful events and experiences. Babies learn to ignore sounds that are not eventful or particularly meaningful.

Infants differentiate mother's voice from others and prefer to listen to mother's voice, shortly after delivery. DeCasper & Fifer observed sucking responses in newborns more often at the introduction of mother's voice as compared with the voice of another mother. As an infant approaches his fourth month of age he may turn his head in the direction of sound however the response is variable. Localizing the source of sounds promotes spacial awareness. By the end of the fourth month the infant consistently demonstrates head turning in response to sound. The infant progressively gains motor control in the neck and becomes strong enough to turn laterally and directly in response to sound by approximately 7 months of age.

However, the turn may not be directed to exact location of source of sound if it is below the infant's eyes. Localization of sound at eye level or below occurs between 7 and 9 months and is quick and defined with head turns. Sounds originating from any plane, above or below baby provoke a direct and briskly defined response of localization by the end of 13 months of age. By the end of the first year of life, babies can associate the sequence of sounds with specific events or experiences and make connections between sounds and people. Babies intentionally produce sounds to communicate. Auditory processing is growing in complexity as memories of experiences involving sounds, events, and significant people become more sophisticated.

Auditory development facilitates and provides the infant feedback for language and speech development. By two months of age, babies are making some sounds more than others. Cooing, laughing, and babbling provide stimulation to an infant who is hearing. Sounds approximating vowels occur between 2-4 months of age and sounds approximating consonants occur by 5 months of age. Exploration of sounds and babbling begins as infants listen to their babbling. Mother's/caregiver's responsiveness to a child's first sounds provides the foundation for further spoken language development. Infants experience a caregiver's repertoire of speech improvisations and imitates. However, babies may or may not understand meaning attached to imitated sounds.

Speech Development

Impact of Hearing Loss on Speech Development

Speech development is very different for infants who are deaf or hard of hearing because their auditory input is limited or distorted due to hearing loss. Consonant sounds do not evolve out of canonical (song-like) babbling for infants with hearing loss as they do for infants who hear. However, babbling level does not predict later speech intelligibility. The ability to produce speech varies between two groups of children: Those children with mild hearing loss who have normal language development typically achieve intelligible speech between 2.5 and 3 years of age while those with moderate to severe hearing loss who have normal language development generally achieve intelligible speech between 3 and 5 years of age. Children with a profound hearing loss have much poorer speech production than those with mild through severe hearing loss.

From 5-12 months infants begin to communicate in gestures, using their hands to indicate intent such as, "gimme up", "bye-bye". Infants may point at objects with arms, hands or fingers to communicate intentions. They may hit or push to express negative feelings. Such gestures and vocalizations can be used to encourage conversations. Conversational turn-taking is learned when caregivers are sensitive to these learning opportunities and respond to the baby thus encouraging interaction. For example, a baby may request to be picked up by raising his arms, offering the opportunity for the caregiver to respond by making a statement such as; "You want to be picked up. What do you want to do?" Then the caregiver proceeds to pick up the infant. A parent's or caregiver's vocal responsiveness followed by pauses supports auditory development.

Caregivers who are engaged with infants participate in conversation while taking turns expressing delight and involvement with baby's experience provide a rich learning medium for language development.

Historically, children with hearing loss experience delays in speech development. However, Obenchain; Menn; & Yoshinaga-Itano (1999) determined that the following speech and language characteristics present at 16-36 months are associated with development of intelligible speech at 36 months in toddlers who have hearing loss other than severe and profound, provided they do not suffer cognitive and motor delays, and whose parents use oral communication:

- high frequency of vocal utterances;

- relatively high proportion of vocal utterances that included intelligible true words
- relatively large lexical inventory or more than 9 spoken words
- large consonant inventory
- high percentage of rising tones;
- high percentage of intonational utterances
- large percentage of syllables containing consonants
- tendency to show intention, even in utterances with no
- semantic content, through gestures.

With early identification, and delivery of appropriate early intervention services prior to 6 months of age, language outcomes for children with hearing loss are similar to peers. Increased language skills are positively associated with speech development. Development of communication skills for infants and toddlers who are deaf/hard of hearing can be enhanced in the natural environment through caregiver interaction. Activities that include smiling, hugging, swinging, clapping, moving objects, and use of light for offering visual cues and reinforcement support the child's development.

Speech Development at a Glance

2 Months : Makes some sounds more than others.

2-4 Months : Sounds approximate consonants.

5 Months : Sounds approximate vowels.

6 Months : Babbling diminishes and consonant-vowel sounds evolve.

10 Months : "Dada" or "mama" spoken.

12-14 Months : Meaningful words spoken Follows simple directions.

Speaks in phrases. Identifies names of people, toys Responds to music.

18 Months : Vocabulary increases from 6 to 10 words.

Visual Development

Vision facilitates infants'/toddlers' exploration in the world, informing spatial awareness and orientation. Information regarding visual details and nuances of people and settings is gathered however vision is the most immature of the senses in newborns. For infants who are deaf, vision is critical in developing communication skills (Easterbrooks, 2002), learning signs, and language. National Institute on Deafness and Other Communication Disorders reported that when children who are deaf are exposed to ASL (American Sign Language) and compared to hearing children exposed to speech, deaf children performed language milestones at approximately concurrent times, within days of one another. In particular, infants who were deaf signed their first word at 12 months and produced two-word sentences at 18 months. Infants who are deaf manually babble (basic signs such as isolated motions and handshapes) experimenting with sign language. In addition, research indicates that when manually babbling infants who are deaf are compared to infants who are hearing, infants who are deaf produce more manual babbles. How does vision develop to support infants in communicating and learning about the world?

Visual development (Berk, 2000) can be described according to the following features: acuity, colour perception, focusing and tracking ability, depth perception, pattern, recognition, and object perception. An infant's ability to differentiate and isolate visual stimuli contributes to understanding the environment and gives meaning to experiences. For infants/ toddlers who are deaf/hard of hearing, possible visual cues to gain attention of the child include, pointing or waving in child's visual field, tapping objects such as the floor or table. The visual field contributes to information received from other modalities such as touch, increasing a child's understanding of his/her environment. However, visual development occurs over many years and is described as it reflects overall age trends.

The retina, responsible for capturing light and containing cells that control messaging to brain, is developmentally incomplete at birth. Muscles responsible for controlling the lens continue to develop and the ability to clearly focus is challenging until 3 months of age. Therefore, newborns see images such as the parents face unclearly; however, they actively scan the environment for novel stimuli.

The visual acuity of a one month old infant is 20/600, indicating that close objects are easier to discriminate. For example, holding an infant 8 inches from a caregiver's face is preferable when interacting. Babies can best experience caregiver's facial expressions at this distance. Talking, smiling, and interacting with baby are visual and auditory activities that support development across visual and auditory modalities. In the first month, newborns enjoy large, bold patterns by scanning their borders. Infants understand that size of objects is stable, and they respond to depth cues such as objects nearing the eyes (Berk, 2000).

By 3 months of age the infant can recognize a photo of his mother and he perceives colour. Visual activities that encourage an infant's ability to make meaning during this early period of development include pointing or showing objects to a child while speaking or signing and shaking or moving the object. By 3 months, baby experiences viewing objects three dimensionally: The brain interprets messaging from each eye and integrates the information thus producing three-dimensional experiences. Patterns with fine detail are recognizable and interesting. Motion and spatial dimension are features of the environment that the child perceives and uses to identify objects. Exploring objects and salient features is cognitively engaging and entertaining to the child (Berk, 2000).

By 5 months the infant uses kinetic cues created by motion, indicative of object depth, to perceive objects three dimensionally. Stationary cues such as object shape, texture, and colour contribute to the infant identifying objects. Colors are categorized, such as varying shades of blues are all recognized as blue (Berk, 2000).

Between 7-10 months of age infants respond to emotional expressions indicating recognition of the difference between a happy and fearful or sad expression (Ludemann, 1991). Interactions with caregivers contribute to visual discrimination and interpretation of events. Objects in motion are tracked. By 8 months of age, visual acuity has increased to 20/100. Objects or individuals such as mother can be tracked as they move. As an eight month old crawls, they will avoid drops at stairs or visual cliffs. By 12 months of age, an infant perceives patterns of movement as meaningful wholes. For example, she/he may associate mother's walking to the door as an indication that another person may appear.

Visual Cues for infants/toddlers who are deaf/hard of hearing For infants who are deaf/hard of hearing, visual cues and experiences support learning and communication development. For example, when the phone rings the caregiver may want to point to the phone indicating that they are going to answer the phone. Signing to the child as they move to the phone provides a visual communication experience. Prendergast & McCollum (1996) noted that mothers who are deaf may be best able to provide the child with access to visual cues with signs. Repeated episodes of such sensory experiences support the growth of brain synapses and pathways, facilitating an infant's communication development.

Visual Development at a Glance

1 Month; Visual acuity is 20/600

3 Months; Ability to focus on objects

Can recognize photo of mother

Perceives colour across the spectrum

Views objects three-dimensionally

Prefers patterns of fine detail.

4-5 Months; Utilizes kinetic cues created by motion,

Organizes colors by category.

6-10 Months; Responds to emotional expressions.

Visual acuity is 20/100

Tracks objects Avoids a drop-off or cliff.

12 Months; Infant perceives patterns of movement as meaningful wholes.

Touch

Babies come into the world with the ability to experience touch, temperature changes, and pain (Berk, 2000). The experience of touch is the most basic of human needs and validates the infant's existence, affirming his presence as valued. Touch provides stimulation and consequently contributes to development. However, each infant is unique in preferences for how he likes to be stroked, held, and patted. Caregivers who explore the use of touch with infants can learn an infant's preference and communicate positive regard using this modality.

Touch mediates an infant's/toddler's experience of the world. As an infant/toddler moves through his environment, objects are explored for kinesthetic properties and categorized accordingly. One of baby's first experiences exploring objects is with his thumb.

Baby's responsiveness to caregiver's touch can soothe or comfort, communicating that the world is safe and caregivers are trustworthy. Massage has been used with infants and toddlers to encourage positive interactions with caregivers thereby supporting the infant's development of self-esteem.

In addition, massage lowers stress hormones, anxiety levels and is often used to improve outcomes for children under treatment for such conditions as diabetes, cancer, and asthma. Massage therapy improves an infant's mood or a toddler's sociability, and attentiveness to auditory-visual stimuli.

Touch Cues for Infants/Toddlers who are Deaf/Hard of Hearing

For infants/toddlers who are deaf and hard of hearing, touch provides cues and information that facilitate understanding of their social environment.

For example, to get an infant's/toddler's attention with a hearing loss, touch maybe use to communicate a need to pay attention and provide direction. Gentle touches on the shoulder can secure the child's attention most effectively. Caregivers need to avoid grabbing, moving or touching the child's heads/ faces in an intrusive manner to gain attention. Touch is particularly effective when employing visual-gestural modes of communication. Given that babies have ready access to the sense of touch more than any other at birth, it perhaps offers the easiest way to communicate caring feelings supportive of emotional well-being (Elliot, 1999).

Sensory Integration

Sensory integration is the ability of the brain to gather, organize, and synthesize environmental information available from the senses to interpret and determine meaning from events. For infants and toddlers who are deaf/hard of hearing, processing limited or distorted auditory stimuli may present sensory integration issues. Upon the recommendation of a health professional, parents of an infant/toddler with hearing loss may employ an occupational therapist to address sensory integration issues. Positive anecdotal accounts of sensory integration therapy do occur; thus, parents may want to further explore sensory integration issues that appear to evolve out of hearing loss. However, a literature review (Griffer, 1999), conducted to explore the efficacy of sensory integration therapy for children with language delays, described a lack of statistically significant data, derived from studies that utilized sound research methods, to support sensory integration therapy for children with language-learning challenges.

11

Personality Development

Personality can be defined as a dynamic and organized set of characteristics possessed by a person that uniquely influences his or her cognitions, motivations, and behaviours in various situations. The word "personality" originates from the Latin *persona*, which means mask. Significantly, in the theatre of the ancient Latin-speaking world, the mask was not used as a plot device to *disguise* the identity of a character, but rather was a convention employed to represent or *typify* that character.

The pioneering American psychologist, Gordon Allport (1937) described two major ways to study personality, the nomothetic and the idiographic. *Nomothetic psychology* seeks general laws that can be applied to many different people, such as the principle of self-actualization, or the trait of extraversion. *Idiographic psychology* is an attempt to understand the unique aspects of a particular individual.

The study of personality has a broad and varied history in psychology, with an abundance of theoretical traditions. The major theories include dispositional (trait) perspective, psychodynamic, humanistic, biological, behaviourist and social learning perspective. There is no consensus on the definition of "personality" in psychology. Most researchers and psychologists do not explicitly identify themselves with a certain perspective and often take an eclectic approach. Some research is empirically driven such as the "Big 5" personality model whereas other research emphasizes theory development such as psychodynamics. There is also a substantial emphasis on the applied field of personality testing. In psychological education and training, the study of the nature of personality and its psychological development is usually reviewed as a prerequisite to courses in abnormal or clinical psychology.

Philosophical Assumptions

Many of the ideas developed by historical and modern personality theorists stem from the basic philosophical assumptions they hold. The study of personality is not a purely empirical discipline, as it brings in elements of art, science, and philosophy to draw general conclusions. The following five categories are some of the most fundamental philosophical assumptions on which theorists disagree:

Freedom Versus Determinism

This is the debate over whether we have control over our own behaviour and understand the motives behind it (Freedom), or if our behaviour is causally determined by forces beyond our control (Determinism). Determinism has been considered unconscious, environmental, or biological by various theories.

Heredity Versus Environment

Personality is thought to be determined largely by genetics and biology, by environment and experiences, or by some combination resulting thereof. There is evidence for all possibilities. Contemporary research suggests that most personality traits are based on the joint influence of genetics and environment. One of the forerunners in this arena is C. Robert Cloninger with the Temperament and Character model.

Uniqueness Versus Universality

The argument over whether we are all unique individuals (Uniqueness) or if humans are basically similar in their nature (Universality). Gordon Allport, Abraham Maslow, and Carl Rogers were all advocates of the uniqueness of individuals. Behaviourists and cognitive theorists, in contrast, emphasized the importance of universal principles such as reinforcement and self-efficacy.

Active Versus Reactive

Do we primarily act through our own initiative (Active), or react to outside stimuli (Reactive)? Behavioural theorists typically believe that humans are passively shaped by their environments, whereas humanistic and cognitive theorists believe that humans are more active.

Optimistic Versus Pessimistic

Personality theories differ on whether people can change their personalities (Optimism), or if they are doomed to remain the same throughout their lives (Pessimism). Theories that place a great deal of emphasis on learning are often, but not always, more optimistic than theories that do not emphasize learning.

Theories of Personality

Critics of personality theory claim personality is "plastic" across time, places, moods, and situations. Changes in personality may indeed result from diet (or lack thereof), medical effects, significant events, or learning. However, most personality theories emphasize stability over fluctuation. The definition of personality that is most widely supported to date is attributed to the neurologist Paul Roe. He stated personality to be "an individual's predisposition to think certain patterns of thought, and therefore engage in certain patterns of behaviour".

Trait Theories

According to the *Diagnostic and Statistical Manual* of the American Psychiatric Association, personality traits are "enduring patterns of perceiving, relating to, and thinking about the environment and oneself that are exhibited in a wide range of social and personal contexts." Theorists generally assume a) traits are relatively stable over time, b) traits differ among individuals (e.g. some people are outgoing while others are reserved), and c) traits influence behaviour.

The most common models of traits incorporate three to five broad dimensions or factors. The least controversial dimension, observed as far back as the ancient Greeks, is simply extraversion and introversion (outgoing and physical-stimulation-oriented vs. quiet and physical-stimulation-averse).

- Gordon Allport delineated different kinds of traits, which he also called dispositions. *Central traits* are basic to an individual's personality, while *secondary traits* are more peripheral. *Common traits* are those recognized within a culture and thus may vary from culture to culture. *Cardinal traits* are those by which an individual may be strongly recognized.

- Raymond Cattell's research propagated a two-tiered personality structure with sixteen "primary factors" (16 Personality Factors) and five "secondary factors."
- Hans Eysenck believed just three traits—extraversion, neuroticism and psychoticism—were sufficient to describe human personality. Differences between Cattell and Eysenck emerged due to preferences for different forms of factor analysis, with Cattell using oblique, Eysenck orthogonal, rotation to analyse the factors that emerged when personality questionnaires were subjected to statistical analysis. Today, the Big Five factors have the weight of a considerable amount of empirical research behind them, building on the work of Cattell and others.
- Lewis Goldberg proposed a five-dimension personality model, nicknamed the "Big Five":

1. Openness to Experience: the tendency to be imaginative, independent, and interested in variety vs. practical, conforming, and interested in routine.
2. Conscientiousness: the tendency to be organized, careful, and disciplined vs. disorganized, careless, and impulsive.
3. Extraversion: the tendency to be sociable, fun-loving, and affectionate vs. retiring, somber, and reserved.
4. Agreeableness: the tendency to be softhearted, trusting, and helpful vs. ruthless, suspicious, and uncooperative.
5. Neuroticism: the tendency to be calm, secure, and self-satisfied vs. anxious, insecure, and self-pitying

The Big Five contain important dimensions of personality. However, some personality researchers argue that this list of major traits is not exhaustive. Some support has been found for two additional factors: excellent/ordinary and evil/decent. However, no definitive conclusions have been established.

John L. Holland's *RIASEC* vocational model, commonly referred to as the Holland Codes, stipulates that six personality traits lead people to choose their career paths. In this circumplex model, the six types are represented as a hexagon, with adjacent types more closely related than those more distant. The model is widely used in vocational counseling.

Trait models have been criticized as being purely descriptive and offering little explanation of the underlying causes of personality. Eysenck's theory, however, does propose biological mechanisms as driving traits, and modern behaviour genetics researchers have shown a clear genetic substrate to them. Another potential weakness of trait theories is that they lead people to accept oversimplified classifications, or worse offer advice, based on a superficial analysis of their personality. Finally, trait models often underestimate the effect of specific situations on people's behaviour. It is important to remember that traits are statistical generalizations that do not always correspond to an individual's behaviour.

Type Theories

Personality type refers to the psychological classification of different types of people. Personality types are distinguished from personality traits, which come in different levels or degrees. For example, according to type theories, there are two types of people, introverts and extraverts. According to trait theories, introversion and extraversion are part of a continuous dimension, with many people in the middle. The idea of psychological types originated in the theoretical work of Carl Jung and William Marston, whose work is reviewed in Dr. Travis Bradberry's *Self-Awareness*. Jung's seminal 1921 book on the subject is available in English as *Psychological Types*.

Building on the writings and observations of Jung, during World War II, Isabel Briggs Myers and her mother, Katharine C. Briggs, delineated personality types by constructing the Myers-Briggs Type Indicator. This model was later used by David Keirsey with a different understanding from Jung, Briggs and Myers. In the former Soviet Union, Lithuanian Auðra Augustinavièiûtë independently derived a model of personality type from Jung's called Socionics.

The model is an older and more theoretical approach to personality, accepting extraversion and introversion as basic psychological orientations in connection with two pairs of psychological functions:

- Perceiving functions: sensing and intuition (trust in concrete, sensory-oriented facts vs. trust in abstract concepts and imagined possibilities)
- Judging functions: thinking and feeling (basing decisions primarily on logic vs. considering the effect on people).

Briggs and Myers also added another personality dimension to their type indicator to measure whether a person prefers to use a judging or perceiving function when interacting with the external world. Therefore they included questions designed to indicate whether someone wishes to come to conclusions (judgment) or to keep options open (perception).

This personality typology has some aspects of a trait theory: it explains people's behaviour in terms of opposite fixed characteristics. In these more traditional models, the sensing/intuition preference is considered the most basic, dividing people into "N" (intuitive) or "S" (sensing) personality types. An "N" is further assumed to be guided either by thinking or feeling, and divided into the "NT" (scientist, engineer) or "NF" (author, humanitarian) temperament.

An "S", by contrast, is assumed to be guided more by the judgment/perception axis, and thus divided into the "SJ" (guardian, traditionalist) or "SP" (performer, artisan) temperament. These four are considered basic, with the other two factors in each case (including always extraversion/introversion) less important. Critics of this traditional view have observed that the types can be quite strongly stereotyped by professions (although neither Myers nor Keirsey engaged in such stereotyping in their type descriptions), and thus may arise more from the need to categorize people for purposes of guiding their career choice.

This among other objections led to the emergence of the five-factor view, which is less concerned with behaviour under work conditions and more concerned with behaviour in personal and emotional circumstances. (It should be noted, however, that the MBTI is not designed to measure the "work self," but rather what Myers and McCaulley called the "shoes-off self.") Some critics have argued for more or fewer dimensions while others have proposed entirely different theories (often assuming different definitions of "personality").

Type A and Type B personality theory: During the 1950s, Meyer Friedman and his co-workers defined what they called Type A and Type B behaviour patterns. They theorized that intense, hard-driving Type A personalities had a higher risk of coronary disease because they are "stress junkies." Type B people, on the other hand, tended to be relaxed, less competitive, and lower in risk. There was also a Type AB mixed profile. Dr. Redford Williams, cardiologist at Duke University, refuted Friedman's theory that Type A personalities have a higher risk of coronary heart disease; however, current research indicates that only the hostility component of Type A may have health implications. Type A/B theory has been extensively criticized by psychologists because it tends to oversimplify the many dimensions of an individual's personality.

Psychoanalytic Theories

Psychoanalytic theories explain human behaviour in terms of the interaction of various components of personality. Sigmund Freud was the founder of this school. Freud drew on the physics of his day (thermodynamics) to coin the term psychodynamics. Based on the idea of converting heat into mechanical energy, he proposed psychic energy could be converted into behaviour. Freud's theory places central importance on dynamic, unconscious psychological conflicts.

Freud divides human personality into three significant components: the id, ego, and super-ego. The id acts according to the *pleasure principle*, demanding immediate gratification of its needs regardless of external environment; the ego then must emerge in order to realistically meet the wishes and demands of the id in accordance with the outside world, adhering to the *reality principle*. Finally, the superego (conscience) inculcates moral judgment and societal rules upon the ego, thus forcing the demands of the id to be met not only realistically but morally. The superego is the last function of the personality to develop, and is the embodiment of parental/social ideals established during childhood. According to Freud, personality is based on the dynamic interactions of these three components. The channeling and release of sexual (libidal) and aggressive energies, which ensues from the "Eros" (sex; instinctual self-preservation) and "Thanatos" (death; instinctual self-annihilation) drives respectively, are major components of his theory. It is important to note that Freud's broad understanding of sexuality included all kinds of pleasurable feelings experienced by the human body.

Freud proposed five psychosexual stages of personality development. He believed adult personality is dependent upon early childhood experiences and largely determined by age five. Fixations that develop during the Infantile stage contribute to adult personality and behaviour.

One of Sigmund Freud's earlier associates, Alfred Adler, did agree with Freud early childhood experiences are important to development, and believed birth order may influence personality development. Adler believed the oldest was the one that set high goals to achieve to get the attention they lost back when the younger siblings were born. He believed the middle children were competitive and ambitious possibly so they are able to surpass the first-born's achievements, but were not as much concerned about the glory. Also he believed the last born would be more dependent and sociable but be the baby. He also believed that the only child loves being the centre of attention and matures quickly, but in the end fails to become independent.

Heinz Kohut thought similarly to Freud's idea of transference. He used narcissism as a model of how we develop our sense of self. Narcissism is the exaggerated sense of one self in which is believed to exist in order to protect one's low self esteem and sense of worthlessness. Kohut had a significant impact on the field by extending Freud's theory of narcissism and introducing what he called the 'self-object transferences' of mirroring and idealization. In other words, children need to idealize and emotionally "sink into" and identify with the idealized competence of admired figures such as parents or older siblings. They also need to have their self-worth mirrored by these people. These experiences allow them to thereby learn the self-soothing and other skills that are necessary for the development of a healthy sense of self.

Another important figure in the world of personality theory was Karen Horney. She is credited with the development of the "real self" and the "ideal self". She believes all people have these two views of their own self. The "real self" is how you really are with regards to personality, values, and morals; but the "ideal self" is a construct you apply to yourself to conform to social and personal norms and goals. Ideal self would be "I can be successful, I am CEO material"; and real self would be "I just work in the mail room, with not much chance of high promotion".

Behaviourist Theories

Behaviourists explain personality in terms of the effects external stimuli have on behaviour. It was a radical shift away from Freudian philosophy. This school of thought was developed by B. F. Skinner who put forth a model which emphasized the mutual interaction of the person or "the organism" with its environment. Skinner believed children do bad things because the behaviour obtains attention that serves as a reinforcer. For example: a child cries because the child's crying in the past has led to attention. These are the *response*, and *consequences*. The response is the child crying, and the attention that child gets is the reinforcing consequence. According to this theory, people's behaviour is formed by processes such as operant conditioning. Skinner put forward a "three term contingency model" which helped promote analysis of behaviour based on the "Stimulus-Response-Consequence Model" in which the critical question is: "Under which circumstances or antecedent 'stimuli' does the organism engage in a particular behaviour or 'response', which in turn produces a particular 'consequence'?"

Richard Herrnstein extended this theory by accounting for attitudes and traits. An attitude develops as the response strength (the tendency to respond) in the presences of a group of stimuli become stable. Rather than describing conditionable traits in non-behavioural language, response strength in a given situation accounts for the environmental portion. Herrstein also saw traits as having a large genetic or biological component as do most modern behaviourists.

Ivan Pavlov is another notable influence. He is well known for his classical conditioning experiments involving dogs. These physiological studies led him to discover the foundation of behaviourism as well as classical conditioning.

Social Cognitive Theories

In cognitive theory, behaviour is explained as guided by cognitions (e.g. expectations) about the world, especially those about other people. Cognitive theories are theories of personality that emphasize cognitive processes such as thinking and judging.

Albert Bandura, a social learning theorist suggested the forces of memory and emotions worked in conjunction with environmental influences. Bandura was known mostly for his "Bobo Doll experiment". During these experiments, Bandura video taped a college student kicking and verbally abusing a bobo doll. He then showed this video to a class of kindergarten children who were getting ready to go out to play. When they entered the play room, they saw bobo dolls, and some hammers. The people observing these children at play saw a group of children beating the doll. He called this study and his findings observational learning, or modelling.

Early examples of approaches to cognitive style are listed by Baron (1982). These include Witkin's (1965) work on field dependency, Gardner's (1953) discovering people had consistent preference for the number of categories they used to categorise heterogeneous objects, and Block and Petersen's (1955) work on confidence in line discrimination judgments. Baron relates early development of cognitive approaches of personality to ego psychology. More central to this field have been:

- Self-efficacy work, dealing with confidence people have in abilities to do tasks;
- Locus of control theory dealing with different beliefs people have about whether their worlds are controlled by themselves or external factors;
- Attributional style theory dealing with different ways in which people explain events in their lives. This approach builds upon locus of control, but extends it by stating we also need to consider whether people attribute to stable causes or variable causes, and to global causes or specific causes.

Various scales have been developed to assess both attributional style and locus of control. Locus of control scales include those used by Rotter and later by Duttweiler, the Nowicki and Strickland (1973) Locus of Control Scale for

Children and various locus of control scales specifically in the health domain, most famously that of Kenneth Wallston and his colleagues, The Multidimensional Health Locus of Control Scale. Attributional style has been assessed by the Attributional Style Questionnaire, the Expanded Attributional Style Questionnaire, the Attributions Questionnaire, the Real Events Attributional Style Questionnaire and the Attributional Style Assessment Test.

Walter Mischel (1999) has also defended a cognitive approach to personality. His work refers to "Cognitive Affective Units", and considers factors such as encoding of stimuli, affect, goal-setting, and self-regulatory beliefs. The term "Cognitive Affective Units" shows how his approach considers affect as well as cognition.

Personal Construct Psychology (PCP) is a theory of personality developed by the American psychologist George Kelly in the 1950s. From the theory, Kelly derived a psychotherapy approach and also a technique called *The Repertory Grid Interview* that helped his patients to uncover their own "constructs" (defined later) with minimal intervention or interpretation by the therapist. The Repertory Grid was later adapted for various uses within organizations, including decision-making and interpretation of other people's world-views. From his 1963 book, *A Theory of Personality*:

- Fundamental Postulate: A person's processes are psychologically channelized by the ways in which the person anticipates events.
- Construction Corollary: A person anticipates events by construing their replications.
- Individuality Corollary: People differ from one another in their construction of events.
- Organization Corollary: Each person characteristically evolves, for convenience in anticipating events, a construction system embracing ordinal relationships between constructs.
- Dichotomy Corollary: A person's construction system is composed of a finite number of dichotomous constructs.
- Choice Corollary: People choose for themselves the particular alternative in a dichotomized construct

through which they anticipate the greater possibility for extension and definition of their system.

- Range Corollary: A construct is convenient for the anticipation of a finite range of events only.
- Experience Corollary: A person's construction system varies as the person successively construes the replication of events.
- Modulation Corollary: The variation in a person's construction system is limited by the permeability of the constructs within whose ranges of conveniences the variants lie.
- Fragmentation Corollary: A person may successively employ a variety of construction subsystems which are inferentially incompatible with each other.
- Commonality Corollary: To the extent that one person employs a construction of experience which is similar to that employed by another, the psychological processes of the two individuals are similar to each other.
- Sociality Corollary: To the extent that one person construes another's construction processes, that person may play a role in a social process involving the other person.

Humanistic Theories

In humanistic psychology it is emphasized people have free will and they play an active role in determining how they behave. Accordingly, humanistic psychology focuses on subjective experiences of persons as opposed to forced, definitive factors that determine behaviour. Abraham Maslow and Carl Rogers were proponents of this view, which is based on the "phenomenal field" theory of Combs and Snygg (1949).

Maslow spent much of his time studying what he called "self-actualizing persons", those who are "fulfilling themselves and doing the best they are capable of doing". Maslow believes all who are interested in growth move towards self-actualizing (growth, happiness, satisfaction) views. Many of these people demonstrate a trend in dimensions of their personalities. Characteristics of self-actualizers according to Maslow include the four key dimensions:

1. Awareness-maintaining constant enjoyment and awe of life. These individuals often experienced a "peak experience". He defined a peak experience as an "intensification of any experience to the degree there is a loss or transcendence of self". A peak experience is one in which an individual perceives an expansion of his or herself, and detects a unity and meaningfulness in life. Intense concentration on an activity one is involved in, such as running a marathon, may invoke a peak experience.
2. Reality and problem centred-they have tendency to be concerned with "problems" in their surroundings.
3. Acceptance/Spontaneity-they accept their surroundings and what cannot be changed.
4. Unhostile sense of humour/democratic-they do not like joking about others, which can be viewed as offensive. They have friends of all backgrounds and religions and hold very close friendships.

Maslow and Rogers emphasized a view of the person as an active, creative, experiencing human being who lives in the present and subjectively responds to current perceptions, relationships, and encounters. They disagree with the dark, pessimistic outlook of those in the Freudian psychoanalysis ranks, but rather view humanistic theories as positive and optimistic proposals which stress the tendency of the human personality toward growth and self-actualization. This progressing self will remain the centre of its constantly changing world; a world that will help mold the self but not necessarily confine it. Rather, the self has opportunity for maturation based on its encounters with this world. This understanding attempts to reduce the acceptance of hopeless redundancy. Humanistic therapy typically relies on the client for information of the past and its effect on the present, therefore the client dictates the type of guidance the therapist may initiate. This allows for an individualized approach to therapy. Rogers found patients differ in how they respond to other people. Rogers tried to model a particular approach to therapy-he stressed the reflective or empathetic response. This response type takes the client's viewpoint and reflects back his or her feeling and the context for it. An example of a reflective response would be,

"It seems you are feeling anxious about your upcoming marriage". This response type seeks to clarify the therapist's understanding while also encouraging the client to think more deeply and seek to fully understand the feelings they have expressed.

Biopsychological Theories

Some of the earliest thinking about possible biological bases of personality grew out of the case of Phineas Gage. In an 1848 accident, a large iron rod was driven through Gage's head, and his personality apparently changed as a result.

In general, patients with brain damage have been difficult to find and study. In the 1990s, researchers began to use Electroencephalography (EEG), Positron Emission Tomography (PET) and more recently functional Magnetic Resonance Imaging (fMRI), which is now the most widely used imaging technique to help localize personality traits in the brain. One of the founders of this area of brain research is Richard Davidson of the University of Wisconsin–Madison. Davidson's research lab has focused on the role of the prefrontal cortex (PFC) and amygdala in manifesting human personality. In particular, this research has looked at hemispheric asymmetry of activity in these regions. Neuropsychological experiments have suggested that hemispheric asymmetry can affect an individual's personality (particularly in social settings) for individuals with NLD (non-verbal learning disorder), which is marked by the impairment of nonverbal information controlled by the right hemisphere of the brain. Progress will arise in the areas of gross motor skills, inability to organize visual-spatial relations, or adapt to novel social situations. Frequently, a person with NLD is unable to interpret non-verbal cues, and therefore experiences difficulty interacting with peers in socially normative ways. One integrative, biopsychosocial approach to personality and psychopathology, linking brain and environmental factors to specific types of activity, is the hypostatic model of personality, created by Codrin Stefan Tapu.

Big Five Personality Traits

In contemporary psychology, the "Big Five" factors (or Five Factor Model; FFM) of personality are five broad domains or dimensions of personality which are used to describe human personality.

The Big five factors are Openness, Conscientiousness, Extraversion, Agreeableness, and Neuroticism (OCEAN, or CANOE if rearranged). The Neuroticism factor is sometimes referred to as Emotional Stability. Some disagreement remains about how to interpret the Openness factor, which is sometimes called "Intellect". Each factor consists of a cluster of more specific traits that correlate together. For example, extraversion includes such related qualities as sociability, excitement seeking, impulsiveness, and positive emotions.

The Five Factor Model is a purely descriptive model of personality, but psychologists have developed a number of theories to account for the Big Five.

Overview

The Big Five factors and their constituent traits can be summarized as follows:

- Openness – (inventive / curious vs. consistent / cautious). Appreciation for art, emotion, adventure, unusual ideas, curiosity, and variety of experience.
- Conscientiousness – (efficient / organized vs. easy-going / careless). A tendency to show self-discipline, act dutifully, and aim for achievement; planned rather than spontaneous behaviour.
- Extraversion – (outgoing / energetic vs. shy / reserved). Energy, positive emotions, surgency, and the tendency to seek stimulation in the company of others.
- Agreeableness – (friendly / compassionate vs. competitive / outspoken). A tendency to be compassionate and cooperative rather than suspicious and antagonistic towards others.
- Neuroticism – (sensitive / nervous vs. secure / confident). A tendency to experience unpleasant emotions easily, such as anger, anxiety, depression, or vulnerability.

The Big Five model is a comprehensive, empirical, data-driven research finding. Identifying the traits and structure of human personality has been one of the most fundamental goals in all of psychology. The five broad factors were discovered and defined by several independent sets of researchers (Digman, 1990). These researchers began by studying known personality traits and then factor-analyzing hundreds of measures of these traits (in self-report and questionnaire data, peer ratings, and objective measures from experimental settings) in order to find the underlying factors of personality.

The initial model was advanced by Ernest Tupes and Raymond Cristal, but failed to reach an academic audience until the 1980s. In 1990, J.M. Digman advanced his five factor model of personality, which Goldberg extended to the highest level of organization (Goldberg, 1993). These five over-arching domains have been found to contain and subsume most known personality traits and are assumed to represent the basic structure behind all personality traits. These five factors provide a rich conceptual framework for integrating all the research findings and theory in personality psychology. The Big Five traits are also referred to as the "Five Factor Model" or FFM, and as the Global Factors of personality.

At least four sets of researchers have worked independently for decades on this problem and have identified generally the same Big Five factors: Tupes & Cristal were first, followed by Goldberg at the Oregon Research Institute, Cattell at the University of Illinois, and Costa and McCrae at the National Institutes of Health. These four sets of researchers used somewhat different methods in finding the five traits, and thus each set of five factors has somewhat different names and definitions. However, all have been found to be highly inter-correlated and factor-analytically aligned.

Because the Big Five traits are broad and comprehensive, they are not nearly as powerful in predicting and explaining actual behaviour as are the more numerous lower-level traits. Many studies have confirmed that in predicting actual behaviour the more numerous facet or primary level traits are far more effective.

When scored for individual feedback, these traits are frequently presented as percentile scores. For example, a Conscientiousness rating in the 80th percentile indicates a relatively strong sense of responsibility and orderliness, whereas an Extraversion rating in the 5th percentile indicates an exceptional need for solitude and quiet. Although these trait clusters are statistical aggregates, exceptions may exist on individual personality profiles. On average, people who register high in Openness are intellectually curious, open to emotion, interested in art, and willing to try new things. A particular individual, however, may have a high overall Openness score and be interested in learning and exploring new cultures but have no great interest in art or poetry.

The most frequently used measures of the Big Five comprise either items that are self-descriptive sentences or, in the case of lexical measures, items that are single adjectives. Due to the length of sentence-based and some lexical measures, short forms have been developed and validated for use in applied research settings where questionnaire space and respondent time are limited, such as the 40-item balanced *International English Big-Five Mini-Markers* or a very brief (10 item) measure of the Big Five domains.

Openness to Experience

Openness to experience is one of five major domains which are used to describe human personality. Openness involves active imagination, aesthetic sensitivity, attentiveness to inner feelings, preference for variety, and intellectual curiosity. A great deal of psychometric research has demonstrated that these qualities are statistically correlated. Thus, openness can be viewed as a global personality trait consisting of a set of specific traits, habits, and tendencies that cluster together.

Openness tends to be normally distributed with a small number of individuals scoring extremely high or low on the trait, and most people scoring near the average. People who score low on openness are considered to be *closed to experience*. They tend to be conventional and traditional in their outlook and behaviour. They prefer familiar routines to new experiences, and generally have a narrower range of interests.

People who are open to experience are no different in mental health from people who are closed to experience. There is no relationship between openness and neuroticism, or any other measure of psychological wellbeing. Being open and closed to experience are simply two different ways of relating to the world.

Measurement

The NEO PI-R personality test measures six *facets* or elements of openness to experience:

1. Fantasy-the tendency toward a vivid imagination and fantasy life.
2. Aesthetics-the tendency to appreciate art, music, and poetry.
3. Feelings-being receptive to inner emotional states and valuing emotional experience.
4. Actions-the inclination to try new activities, visit new places, and try new foods.
5. Ideas-the tendency to be intellectually curious and open to new ideas.
6. Values-the readiness to re-examine traditional social, religious, and political values.

Openness has also been measured, along with all the other Big Five personality traits, on Goldberg's International Personality Item Pool (IPIP). The Myers-Briggs Type Indicator (MBTI) measures the preference of "intuition," which is related to openness to experience.

According to research by Sam Gosling, it is possible to assess openness by examining people's homes and work spaces. Individuals who are highly open to experience tend to have distinctive and unconventional decorations. They are also likely to have books on a wide variety of topics, a diverse music collection, and works of art on display.

Psychological Aspects

Openness to experience correlates with creativity, as measured by tests of divergent thinking. Openness is also associated with crystallized intelligence, but not fluid intelligence. These mental abilities may come more easily when people are dispositionally curious and open to learning. However, openness is only weakly related to general intelligence. Openness to experience is related to need for cognition, a motivational tendency to think about ideas, scrutinize information, and enjoy solving puzzles. There are social and political implications to this personality trait. People who are highly open to experience tend to be politically liberal and tolerant of diversity. As a consequence, they are generally more open to different cultures and lifestyles. They are lower in ethnocentrism and right-wing authoritarianism.

Genes and Physiology

Openness to experience, like the other traits in the five factor model, is believed to have a genetic component. Identical twins (who have the same DNA) show similar scores on openness to experience, even when they have been adopted into different families and raised in very different environments. One genetic study with 86 subjects found Openness to experience related to the 5-HTTLPR polymorphism associated with the serotonin transporter gene.

Higher levels of openness have been linked to activity in the ascending dopaminergic system and the dorsolateral prefrontal cortex. Openness is the only personality trait that correlates with neuropsychological tests of dorsolateral prefrontal cortical function, supporting theoretical links among openness, cognitive functioning, and IQ.

Geography

Researchers have found that people who live on islands tend to be less open to experience than those living on the mainland, and that people whose ancestors had inhabited the island for twenty generations tend to be less open to experience than more recent arrivals. Additionally, people who emigrate from islands to the mainland tend to be more open to experience than people that stay on islands, and those that immigrate to islands.

People living in the eastern and western parts of the United States tend to score higher on openness to experience than those living in the midwest. The highest average scores on openness are found in the states of New York, Oregon, Massachusetts, Washington, and California. Lowest average scores are found in North Dakota, Wyoming, Alaska, Alabama, and Wisconsin.

Drug Use

Psychologists in the early 1970s used the concept of openness to experience to describe people who are more likely to use marijuana. Openness was defined in these studies as high creativity, adventuresomeness, internal sensation novelty seeking, and low authoritarianism. Several correlational studies confirmed that young people who score high on this cluster of traits are more likely to use marijuana. More recent research has replicated this finding using contemporary measures of openness.

Openness is a general appreciation for art, emotion, adventure, unusual ideas, imagination, curiosity, and variety of experience. The trait distinguishes imaginative people from down-to-earth, conventional people. People who are open to experience are intellectually curious, appreciative of art, and sensitive to beauty. They tend to be, compared to closed people, more creative and more aware of their feelings. They are more likely to hold unconventional beliefs.

People with low scores on openness tend to have more conventional, traditional interests. They prefer the plain, straightforward, and obvious over the complex, ambiguous, and subtle. They may regard the arts and sciences with suspicion or even view these endeavors as uninteresting.

Sample Openness Items

- I have a rich vocabulary.
- I have a vivid imagination.
- I have excellent ideas.
- I spend time reflecting on things.
- I use difficult words.
- I am not interested in abstractions. (*reversed*)
- I do not have a good imagination. (*reversed*)
- I have difficulty understanding abstract ideas. (*reversed*)

Conscientiousness

Conscientiousness is a tendency to show self-discipline, act dutifully, and aim for achievement. The trait shows a preference for planned rather than spontaneous behaviour. It influences the way in which we control, regulate, and direct our impulses. Conscientiousness includes the factor known as Need for Achievement (NAch). Conscientiousness is the trait of being painstaking and careful, or the quality of acting according to the dictates of one's conscience. It includes such elements as self-discipline, carefulness, thoroughness, organization, deliberation (the tendency to think carefully before acting), and need for achievement.

It is an aspect of what has traditionally been called character. Conscientious individuals are generally hard working and reliable. When taken to an extreme, they may also be workaholics, perfectionists, and compulsive in their behaviour. People who are low on conscientiousness are not necessarily lazy or immoral, but they tend to be more laid back, less goal oriented, and less driven by success.

Personality Models

Conscientiousness is one of five superordinate traits in the "Big Five model" of personality which also consists of extraversion, neuroticism, openness to experience, and agreeableness. Two personality tests that assess these traits are Costa and McCrae's NEO PI-R and Goldberg's NEO-IPIP. According to these models, conscientiousness is considered to be a continuous dimension of personality, rather than a categorical "type" of person. Scores in conscientiousness follow a normal distribution.

Conscientiousness is related to impulse-control, but it should not be confused with the problems of impulse control found in neuroticism. People high on *neurotic* impulsiveness find it difficult to resist temptation or delay gratification. Individuals who are low on *conscientious* self-discipline are unable to motivate themselves to perform a task that they would like to accomplish. These are conceptually similar but empirically distinct.

The trait cluster of conscientiousness overlaps with other models of personality, such as C. Robert Cloninger's Temperament and Character Inventory, in which it is called *self-directedness*. It also includes the specific traits of *rule consciousness* and *perfectionism* in Cattell's 16 PF model. Many of the behaviours associated with conscientiousness fall under the broad category of emotional intelligence. Traits associated with conscientiousness are frequently assessed by self-report integrity tests given by various corporations to prospective employees.

Behaviour

People who score high on the trait of conscientiousness tend to be more organized and less cluttered in their homes and offices. For example, their books tend to be neatly shelved in alphabetical order, or categorized by topic, rather than scattered around the room. Their clothes tend to be folded and arranged in drawers or closets instead of lying on the floor. The presence of planners and to-do lists are also signs of conscientiousness. Their homes tend to have better lighting than the homes of people who are low on this trait.

Conscientiousness is related to successful academic performance in students. Low levels of conscientiousness are strongly associated with procrastination. A considerable amount of research indicates that conscientiousness is one of the best predictors of performance in the workplace. and indeed that after general mental ability is taken into account, the other four of the Big Five personality traits do not aid in predicting career success. Conscientious employees are generally more reliable, more motivated, and harder working. Furthermore, conscientiousness is the only personality trait that correlates with performance across all categories of jobs. However, agreeableness and emotional stability may also be important, particularly in jobs that involve a significant amount of social interaction.

Although conscientiousness is generally seen as a positive trait to possess, recent research has suggested that in some situations it may be harmful for well-being. In a prospective study of 9570 individuals over four years, highly conscientiousness people suffered more than twice as much if they became unemployed. The authors suggested this may be due to conscientious people making different attributions about why they became unemployed, or through experiencing stronger reactions following failure. This finding is consistent with perspectives which see no trait as inherently positive or negative, but rather the consequences of the trait being dependant on the situation and concomitant goals and motivations.

Sample Conscientiousness Items

- I am always prepared.
- I am exacting in my work.

- I follow a schedule.
- I get chores done right away.
- I like order.
- I pay attention to details.
- I leave my belongings around. (*reversed*)
- I make a mess of things. (*reversed*)
- I often forget to put things back in their proper place. (*reversed*)
- I shirk my duties. (*reversed.*

Extraversion

Extraversion is characterized by positive emotions, surgency, and the tendency to seek out stimulation and the company of others. The trait is marked by pronounced engagement with the external world. Extraverts enjoy being with people, and are often perceived as full of energy. They tend to be enthusiastic, action-oriented individuals who are likely to say "Yes!" or "Let's go!" to opportunities for excitement. In groups they like to talk, assert themselves, and draw attention to themselves.

Introverts lack the social exuberance and activity levels of extraverts. They tend to seem· quiet, low-key, deliberate, and less involved in the social world. Their lack of social involvement should not be interpreted as shyness or depression. Introverts simply need less stimulation than extraverts and more time alone. They may be very active and energetic, simply not socially.

Sample Extraversion Items

- I am the life of the party.
- I don't mind being the centre of attention.
- I feel comfortable around people.
- I start conversations.
- I talk to a lot of different people at parties.
- I am quiet around strangers. (*reversed*)
- I don't like to draw attention to myself. (*reversed*)
- I don't talk a lot. (*reversed*)

  I have little to say. (*reversed*).

Agreeableness

Agreeableness is a tendency to be compassionate and cooperative rather than suspicious and antagonistic towards others. The trait reflects individual differences in general concern for social harmony. Agreeable individuals value getting along with others. They are generally considerate, friendly, generous, helpful, and willing to compromise their interests with others. Agreeable people also have an optimistic view of human nature. They believe people are basically honest, decent, and trustworthy.

Disagreeable individuals place self-interest above getting along with others. They are generally unconcerned with others' well-being, and are less likely to extend themselves for other people. Sometimes their skepticism about others' motives causes them to be suspicious, unfriendly, and uncooperative.

Sample Agreeableness Items :

- I am interested in people.
- I feel others' feelings.
- I have a soft heart.
- I make people feel at ease.
- I sympathize with others' feelings.
- I take time out for others.
- I am not interested in other people's problems. (*reversed*)
- I am not really interested in others. (*reversed*)
- I feel little concern for others. (*reversed*)
- I insult people. (*reversed*)
- I like being isolated. (*reversed*).

Neuroticism

Neuroticism is the tendency to experience negative emotions, such as anger, anxiety, or depression. It is sometimes called emotional instability. Those who score high in neuroticism are emotionally reactive and vulnerable to stress. They are more likely to interpret ordinary situations as threatening, and minor frustrations as hopelessly difficult. Their negative emotional reactions tend to persist for unusually long periods of time, which means they are often in a bad mood. These problems in emotional regulation can diminish the ability of a person scoring high on neuroticism to think clearly, make decisions, and cope effectively with stress.

At the other end of the scale, individuals who score low in neuroticism are less easily upset and are less emotionally reactive. They tend to be calm, emotionally stable, and free from persistent negative feelings. Freedom from negative feelings does not mean that low scorers experience a lot of positive feelings.

Sample neuroticism items:

- I am easily disturbed.
- I change my mood a lot.
- I get irritated easily.
- I get stressed out easily.
- I get upset easily.
- I have frequent mood swings.
- I often feel blue.
- I worry about things.
- I am relaxed most of the time. (*reversed*)
- I seldom feel blue. (*reversed*).

History

Early Trait Research

Sir Francis Galton was the first scientist to recognize what is now known as the Lexical Hypothesis. This is the idea that the most salient and socially relevant personality differences in people's lives will eventually become encoded into language. The hypothesis further suggests that by sampling language, it is possible to derive a comprehensive taxonomy of human personality traits. In 1936, Gordon Allport and H. S. Odbert put this hypothesis into practice. They worked through two of the most comprehensive dictionaries of the English language available at the time and extracted 17,953 personality-describing words. They then reduced this gigantic list to 4,504 adjectives which they believed were descriptive of observable and relatively permanent traits.

Raymond Cattell obtained the Allport-Odbert list in the 1940s, added terms obtained from psychological research, and then eliminated synonyms to reduce the total to 171. He then asked subjects to rate people whom they knew by the adjectives on the list and analyzed their ratings. Cattell identified 35 major clusters of personality traits which he referred to as the "personality sphere." He and his associates then constructed personality tests for these traits. The data they obtained from these tests were analyzed with the emerging technology of computers combined with the statistical method of factor analysis. This resulted in sixteen major personality factors, which led to the development of the 16PF Personality Questionnaire.

In 1961, two Air Force researchers, Ernest Tupes and Raymond Christal, analyzed personality data from eight large samples. Using Cattell's trait measures, they found five recurring factors, which they named "Surgency", "Agreeableness", "Dependability", "Emotional Stability", and "Culture". This work was replicated by Warren Norman, who also found that five major factors were sufficient to account for a large set of personality data. Norman named these factors Surgency, Agreeableness, Conscientiousness, Emotional Stability, and Culture. Raymond Cattell viewed these developments as an attack on his 16PF model and never agreed with the growing Five Factor consensus. He refers to "...the five factor heresy" which he considers "...is partly directed against the 16PF test". Responding to Goldberg's article in the American Psychologist, 'The Structure of Phenotypic Personality Traits', Cattell stated, "No experienced factorist could agree with Dr Goldberg's enthusiasm for the five factor personality theory". This determined rejection of the FFM challenge to his 16 factor model is presented in an article published towards the end of his life and entitled 'The fallacy of five factors in the personality sphere', Cattell, R. B. (1995), *The Psychologist, The British Psychological Society*, May Issue pp 207–208.

Hiatus in Research

For the next two decades, the changing zeitgeist made publication of personality research difficult. In his 1968 book *Personality and Assessment*, Walter Mischel asserted that personality tests could not predict behaviour with a correlation of more than 0.3. Social psychologists like Mischel argued that attitudes and behaviour were not stable, but varied with the situation. Predicting behaviour by personality tests was considered to be impossible.

Emerging methodologies challenged this point of view during the 1980s. Instead of trying to predict single instances of behaviour, which was unreliable, researchers found that they could predict patterns of behaviour by aggregating large numbers of observations. As a result correlations between personality and behaviour increased substantially, and it was clear that "personality" did in fact exist. Personality and social psychologists now generally agree that both personal and situational variables are needed to account for human behaviour. Trait theories became justified, and there was a resurgence of interest in this area.

By 1980, the pioneering research by Tupes, Christal, and Norman had been largely forgotten by psychologists. Lewis Goldberg started his own lexical project, independently found the five factors once again, and gradually brought them back to the attention of psychologists. He later coined the term "Big Five" as a label for the factors.

Validity of the Big Five

In a 1981 symposium in Honolulu, four prominent researchers, Lewis Goldberg, Naomi Takemoto-Chock, Andrew Comrey, and John M. Digman, reviewed the available personality tests of the day. They concluded that the tests which held the most promise measured a subset of five common factors, just as Norman had discovered in 1963. This event was followed by widespread acceptance of the five factor model among personality researchers during the 1980s. In 1984 Peter Saville and his team included the five-factor "Pentagon" model with the original OPQ. Pentagon was closely followed by the NEO five-factor personality inventory, published by Costa and McCrae in 1985.

One of the most significant advances of the five-factor model was the establishment of a common taxonomy that demonstrates order in a previously scattered and disorganized field. What separates the five-factor model of personality from all others is that it is not based on the theory of any one particular psychologist, but rather on language.

A number of meta-analyses have confirmed the predictive value of the Big Five across a wide range of behaviours. Saulsman and Page examined the relationships between the Big Five personality dimensions and each of the 10 personality disorder categories in the *Diagnostic and Statistical Manual of Mental Disorders* (DSM-IV). Across 15 independent samples, the researchers found that each disorder displayed a unique and predictable five-factor profile. The most prominent and consistent personality predictors underlying the disorders were positive associations with Neuroticism and negative associations with Agreeableness. In the area of job performance, Barrick and Mount reviewed 117 studies utilizing 162 samples with 23,994 participants. They found that conscientiousness showed consistent relations with all performance criteria for all occupational groups. Extraversion was a valid predictor for occupations involving social interaction (e.g. management and sales). Furthermore, extraversion and openness to experience were valid predictors of training proficiency criteria.

Selected Scientific Findings

Ever since the 1990s when the consensus of psychologists gradually came to support the Big Five, there has been a growing body of research surrounding these personality traits.

Heritability

All five factors show an influence from both heredity and environment. Twin studies suggest that these effects contribute in roughly equal proportion. Of four recent twin studies the mean estimated broad heritabilities on self-report measures for the Big Five traits were as follows:

Openness: 57%

Conscientiousness: 49%

Extraversion: 54%

Agreeableness: 42%

Neuroticism: 48%

Development

Many studies of longitudinal data, which correlate people's test scores over time, and cross-sectional data, which compare personality levels across different age groups, show a high degree of stability in personality traits during adulthood. More recent research and meta-analyses of previous studies, however, indicate that change occurs in all five traits at various points in the lifespan. The new research shows evidence for a maturation effect. On average, levels of Agreeableness and Conscientiousness typically increase with time, whereas Extraversion, Neuroticism, and Openness tend to decrease. In addition to these group effects, there are individual differences: different people demonstrate unique patterns of change at all stages of life.

Gender Differences

Cross-cultural research from 26 nations ($N = 23{,}031$ subjects) and again in 55 nations ($N = 17{,}637$ subjects) has shown a universal pattern of sex differences on responses to the Big Five Inventory. Women consistently report higher Neuroticism and Agreeableness, and men often report higher Extraversion and Conscientiousness. Sex differences in personality traits are larger in prosperous, healthy, and egalitarian cultures in which women have more opportunities that are equal to those of men; both men and women tend to grow more extraverted and conscientious and less neurotic and agreeable as cultures grow more prosperous and egalitarian, but the effect is stronger for men.

Birth Order

The suggestion has often been made that individuals differ by the order of their births. Frank J. Sulloway argues that birth order is correlated with personality traits. He claims that firstborns are more conscientious, more socially dominant, less agreeable, and less open to new ideas compared to laterborns.

However, Sulloway's case has been called into question. One criticism is that his data confounds family size with birth order. Subsequent analyses have shown that birth order effects are only found in studies where the subjects' personality traits are rated by family members (such as siblings or parents) or by acquaintances familiar with the subjects' birth order. Large scale studies using random samples and self-report personality tests like the NEO PI-R have found no significant effect of birth order on personality.

Cross-cultural Research

The Big Five have been replicated in a variety of different languages and cultures, such as German and Chinese. Thompson has demonstrated the Big Five structure across several cultures using an international English language scale.

Recent work has found relationships between Geert Hofstede's cultural factors, Individualism, Power Distance, Masculinity, and Uncertainty Avoidance, with the average Big Five scores in a country. For instance, the degree to which a country values individualism correlates with its average Extraversion, while people living in cultures which are accepting of large inequalities in their power structures tend to score somewhat higher on Conscientiousness. The reasons for these differences are as yet unknown; this is an active area of research.

Additionally, there has been an introduction of a correlation between leadership and Taoist (or Daoist) Big Five and Water-like (W-L) Leadership/Personality as discussed by the Chinese psychologist Yueh-Ting Lee.

Non-humans

The big five personality factors have been assessed in some non-human species. In one series of studies, human ratings of chimpanzees using the Chimpanzee Personality Questionnaire (CPQ) revealed factors of extraversion, conscientiousness and agreeableness – as well as an additional factor of dominance – across hundreds of chimpanzees in zoological parks, a large naturalistic sanctuary and a research laboratory. Neuroticism and Openness factors were found in an original zoo sample, but did not replicate in a new zoo sample or to other settings (perhaps reflecting the design of the CPQ).

Criticisms

Much research has been conducted on the Big Five. This has resulted in both criticism and support for the model. Critics argue that there are limitations to the scope of Big Five as an explanatory or predictive theory. It is argued that the Big Five does not explain all of human personality. The methodology used to identify the dimensional structure of personality traits, factor analysis, is often challenged for not having a universally-recognized basis for choosing among solutions with different numbers of factors. Another frequent criticism is that the Big Five is not theory-driven. It is merely a data-driven investigation of certain descriptors that tend to cluster together under factor analysis.

Limited Scope

One common criticism is that the Big Five does not explain all of human personality. Some psychologists have dissented from the model precisely because they feel it neglects other domains of personality, such as Religiosity, Manipulativeness/ Machiavellianism, Honesty, Self-Awareness, Thriftiness, Conservativeness, Critical Judgement, Masculinity/Femininity, Snobbishness, Sense of humour, Identity, Self-concept, and Motivation. Correlations have been found between some of these variables and the Big Five, such as the inverse relationship between political conservatism and Openness; although variation in these traits is not well explained by the Five Factors themselves. McAdams has called the Big Five a "psychology of the stranger," because they refer to traits that are relatively easy to observe in a stranger; other aspects of personality that are more privately held or more context-dependent are excluded from the Big Five.

In many studies, the five factors are not fully orthogonal to one another; that is, the five factors are not independent. Negative correlations often appear between Neuroticism and Extraversion, for instance, indicating that those who are more prone to experiencing negative emotions tend to be less talkative and outgoing. Orthogonality is viewed as desirable by some researchers because it minimizes redundancy between the dimensions. This is particularly important when the goal of a study is to provide a comprehensive description of personality with as few variables as possible.

Methodological Issues

The methodology used to identify the dimensional structure of personality traits, factor analysis, is often challenged for not having a universally-recognized basis for choosing among solutions with different numbers of factors. That is, a five factor solution depends on some degree of interpretation by the analyst. A larger number of factors may, in fact, underlie these five factors. This has led to disputes about the "true" number of factors. Big Five proponents have responded that although other solutions may be viable in a single dataset, only the five factor structure consistently replicates across different studies.

A methodological criticism often directed at the Big Five is that much of the evidence relies on self report questionnaires; self-report bias and falsification of responses are difficult to deal with and account for. This becomes especially important when considering why scores may differ between individuals or groups of people – differences in scores may represent genuine underlying personality differences, or they may simply be an artifact of the way the subjects answered the questions. The five factor structure has been replicated in peer reports. However, many of the substantive findings rely on self-reports.

Theoretical Status

A frequent criticism is that the Big Five is not based on any underlying theory; it is merely an empirical finding that certain descriptors cluster together under factor analysis. While this does not mean that these five factors don't exist, the underlying causes behind them are unknown. Sensation seeking and cheerfulness are not linked to Extraversion because of an underlying theory; this relationship is an empirical finding to be explained.

Jack Block's final published work before his death in January 2010 drew together his lifetime perspective on the five factor model

He summarised his critique of the model in terms of:

- the atheoretical nature of the five-factors
- their cloudy measurement
- the model's inappropriateness for studying early childhood
- the use of factor analysis as the exclusive paradigm for conceptualizing personality
- the continuing non-consensual understandings of the five-factors
- the existence of various unrecognised but successful efforts to specify aspects of character not subsumed by the five-factors.

He went on to suggest that repeatedly observed higher order factors hierarchically above the proclaimed five may promise deeper biological understanding of the origins and implications of these superfactors.

General Aspects of Personality Development

Personality is the overall impression that a person creates on others. It is the integrated image of all the psychological, intellectual, emotional and physical characteristics of an individual as they are presented to other people. A good personality is vital for success in the professional as well as personal life. It depends on a number of qualities but few of the important ones are given below. Awareness of these qualities along with self-appraisal and efforts for improvement of shortcomings can greatly help in the development of a good personality.

1) Physical appearance
2) Communication skills
3) Knowledge
4) Skills – Professional and Personal
5) Self-confidence
6) Personal qualities
7) Health
8) Activities and Interests
9) Achievement and success.

A brief insight to the above qualities is given in the following paragraphs:

Physical Appearance

Visual impact is the first impression that you make on others. Factors which help are cleanliness, proper clothing, smartness and cheerfulness. Try to be at your visual best always.

Communication Skills

Communication skills play a very important role in your personality rating. Communication Skills comprises of speaking ability, comprehension, voiceculture as well as writing skills. Also, if you are a good conversationalist as well as a good listener and genuinely interested in other people, you can win many friends and make a good impression on others.

Knowledge

A wide and prospective knowledge in addition to depth in your own field of study greatly helps in the building up of your personality. This needs wide reading and assimilation, observation and inquisitiveness to learn and also interaction with learned experienced people.

Skills-(Professional and Personal)

Development o pertinent skills needed for your professional work and personal life greatly enhances your personality. Some of the important ones are leadership skills, organizations skills, practical skills in your field, human management skills, entertainment skills including some basic skills like first-aid, cooking, driving etc.

Self-confidence

It is the confidence in one's own abilities which helps in taking up responsibilities and initiative things. Self-confidence can greatly perk up your image and help you in giving a dynamic personality.

Courage, logical analysis and successful experiences greatly help in boosting up your self-confidence.

Personal Qualities

To a great extent, it is the personal qualities which constitute and give shape to your personality. Some of the important qualities which help towards a good personality build-up are the following: character and morality; etiquette and manners; discipline; work ethics; time management; friendliness and love: humour; optimism and cheerful attitude: helpful nature: humidity; maturity and emotional stability.

Health

Good and robust health is an essential and necessary quality for a good personality. Without good health you become ineffective even if you possess all other qualities and achievements.

Activities and Intersts

An active interest in a wide variety of things like sports, cultural activities, social activities, as well as interest in some hobbies go a long way in giving an all round personality to an individual.

Achievements and Success

Finally, achievements and success are factors which enhances your personality and image. They in turn bring popularity and more opportunities. They are great motivating factors which will give a boost to your personality.

Personality development is the developing a personality cult so as to create a strong positive impression about self with the targeted group, or in general; and more pertinent aspect of such personality is to maintain and prove in a long run.

Ten Imp. Points for an Ultimate Personality:

- Appearance.
- Intelligence.
- Smartness.
- Trustworthy, High integrity and Responsible.
- Knowledge, in depth.
- Management.
- Efficiency.
- Economic independence.
- Morality / Character.
- Being beneficial / advantageous.

Strong negative aspects to spoil personality:

- Unhygienic
- Hurting attitude.
- Useless approach.
- Non-beneficial communication.
- Untrustworthy, Irresponsible, Lack of integrity.
- Below average performance.
- Powerless egoism.
- Financial indiscipline.

- Mismanagements.
- Uncontrolled burst of negative emotions.

The four aspects influencing personality are:

Physical, Social, Psychological and Philosophical

Physical personality depends upon pleasing personality indirectly supported by health, strength and withstanding capacity.

Social personality's main factors are: social values, communication skill, attitude and economic independence especially in relation with wealth.

Psychological personality is in tune with personal values, approach, thinking pattern, emotional management and influenced by knowledge, intelligence and smartness.

Philosophical personality is on account of maturity of values.

Main factors for developing a strong personality in social environment:

1. Pleasing appearance.
2. Beneficial communication.
3. Adapting and adhering to social values in interactions.
4. Developing confidence of
   (a) Sincerity, integrity and trust.
   (b) Completing duties, fulfilling responsibilities in time.
   (c) Economic independent, but not being miser.
5. Additional spices for the best impression:
   (a) Awareness and alertness.
   (b) Useful application of: knowledge in depth, positive intelligence and defensive smartness.
   (c) Self-Confidence, Initiative, dynamism, leadership qualities, will-power and self-discipline.
   (d) Adaptive to moral values.

Main factors for developing a strong personality in working field:

1. Sincerity, integrity and trust.
2. Awareness, alertness and grasping capacity.
3. Beneficial communication skill.

4. Useful application of required knowledge in depth, positive intelligence and defensive smartness.
5. Non dependence of economic condition other than for rightful privileges.
6. Completing duties and fulfilling responsibilities in time and absolute accountability.
7. Pleasing appearance with good health.
8. Social interactions in tune with institutional decorum.
9. Sensible thinking inspite of emotionally charged, or embarrassing, circumstances.
10. Dynamism in positive approaches, initiative in new skills and adaptive to institutional policies.
11. Being in tune with changing times; especially so with changing technologies in the respective line.
12. Not to be with:
    (i) Creating helplessness, self satisfaction at others' cost, egoism, sadism, criticism, putting blame on others to escape, irritating communication, untrustworthiness.
    (ii) Laziness, lethargic attitude, falling into helplessness, unusual attitude, useless/boom-ranging approaches, irresponsibility, ignorance, borrowings, unhygienic/disliking appearance.

Main factors for Self development:

1. Self-discipline especially against temptations.
2. Not telling lies.
3. Attainment of maturity in distinguishing good and bad, and development of discipline to do such good and will-power to stand against such bad.
4. Performance of accepted role-play with fulfilling duty, responsibility and accountability.
5. Love and gratitude.
6. Using sensibility rather than becoming emotional.
7. Listen and gather but take your own decision.
8. Don't accept failures, but rectify mistakes in such failures.
9. Skill to do, will to achieve and thrill to help.

10. Try to create happiness around you even at your own personal cost.
11. Helping should always be motto of life without expectation in return.
12. Be selfish within such level of: don't give away your owns if meant for fulfilling your duties.
13. Thinking should be positive so that your attitude and approaches will also be positive.
14. Learn useful knowledge, develop positive intelligence and equip with defensive smartness.
15. Time shall be managed to such optimum level either for usefulness, or for relaxation.
16. Have such hobbies so as to convert the remaining time to be useful.
17. Dependence should be a strategy to get the things done.

Other notable points:-

1. Favourable social interactions are possible by pleasing appearance, beneficial communication, happy creating attitude, and mutually useful approach with maturity in social values.
2. In-depth knowledge should be useful.
3. Criticism is the self-defensive mechanism to cover up one's own inefficiency.
4. Not telling a lie is not wrong but it doesn't mean to tell the truth; however, not telling truth should be for a positive aspect without absolute selfishness.

In other words, personality development depends on:

- Character and Conduct.
- Theory of relativity, Perceptions and Values.
- Awareness and alertness.
- Health, wealth, in-depth knowledge, positive intelligence and defensive smartness.
- Self-Confidence, Will-Power and Self-Discipline.
- Duty, responsibility and accountability.
- Moral Values.

Understanding the Personality Development of Children

Children are not just little adults. They go through typical characteristics of growth—intellectually, emotionally, and socially—on their way to becoming adults. When parents realize these things, there is less strain on both parents and children. Family home evenings can be more enjoyable and successful when a child's personality development is considered. Remembering that a child does not think like an adult, have the same attention span, or see the world the same way adults do, can help a parent plan a home evening everyone can enjoy.

Sometimes we may think that children are too young to understand a gospel principle or that we really don't have much influence with our older children. But Joseph Smith taught that "all the minds and spirits that God ever sent into the world are susceptible of enlargement".

The Spirit of Christ is striving to help each of Heavenly Father's spirit children. In addition, Satan cannot tempt little children until they reach the age of accountability. Therefore, parents have a powerful ally in God and a clear opportunity to help their children develop a sure and safe foundation for future gospel living.

Although Satan cannot tempt little children directly, their innocence and trust make them very open to suggestions and to the influences of others. They look to their parents, older brothers and sisters, and other children and adults for examples and models of behaviour to follow. For these reasons, childhood is a crucial time for laying the proper foundation.

Parents need to be constantly alert to the influences around their children and work hard to teach them the gospel. Parents often unknowingly lead children astray through uncaring, unthinking, and inconsistent behaviour. Perhaps this is one reason why the Lord has said that the iniquity of the fathers will be visited upon the children and why he holds parents responsible if they have not taught their children the things they must know.

The following chart lists some common characteristics of children's behaviour, arranged by broad age groupings, with reasons for that behaviour and the implications that behaviour may have on planning enjoyable and productive family home evenings. However, when considering any growth or behaviour chart, remember that not every child will necessarily fit into described patterns. Individual children grow and develop differently and at different speeds. For instance, all children in one family will not walk or talk at the same age. Each child should be respected as an individual. The descriptions in this chart identify general behaviour only, and you will note that the age groupings overlap.

Personality Disorders in Children

Personality disorders are pervasive chronic psychological disorders, which can greatly affect a person's life. Having a personality disorder can negatively affect one's work, one's family, and one's social life. Personality disorders exists on a continuum so they can be mild to more severe in terms of how pervasive and to what extent a person exhibits the features of a particular personality disorder. While most people can live pretty normal lives with mild personality disorders (or more simply, personality traits), during times of increased stress or external pressures (work, family, a new relationship, etc.), the symptoms of the personality disorder will gain strength and begin to seriously interfere with their emotional and psychological functioning.

Those with a personality disorder possess several distinct psychological features including disturbances in self-image; ability to have successful interpersonal relationships; appropriateness of range of emotion, ways of perceiving themselves, others, and the world; and difficulty possessing proper impulse control. These disturbances come together to create a pervasive pattern of behaviour and inner experience that is quite different from the norms of the individual's culture and that often tend to be expressed in behaviours that appear more dramatic than what society considers usual. Therefore, those with a personality disorder often experience conflicts with other people and vice-versa.

'Personality Disorder' is a controversial diagnosis, covering a wide range of different attitudes and behaviours and affecting an estimated 10% of the general population. The term is generally used to describe behaviours that do not fit into any other obvious diagnostic category, but where the person nevertheless has difficulty coping with life and where that behaviour persistently causes distress to themselves or others. Common problems include having difficulty in sustaining relationships and interpreting social cues. At present there is no consensus as to its causes or treatment.

As the name implies a 'personality' disorder is about problems arising from a persons character. In effect who they are and how they behave are at odds with commonly held social and emotional expectations of what is regarded as 'normal'. What is regarded as 'normal, of course varies from culture to culture and the diagnosis has to be made within the context of the rules, obligations and social expectations held within a particular community. For example, behaviours valued in a battleground are not seen as appropriate during peace time.

There are various different types of personality disorders but all of them share the following features:

- Most often the first signs of a personality disorder appear in late childhood or adolescence and continue during adulthood.
- Personality disorders in children or adolescence are sometimes described as conduct disorders. However most conduct disorders in children do not necessarily lead to personality disorders in adults.
- Someone with a personality disorder holds attitudes and behaves in ways that can cause considerable problems for themselves and others. For example the way they perceive the world; the way they think; the way they relate to other people; the way they do or don't get upset.
- People diagnosed with personality disorder may be inflexible in that they may have a narrow range of attitudes, behaviours and coping mechanisms
- These ways of behaving are long standing.

Other key points:

- Most people diagnosed with a personality disorder fit the criteria for at least two different types of personality disorder

- Most people diagnosed with a personality disorder are not dangerous
- Dangerousness is most often but not exclusively associated with anti-social or psychopathic disorder
- People diagnosed as borderline or paranoid personality disorder may be at higher risk of self harm and/or suicide than other people
- People with personality disorders have multiple needs and vulnerabilities.

Causes of Personality Disorders

To date there has been very little research into the causes of personality disorders. It is generally assumed that there are a number of possible causes including problems in early childhood such as abuse, inadequate parenting, neglect and trauma. Neurological and genetic factors such as brain damage or low levels of serotonin may also play a part.

Related Information

Schizophrenia : If you have a personality disorder you may also have other mental health problems, such as depression, anxiety, panic disorders, eating disorders, deliberate self-harm, substance misuse, and manic depression. It is not known if the personality disorder causes these other problems or if they simply exist side by side and are unrelated.

It can be very difficult to diagnose personality disorders because of other mental health problems, which often hide the personality disorder. It is also possible to misdiagnose someone as having a personality disorder if they have a syndrome with similar symptoms e.g. post-traumatic stress syndrome or Asperger's syndrome.

Classification of Personality Disorders

Two different classification systems are used for personality disorders:

Diagnostic Criteria: DSM Classification System

Diagnostic criteria for personality disorder refer to behaviours or traits that are characteristic of the person's recent and long term functioning since early childhood.

Personality disorder describes a constellation of behaviours or traits that cause either significant impairment in social or occupational functioning or subjective distress.

Diagnostic Criteria: ICD Classification System

Diagnostic criteria include variety of conditions which indicate a person's characteristic and enduring patterns of inner experience (cognition and affect) and behaviour(s) that differ markedly from a culturally expected and accepted range.

Types of Personality Disorder

According to the DSM system, there are three main clusters of personality disorder.

Cluster A:

- Paranoid Personality Disorder
- Schizoid Personality Disorder
- Schizotypal Personality Disorder.

Cluster B:

- Anti Social Personality Disorder
- Emotionally Unstable Personality Disorder
- Histrionic Personality Disorder
- Narcissistic Personality Disorder.

Cluster C:

- Anxious Personality Disorder
- Dependant Personality Disorder
- Obsessive Compulsive Personality Disorder.

Treatments and Self Management Strategies

At present very little is known about the long term benefits of different forms of treatments for personality disorders. This is because very little research has been undertaken. The research that has been undertaken to date suggests that most forms of personality disorder may be treatable or manageable, especially the more moderate forms, but no single treatment or management strategy will be effective in all cases.

Personality disorders may be difficult to treat because they involve lifelong, pervasive attitudes and behaviours and because people with personality disorders often have other mental health problems. When a treatment is seen to fail it is often the patient who is blamed for not fitting the programme rather than the service admitting that it has not met the individual's need.

In the UK treatment for personality disorders varies considerably, depending to a large extent on whether people are in a general NHS setting, an in-patient psychiatric unit, special hospital or in the prison system. The availability of appropriate resources including qualified staff, therapeutic environments and management support for innovative treatments is also a major issue.

Medication (Pharmacological Treatments)

Short term treatments may include anxiolytic or neuroleptic drugs which are given for short periods or at times of severe stress. Long term treatments may involve the use of neuroleptics which can be helpful in cases of paranoid and schizotypal personality disorders. However it is possible that the medication is being used to control risk and stress, rather than having any long term impact on the personality disorder itself.

Psychodynamic Treatment

This treatment emphasises personality structure and development. It aims to provide insight for people allowing them to understand their feelings and to find better coping mechanisms. This approach has had limited success and is likely to be less successful for those with addiction and/or antisocial personality disorder.

Cognitive and Behavioural Therapy

Cognitive and behavioural therapies cover a wide range of treatments such as Cognitive Therapy, Dialectical Behaviour Therapy, Interpersonal Psychotherapy and Cognitive Analytic Therapy. Most cognitive behavioural approaches address specific aspects of thoughts, feelings, behaviour or attitude, and do not claim to treat the entire personality disorder of the person. Research suggests that there are some short term benefits to these approaches but more research is required into the long term benefits.

Therapeutic Communities

The Therapeutic Community (TC) approach involves living in a therapeutic community for several months. Engagement in therapy is voluntary and responsibility for the day to day running of the TC is shared between patients and staff. Members of the TC are encouraged to talk about their feelings, and particularly their feelings about each others' behaviour. This encourages them to think about the affect of their own behaviour on other people. The results of TC are still under scrutiny.

Individual Differences

That people differ from each other is obvious. How and why they differ is less clear and is the subject of the study of Individual differences (IDs). Although to study individual differences seems to be to study variance, how are people different, it is also to study central tendency, how well can a person be described in terms of an overall within-person average. Indeed, perhaps the most important question of individual differences is whether people are more similar to themselves over time and across situations than they are to others, and whether the variation within a single person across time and situation is less than the variation between people. A related question is that of similarity, for people differ in their similarities to each other. Questions of whether particular groups (e.g., groupings by sex, culture, age, or ethnicity) are more similar within than between groups are also questions of individual differences.

Personality psychology addresses the questions of shared human nature, dimensions of individual differences and unique patterns of individuals. Research in IDs ranges from analyses of genetic codes to the study of sexual, social, ethnic, and cultural differences and includes research on cognitive abilities, interpersonal styles, and emotional reactivity. Methods range from laboratory experiments to longitudinal field studies and include data reduction techniques such as Factor Analysis and Principal Components Analysis, as well as Structural Modelling and Multi-Level Modelling procedures. Measurement issues of most importance are those of reliability and stability of Individual Differences.

Research in Individual Differences addresses three broad questions: 1) developing an adequate descriptive taxonomy of how people differ; 2) applying differences in one situation to predict differences in other situations; and 3) testing theoretical explanations of the structure and dynamics of individual differences.

Taxonomies of Individual Differences

Taxonomic work has focused on categorizing the infinite ways in which individuals differ in terms of a limited number of latent or unobservable constructs. This is a multi-step, cyclical process of intuition, observation, deduction, induction, and verification that has gradually converged on a consensual descriptive organization of broad classes of variables as well as on methods for analyzing them. Most of the measurement and taxonomic techniques used throughout the field have been developed in response to the demand for selection for schooling, training, and business applications.

Test Theory

Consider the case of differences in vocabulary in a particular language (e.g., English). Although it is logically possible to organize people in terms of the specific words they know in English, the more than 2^(500,000) possible response patterns that could be found by quizzing people on each of the more than 500,000 words in English introduces more complexity rather than less. Classical Test Theory (CTT) ignores individual response patterns and estimates an individual's total vocabulary size by measuring performance on small samples of words. Words are seen as random replicates of each other and thus individual differences in total vocabulary size are estimated from observed differences on these smaller samples. The Pearson Product Moment Correlation Coefficient (r) compares the degree of covariance between these samples with the variance within samples. As the number of words sampled increases, the correlation of the individual differences within each sample and with those in the total domain increases accordingly.

Estimates of ability based upon Item Response Theory (IRT) take into account parameters of the words themselves (i.e., the difficulty and discriminability of each word) and estimate a single ability parameter for each individual. Although CTT and IRT estimates are highly correlated, CTT statistics are based on decomposing the sources of variance within and between individuals while IRT statistics focus on the precision of an individual estimate without requiring differences between individuals. CTT estimates of reliability of ability measures are assessed across similar items (internal consistency), across alternate forms, and across different forms of assessment as well as over time (stability). Tests are reliable to the extent that differences within individuals are small compared to those between individuals when generalizing across items, forms, or occasions. CTT reliability thus requires between subject variability. IRT estimates, on the other hand, are concerned with the precision of measurement for a particular person in terms of a metric defined by item difficulty.

The test theory developed to account for sampling differences within domains can be generalized to account for differences between domains. Just as different samples of words will yield somewhat different estimates of vocabulary, different cognitive tasks (e.g., vocabulary and arithmetic performance) will yield different estimates of performance. Using multivariate procedures such as Principal Components Analysis or Factor Analysis, it is possible to decompose the total variation into between domain covariance, within domain covariance, and within domain variance. One of the most replicable observations in the study of individual differences is that almost all tests thought to assess cognitive ability have a general factor (g) that is shared with other tests of ability. That is, although each test has specific variance associated with content (e.g., linguistic, spatial), form of administration (e.g., auditory, visual), or operations involved (e.g., perceptual speed, memory storage, memory retrieval, abstract reasoning), there is general variance that is common to all tests of cognitive ability.

Personality and Ability

Although to some the term personality refers to all aspects of a person's individuality, typical usage divides the field into studies of ability and personality. Tests of ability are viewed as maximal performance measures. Ability is construed as the best one can do on a particular measure in a limited time (speed test) or with unlimited time (power test). Personality measures are estimates of average performance and typically include reports of preferences and estimates of what one normally does and how one perceives oneself and is perceived by others.

The same procedures used to clarify the structure of cognitive abilities have been applied to the question of identifying the domains of personality. Many of the early and current personality inventories use self-descriptive questions (e.g., do you like to go to lively parties; are you sometimes nervous) that are rationally or theoretically relevant to some domain of interest for a particular investigator.

Although there is substantial consistency across inventories developed this way, some of this agreement could be due to conceptually overlapping item pools. Other researchers have advocated a lexical approach to the taxonomic problem, following the basic assumption that words in the natural language describe all important individual differences. This shifts the taxonomic question from how are individuals similar and different from each other to how are the words used to describe individuals (e.g., lively, talkative, nervous, anxious) similar and different from each other.

Dimensional analyses of tests developed based on lexical, rational, or theoretical bases suggest that a limited number (between three and seven) of higher order trait domains adequately organize the thousands of words that describe individual differences and the logically infinite way that these words can be combined into self or peer report items. The broadest domains are those of introversion-extraversion and emotional stability-neuroticism, with the domains of agreeableness, conscientiousness and intellectual openness or culture close behind. These domains can be seen as asking the questions that one wants to know about a stranger or a potential mate: are they energetic and dominant (extraverted), emotionally stable (low neurotic), trustworthy (conscientious), loveable (agreeable), and interesting (intelligent and open).

Measures of ability and personality reflect observations aggregated across time and occasion and require inferences about stable latent traits thought to account for the variety of observed behaviours. However there are other individual differences that are readily apparent to outside observers and require little or no inference about latent traits. The most obvious of such variables include sex, age, height, and weight. Differences that require some knowledge and inference are differences in ethnicity and social economic status. These obvious group differences are sometimes analyzed in terms of the more subtle measures of personality and ability or of real life outcomes (e.g, sex differences in neuroticism, mathematics ability, or income).

Predictive Validity

Individual differences are important only to the extent that they make a difference. Does knowing that people differ on a trait X help in predicting the likelihood of their doing behaviour Y? For many important outcome variables the answer is a resounding yes. In their review of 85 years of selection in personnel psychology, Frank Schmidt and John Hunter show how differences in cognitive ability predict differences in job performance with correlations averaging about.50 for mid complexity jobs. These correlations are moderated by job complexity and are much higher for professional-managerial positions than they are for completely unskilled jobs. In terms of applications to personnel psychology, a superior manager (one standard deviation above the mean ability for managers) produces almost 50% more than an average manager. These relationships diminish as a function of years of experience and degree of training. General mental ability (g) also has substantial predictive powers in predicting non-job related outcomes, such as likelihood of completing college, risk for divorce and even risk for criminality.

The non-cognitive measures of individual differences also predict important real life criteria. Extraversion is highly correlated with total sales in dollars among salespeople. Similarly, impulsivity can be used to predict traffic violations. Conscientiousness, when added to g substantially increases the predictability of job performance. Although the size of the correlation is much lower, conscientiousness measured in adolescence predicts premature mortality over the next fifty years.

Sources of Individual Differences

The taxonomic and predictive studies of individual differences are descriptive organizations of thoughts, feelings, and behaviours that go together and how they relate to other outcomes. But this categorization is descriptive rather than causal and is analogous to grouping rocks in terms of density and hardness rather than atomic or molecular structure. Causal theories of individual differences are being developed but are in a much earlier stage than are the descriptive taxonomies.

Descriptive taxonomies are used to organize the results of studies that examine genetic bases of individual differences. By applying structural modelling techniques to the variances and covariances associated with various family constellations it is possible to decompose phenotypic trait variance into separate sources of genetic and environmental variance. The most common family configurations that are used are comparisons of identical (monozygotic) with fraternal (dizygotic) twins. Additional designs include twins reared together or apart, and biological versus adoptive parents, children and siblings. Conclusions from behavioural genetics for most personality traits tend to be similar: Across different designs, with different samples from different countries, roughly 40-60% of the phenotypic variance seems to be under genetic control with only a very small part of the remaining environmental variance associated with shared family environmental effects. Additional results suggest that genetic sources of individual differences remain important across the lifespan. However, this should not be taken to mean that people do not change as they mature but rather that the paths one takes through life are similar to those taken by genetically similar individuals.

Genes do not code for thoughts, feelings or behaviour but rather code for proteins that regulate and modulate biological systems. Although promising work has been done searching for the biological bases of individual differences it is possible to sketch out these bases only in the broadest of terms. Specific neurotransmitters and brain structures can be associated with a broad class of approach behaviours and positive affects while other neurotransmitters and structures can be associated with a similarly broad class of avoidance behaviours and negative affects. Reports relating specific alleles to specific personality traits emphasize that the broad personality traits are most likely under polygenic influence and are moderated by environmental experience.

Subtle differences in neurotransmitter availability and re-uptake vary the sensitivity of individuals to cues about their environment that predict future resource availability and external rewards and punishments. It is the way these cues are detected, atttended to, stored, and integrated with previous experiences that makes each individual unique. Current work on the bases of individual differences is concerned with understanding this delicate interplay of biological propensities with environmental opportunities and constraints as they are ultimately represented in an individual's information processing system. With time we can expect to increase our taxonomic and predictive power by using these causal bio-social theories of individual differences.

Ages & Stages-Individual Differences

Developmental milestones give a general idea about what to expect from children of different ages. However, there will always be differences between individual children. Some children begin to walk at 10 months, some at 15 months. Some toddle along quickly and smoothly, getting the "hang of it" right away. Others fall down a lot, hesitate, or even give up for a few days. Some children talk before they are 2, others talk very little before they are 3 or so. Some will always be quiet people. Some abilities become clear in one child, but may never be very strong in another.

Recognize the individual in the child and look for differences based on the following:

Sense of Security

Some children need more consistency, more reassurance, and more confidence and trust-building than others. Insecurity sometimes can cause a child to withdraw or behave aggressively.

Activity Level

Some children need more active play than others. They need the opportunity to move around, jump, run, and bounce many times throughout the day. Other children need more quiet time or more rest.

Response to Stimulation

Children are inherently different in their tolerance to noise, activity, visual stimulation, or changes in the environment. An environment that is sensitive to this need in children will provide interesting activities as well as a quiet place to get away from the action.

Thinking Style

Some children think quietly through possible solutions to a problem; others push in and try the first idea that occurs to them. Some children are interested in experimenting to find out how objects work; others choose to ask friends or adults for help. Developmental guidelines should be used as a general rule of thumb. In your work with children, do not confuse earlier or faster development with better development. Early talking by a 1-year-old does not mean that the child will be a chatterbox or a brilliant conversationalist at age 10. Later talking may mean that a toddler is putting more energy into physical growth and motor exploration right now.

Problems of Backward, Problematic and Gifted Children

The characteristics of gifted children often lead to social and emotional problems that can affect their emotional and social development. To understand your gifted child completely, it's a good idea to see how your child's giftedness can influence his or her behaviour.

Problems Resulting from Asynchronous Development

1. Gifted children can intellectually understand abstract concepts but may be unable to deal with those concepts emotionally, leading to intense concerns about death, the future, sex, and other such issues.
2. Gifted children's physical development may lead to an inability to complete a task they are capable of intellectually envisioning. (Perfectionism may play a role in this frustration as well.)

3. A gifted child may be able to participate in adult conversations about issues such as global warming or world hunger one minute and the next minute cry and whine because a sibling took a favourite toy.

Problems Resulting from Advanced Verbal and Reasoning Ability

1. Gifted children can be argumentative and/or manipulative. (Adults often remark that theses children are little lawyers!) Parents and other adults need to remember that, although credit should be given for logical and convincing arguments, a child is still a child and requires appropriate discipline, no matter how clever or cute the behaviour may look. Children who see that they can manipulate adults can feel very insecure.
2. Gifted children can be manipulative. (Parents and other adults need to take care that they don't allow this manipulation.)
3. A gifted child may try to outsmart parents and teachers.
4. Sophisticated vocabulary and advanced sense of humour can cause gifted children to be misunderstood, which can make them feel inferior and rejected. (This is one reason gifted children prefer to be around older children and adults.)

Problems Resulting from Perfectionism and Emotional Sensitivities

1. Perfectionism can lead to fear of failure, in turn causing a gifted child to avoid failure by refusing to even try something (including doing a homework assignment!)
2. Keen observation, imagination, and ability to see beyond the obvious can cause a gifted child to appear shy, holding back in new situations in order to consider all the implications.
3. A gifted child may require full details before answering questions or offering help, making him or her appear socially shy.

4. Intense sensitivity can cause gifted children to take criticism, or even general anger, very personally. Childhood slights do not roll off their backs.
5. Sensitivity and well-developed sense of right and wrong can lead to concern over wars, starving children, pollution and other injustice and violence. If they are overloaded with images and discussions of these issues, they can become introverted and withdrawn or even suffer from "existential depression."

Virtually all the characteristics of giftedness can make gifted children feel "different," even at a very early age. It's important, therefore, to get them together with children like them and with people who understand them.

Bibliography

Allport, Gordon: *Becoming: Basic Considerations for a Psychology of Personality,* Yale Univ. Press, New Haven, 1955.

Arndt, William B. Jr. : *Theories of Personality*, Macmillan, New York, 1974.

Bandura, Albert : *Adolescent Aggression*, N.Y. Ronald Press, New York. 1959.

Barry, K.: *The Prostitution of Sexuality*, New York, New York University Press, 1995.

Bell, A., Weinberg, M., Hammersmith, S.: *Homosexualities: A Study of Diversity among Men and Women*. New York: Basic Books, 1978.

Bhaskar, Raj : *Fundamentals of Child Psychology*, Swastik Pub, Delhi, 2008.

Bieber, I.: *Homosexuality: A Psychoanalytic Study of Male Homosexuals*. New York: Basic Books, 1962.

Carr, W. & Kemmis, S. : *Becoming Critical: Education, Knowledge and Action Research*, London, Falmer, 1986.

Fisher, William C. : *Working Toward Sustainable Development: The Narmada Dam Project*, Armonk, New York, 1994.

Galbraith, M.W. : *Education Through Community Organizations*, San Francisco, Jossey-Bass, 1990.

George, I.: *Child labour and child work*, New Delhi, Ashish Publishing House, 1990.

Georgi, A. : *Psychology as a Human Science*, Harper & Row, New York, 1970.

Grace, G. : *School Leadership: Beyond Educational Management*, London, Falmer, 1995.

Green, R.: *Sexual Identity Conflict in Children and Adults.* Baltimore: Penguin, 1974.

Hans, E. : *Psychoticism as a Dimension of Personality*, Pergamon, Elsevier Science Inc, Amsterdam, 1997.

Harry, J.: *Gay Children Grown up: Gender Culture and Gender Deviance*. New York: Praeger, 1983.

Kegan, Robert. : *In over Our Heads: The Mental Demands of Modern Life*, Cambridge, Harvard University Press, 1994.

Lee, Jeong-kyu : *Historic Factors Influencing Korean Higher Education,* Seoul, Jimoondang, 2000.

Maslow, A. H. : *Motivation and Personality,* Harper & Bros, New York, 1954.

May, Rollo : *Psychology and the Human Dilemma*, Norton, New York, 1996.

Millican, J. : *Adult Literacy, A Handbook for Development Education*, Oxford, Oxfam, 1995.

Mittal, Sujata : *Experimental Child Psychology*, Isha Books, Delhi, 2005.

Moberly, E.: *Homosexuality: A New Christian Ethic*. Cambridge: James Clarke, 1983.

Prasad, Deepesh Chandra : *A-Z Handbook of Child Psychology*, Khel Sahitya Kendra, Delhi, 2006.

Rekers, G.: *Handbook of Childhood and Adolescent Sexual Problems*. NY: Lexington Books, 1995.

Sharma, B. : *Child Labour and Urban Informal Sector*, New Delhi, Deep and Deep Publications, 1990.

Sharma, K K : *Methods in Child Psychology*, Sublime, Delhi, 2001.

Sharma, R. N. : *Child Psychology and Child Development*, Shubhi Pub, Delhi, 2006.

Shyam, Radhey and Khan, Azizuddin : *Clinical Child Psychology*, Kalpaz, Delhi, 2009.

Thomas, A. : *Educating Children at Home,* London, Cassell, 1998.

William, D. : *Social and Personality Development, Infancy through Adolescence,* New York: Norton, 1983.

Index

A

Achievements, 36, 40, 246, 272, 273.
Administration, 285.
Aesthetic Development, 116.
Auditory Development, 230, 231, 232.

B

Brain Development, 94, 95, 96, 106, 107, 108, 109.

C

Child Development, 2, 5, 11, 12, 23, 91, 92, 122, 142, 143.
Cognitive Development, 48, 80, 81, 96, 98, 118, 141.
Cognitive Dissonance Theory, 181, 184.
Communication, 26, 33, 43, 85, 86, 97, 122, 166, 230, 232, 233, 234, 236, 237, 271, 273, 274, 275, 276.
Contribution, 63, 64, 68.
Cultures, 7, 50, 52, 121, 138, 217, 220, 224, 255, 279, 292.

D

Democracy, 202.
Developmental Disabilities, 96.
Developments, 87, 113, 222, 232, 288.
Distribution, 68, 259.
Domestic Violence, 121.

E

Emotional Development, 27, 39, 40, 100, 105.
Emotional Intelligence, 175, 259.
Emotional Preparation, 34.

F

Family Environment, 64, 67, 70.
Freedom, 141, 201, 202, 208, 223, 225, 226, 240, 263.

H

Human Development, 44, 110, 158.

I

Industry, 125.
Intellectual Development, 87, 89, 90, 91, 92.
Internal Physiological Changes, 25.

J

Jurisdictions, 50, 51, 52.

L

Language Development, 86, 117, 118, 149, 228, 230, 231, 232.
Leadership, 48, 127, 268, 272, 274.

M

Management, 75, 77, 103, 176, 266, 272, 273, 274, 281, 282.
Mental Development, 87.
Mental Disorders, 266.
Moral Development, 119, 120, 121, 122.
Motivational Factors, 75.
Motor Development, 29, 79.
Multimedia Learning, 159.

N

Networks, 98, 185, 209, 210, 212.

O

Operations, 81, 88, 213, 285.
Organizations, 11, 26, 53, 75, 76, 77, 150, 160, 249, 272, 288.

P

Perceptual Development, 228, 229.
Performance, 48, 79, 89, 117, 151, 152, 153, 158, 159, 194, 197, 203, 207, 209, 260, 266, 273, 275, 284, 285, 286, 287.
Personality Development, 47, 246, 273, 276, 277.
Personality Disorders, 278, 279, 280, 281, 282.
Personality Traits, 62, 63, 240, 241, 242, 243, 252, 254, 256, 260, 263, 264, 266, 267, 268, 269, 278, 288, 289.
Philosophical Assumptions, 240.
Physical Development, 43, 47, 100, 138, 290.
Policy, 53, 93, 208.
Political Party, 65.
Precocious Puberty, 44, 45.
Predictive Validity, 287.
Prenatal Development, 1, 11, 63.
Production, 13, 45, 56, 86, 232.
Projects, 36.
Punishment, 36, 42, 43, 76, 120, 122, 156, 175, 177, 182, 183.

S

Scientific Approach, 62.
Security, 71, 75, 76, 80, 105, 123, 125, 186, 204, 209, 292.
Sexual Development, 110, 129, 130.
Social Class, 2.
Social Development, 1, 47, 120, 123, 124, 125, 126, 127, 128, 190, 290.
Social Relations, 221.
Society, 11, 42, 44, 47, 49, 50, 51, 53, 56, 107, 116, 119, 120, 207, 264, 278.
Speech Development, 231, 232, 233.

T

Technology, 264.
Toddler, 11, 28, 32, 34, 35, 37, 38, 138, 140, 149, 211, 215, 237, 238, 290.
Traditions, 128, 129, 223, 239.
Treatments, 281, 282.

V

Violence, 43, 121, 122, 128, 221, 227, 292.
Visual Development, 233, 236.

□□□